MODERN LEGAL STUDIES

# Rethinking Housing Law

## AUSTRALIA
The Law Book Company
Brisbane ● Sydney ● Melbourne ● Perth


## CANADA
Ottawa ● Toronto ● Calgary ● Montreal ● Vancouver


## AGENTS
Steimatzky's Agency Ltd, Tel Aviv;
N.M. Tripathi (Private) Ltd, Bombay;
Eastern Law House (Private) Ltd, Calcutta;
M.P.P. House, Bangalore;
Universal Book Traders, Delhi;
Aditya Books, Delhi;
MacMillan Shuppan KK, Tokyo;
Pakistan Law House, Karachi, Lahore

MODERN LEGAL STUDIES

# Rethinking Housing Law

ANN STEWART

LONDON
SWEET & MAXWELL
1996

Published by
Sweet & Maxwell Limited of
100 Avenue Road,
London NW3 3PF

Typeset by LBJ Enterprises Ltd.
of Aldermaston and Chilcompton
Printed in Great Britain by
Clays Ltd, St Ives plc

A CIP catalogue record
for this book is available
from the British Library

ISBN 0–421–526408

No natural forests were destroyed to make this product:
only farmed timber was used and re-planted.

# Preface

This book attempts to provide an alternative way of considering some of the social and legal issues associated with the provision of housing. Housing law cannot exist within the parameters of traditional legal scholarship: it is the subject matter of public law, property and land law, landlord and tenant law, welfare and family law. It is straying into the area of company and commercial law as the provision and financing of housing increasingly becomes a matter for the market. We are witnessing the transformation of mutual building societies into banks at the present time and local housing authorities are likely to become companies in the near future. This book offers a way of thinking about the legal implications of these changes which to some extent transcend the traditional legal boundaries.

This book does not cover some of the traditional subject areas of housing law texts, such as homelessness and housing standards. There are a number of excellent text books specifically on these subjects and on the law relating to housing more generally.

The period under review in the book has seen major changes in the provision of housing. Council housing was once the flagship of the local welfare state. Its demise is now more than imaginable, even in the great northern cities. Home ownership as a personal and financial disaster affecting millions was equally unimaginable 10 years ago. Another aim of this book is to try to provide a framework in which to understand the legal consequences of these changes.

I hope the book will be of use to the broad church of housing specialists as well as to students interested in the legal regulation of housing.

Finally, I would like to thank the following people who have provided valuable support and assistance at different times and in different ways: Patrick McAuslan, Hugh Beale, Geoff Green, George Stewart and William Stewart but my special thanks go to Andy Cartwright without whom this book would never have been finished.

Ann Stewart
University of Warwick

# Contents

# Table of Cases

# Table of Statutes

xvii

# Chapter 1

# Introduction

I would like to tell a story. It concerns the creation of a "new" subject called housing law. In the 1970s, the subject was an orphan. Its elderly parents had been a property lawyer and a local government officer who had never had much of a meeting of minds. It was adopted by young and politically progressive parents.

One worked in law centres and legally aided private practice, the other in the new university law schools. Its formative years were spent while both parents were reasonably close and shared roughly similar views, at least on important matters such as values. During adolescence, its parents drifted apart, while experiencing their mid-life crisis accentuated by uncertainty in the broader worlds in which they worked. In early adulthood, being young and keen on action, the subject sought new friends of its own age among other orphaned and adopted subjects such as housing and urban studies but found that they did not share many common interests. It also sought out its relatives who were making careers as successful lawyers. It established an uneasy companionship with some of these but often felt ill at ease because of its background. Now it is uncertain about its identity but is comforted by the observation that most of its contemporaries are experiencing similar crises.

W.I. Jennings writing in 1935 knew what housing law was intended to achieve. "Fundamentally, its purpose is to improve the standard of housing accommodation of the working classes"[1]. "For

---

[1] Jennings "Courts and Administrative Law—The Experience of English Housing Legislation", *Harvard Law Review* Vol. 49 p. 426 at 432.

this purpose several devices have been invented and several different kinds of authorities have been given powers. An analysis of powers along traditional lines does not help."[2] He describes the methods available to achieve clearance through the use of the clearance order and the compulsory purchase of land:

"Here is a pretty mixture of the legislative, administrative, and judicial. Is a clearance order legislation? Is the holding of a public local inquiry a judicial function? Does the local authority in interpreting the Act exercise a judicial function? Is the arbitrator on a compulsory purchase order exercising a judicial function? Is the county court in assessing expenses exercising an administrative function?"[3]

Jennings uses the questions as a context in which to discuss the role of the courts in interpreting these powers. He sees the judges applying "common law principles" such as freedom of contract and the primacy of private property rights in their interpretation of the statutes in such a way that they interfere with the activities of the public bodies to the detriment of the social good:

"The whole purpose of the Housing Acts is to remedy social evils by interfering with the rights of landowners. . . . Nevertheless, since 1928 the courts have frequently. . . . cut down the powers of local authorities. The result is that the statute law of housing is becoming more and more detailed, and is therefore bound to give rise to increasing difficulties of interpretation."[4]

He recognises that what goes on in the courts is only the tip of the proverbial iceberg:

"The civil law and the criminal law are administered in courts; administrative law is administered outside, and the function of the courts is one of control only."[5]

This leads to a lack of competence or at least intuitive understanding in the judges of the ways of the administration and a tendency for

---

[2] *ibid.*
[3] *ibid.* p. 433.
[4] *ibid.* p. 451.
[5] *ibid.* p. 453.

them to rely on what they do understand: the principles of the common law. What administrative lawyers want is "not that judges shall pervert legislation in favour of a 'bureaucracy' but that they shall not interpret it against public policy in the interests of private property."[6]

Jenning's article provides a starting point for this book in two ways: it offers continuity and contrast. The world that Jennings describes seems a great deal simpler and more certain than the present. This is only partly due to the quality of his analysis. Jennings was writing before the expansion of state activity which constituted the post-war welfare state. This produced a very substantial increase in housing powers primarily granted to local authorities to provide and then manage housing. The objectives of the legislation became increasingly complex and interactive.

By the 1970s, there were clearance and rehabilitation schemes, powers not only to provide dwellings but to sell some and to purchase others. Local authorities had powers to grant mortgages to those wishing to purchase a dwelling and to take over mortgages from those with existing mortgages with other mortgagees. Authorities could provide financial support to housing associations to supply rented dwellings but could acquire dwellings compulsorily from other private landlords. They owed duties to those deemed by legislation to be homeless. The financial regimes necessary to support myriad housing activities were increasingly complex. State activity spread across the whole spectrum of housing provision to offer financial support to home purchasers through tax relief on mortgage interest and to private sector tenants through means tested allowances.

Jennings expresses no anxiety about the activity of the state. He perceives a clear distinction between the public and the private spheres. For him the tension was between the courts, with their tendency to support the interests of those with private property, and the administration, which represented the public good. Not so today, state activity and its relationship with civil society has become highly problematic. Commentators from a wide range of perspectives describe a crisis of legitimacy.

---

[6] *ibid.* p. 454.

This phenomenon can be discussed on a number of levels. It provides the backcloth for two separate but related aspects of this book: the material context of contemporary housing policy and the analytical framework which informs the legal discussion. In this section I intend to discuss very briefly the politico-economic aspects of the crisis of legitimacy. Gamble writing of this phenomenon calls it a crisis of hegemony. Hegemony exists "when the political leadership of a group or a nation is exercised with minimal dispute and resistance."[7] He describes its breakdown both at national and international levels:

> "At a national level it occurred when the policies and institutions of postwar social democracy began to be discredited. The authority of the social democratic state in the fields of citizenship, representation and economic management was undermined."[8]

Successive governments have made claim to be able to manage the economy in order to provide sustained prosperity. By the 1970s it had become obvious that this was no longer happening: the state could no longer deliver the goods. Collaterally, there has developed a more general scepticism with the institutions of social democracy. The public sector with its responsibilities for a wide range of activities, such as programmes to combat unemployment and to guarantee welfare by ensuring minimum standards of support for all citizens has been questioned in number of ways.[9] First, it has become increasingly difficult to meet the expectations many of which were contradictory, raised by a vast array of interest groups, through the vehicle of the state. In the area of housing, tenants of public landlords increasingly expect to have the dwelling of their choice maintained to a high standard even though they are unable to pay an economic rent. At the same time more and more see it as their right to be able to own a home while having comparatively limited financial means.

Homelessness is viewed generally as a national evil to be remedied by the state at a time when families are not only disintegrating through violence and abuse but also through the desire of women

---

[7] Gamble, *The Free Economy and Strong State* 1988).
[8] Gamble, *The Free Economy and Strong State* (1988), p. 1.
[9] *ibid.* p. 12.

and young people to escape its structures. Access to paid employment and to decent housing are uncoupled. The financial burden on the state to meet expectations rose steadily in the immediate post-war period and then dramatically in the sixties and seventies so that housing expenditure by the late seventies accounted for a quarter of all public expenditure and seemed unstoppable. Yet housing needs were not satisfied. The politics of housing became increasingly contested requiring the state to make choices which further undermined its credibility.

The institutions of social democracy were also perceived to be failing in a different but related way through their inability to translate policy into practice. Local government has been the target of much of this attack which has come not only from critics on the left and right of politics but also from the users of services. On one level, accountability and participation are seen as inadequate, on another, administrators are seen as inefficient and ineffective and there is general uncertainty over the boundary between politics and administration. No where is this clearer than in the area of housing. Local authority housing departments have been seen as paternalistic, inefficient and unresponsive to tenants needs. Councillors on the housing committee have been seen as usurping their position to obtain political gains and imposing their own views and standards on those whom they house, yet unable to provide decent accommodation to their electors. This is a long way from the world of Jennings and his conception of the public good.

The political response to this crisis in Britain was Thatcherism. There is much debate about the meaning of this term but in general it has involved a rhetoric of rolling back the state to allow the market greater control over a wide range of economic and social relationships. The aim seems to have been to shift the responsibility for meeting and reconciling contradictory interests to the market, thereby depoliticising the process of choice. It also involves the attempt to transform existing institutions so that they adopt a market orientation. This restructuring is directed at the perceived failure of the institutions to implement policies satisfactorily. Gamble describes the project in the following terms:

> "A central goal has been to discredit the social democratic concept of universal citizenship rights, guaranteed and enforced through public

agencies, and to replace it with a concept of citizenship rights achieved through property ownership and participation in markets. In this way a class of sub-citizens is created, consisting of those who, being unable to participate in markets, are forced to remain dependent upon the state. Such dependency becomes a stigma, and allows the demands of these groups to be disregarded."[10]

While there is considerable disagreement on the degree of coherence within the policies of the Thatcherite project, its impact in the housing area is clear to see, particularly since the mid-eighties. The extension of the home owning democracy through the sale of council houses has been one of the most successful policies irrespective of the difficulties encountered over the recession in the property market in the early nineties. The gradual erosion in the council sector, described in the housing literature as residualisation, is producing a perception that it is only for those who cannot go elsewhere, essentially for those with no or very limited access to the labour market. Demands for resources to improve conditions and to increase supply to the sector have been easily resisted in recent years. Responsibility for homelessness is being restructured. Increasingly it is being separated into different categories and the responsibility of the state reduced, for instance young people become the responsibility of their parents irrespective of the reality of any relationship. Homelessness is being redefined as destitution and fecklessness and therefore able to be ignored. Rents in all sectors are now based to a greater extent on a market basis. Opposition to the concept of private renting is being eroded. It would however be highly misleading to see these developments as a uniform success story for the Thatcherite project or as a phenomenon which has outlived its creator. Citizenship is presently under reconstruction within a market philosophy rather than within the political framework of the social democratic state.

Jenning's article on housing law is immediately recognisable to a lawyer sixty years later. Unlike much material which we may read at such distance it does not seem dated. This desire to understand law through the way that judges construe statutes and interpret cases still constitutes the orthodoxy. Yet, the growth in state activity in the

---

[10] Gamble, *op. cit.* p. 16.

post-war period in its welfare state form and the problems described in the previous section have provoked very considerable debate about the nature of law and its uses in modern society. Thus the crisis of the political world is embedded in these theoretical discussions about law.[11]

De Sousa Santos sets out one way of seeing the issues:

"I would like to suggest that law has . . . undergone three meta-morphoses in the modern era . . . In the seventeenth and eighteenth centuries . . . the new theories of natural law and the liberal political philosophy were a magnificent new creation of values and beliefs that testified to the emergence and consolidation of bourgeois society. But as the nineteenth century wore on . . . law was resisting against the demands which the social question had given rise to and which were being pressed into the political agenda by emergent social and political forces, . . . after the Second World War, the law . . . gave up resistance in docile submission to the whole range of values and beliefs . . . that the different social and political forces imposed upon it."[12]

The state and its legal order does far more than provide a "neutral" system of rules.[13] Thus this loading of law with a variety of values and beliefs is strongly associated with the increasing intrusion of law into social life. Teubner calls it "materialisation" of formal law.[14] Ewald refers to it as "social law": "a law of preferences, a law of non-reciprocity, a law of positive discriminations."[15] No-one is autonomous: no-one exists except in as far as s/he represents an interest, and interests are determined through the classification and gradation of each in relation to others.[16]

The reach of regulation not only extends into new areas but its boundaries become unclear as state regulation intertwines with other modes of regulation such as business self regualtion.

---

[11] Cotterell, *The Sociology of Law* (1992).
[12] De Sousa Santos, "Law : A Map of Misreading. Towards a Post Modern Conception of Law", *Journal of Law and Society*, Vol. 14, No. 3, pp. 279–302.
[13] Cotterell, *op. cit.* p. 209.
[14] Teubner, "The Transformation of Law in the Welfare State "in G. Teubner (ed.) *Dilemmas of Law in the Welfare State* (1986), pp. 3–10.
[15] Ewald, "A Concept of Social Law" in G. Teubner (ed.) *Dilemmas of Law in the Welfare State* (1986), pp. 41–75.
[16] Ewald, *op. cit.*, p. 46.

"Law seems to extend its regulatory scope deeper into society but much of this extension is by means that cannot be understood as the application of Weberian formal rationality or the fulfilment of the promise of the rule of law."[17]

The effects upon the form of law "range from a weakening of the idea of generality to changes in methods of interpretation."[18] Comprehensive regulation appears to require discretionary decision-making by officials which undermines the liberal dichotomy of the public and the private. Galligan see it thus,

"The legal framework has become increasingly characterized by the combination of broad statutory provisions and the vesting in officials of wide discretionary powers. The result has been that State regulation enters into areas traditionally thought of as private, in order to impose within these domains certain conceptions of the public good."[19]

Private rights guaranteed by explicit legal norms and enforceable by legal institutions give way to power exercised by officials according to a wide sense of the public interest.

"The risk is that courts with their characteristic methods of control and accountability are either pushed to the margin of public affairs and become ineffectual, or that the exercise of legal control itself becomes discretionary, sectional and subjective in the same way as the institutions that it seeks to control."[20]

At a more abstract level, De Sousa Santos describes the consequences as interlegality.

"[D]ifferent legal spaces superimposed, interpenetrated, and mixed in our minds as much as in our actions. . . . Our legal life is constituted by an intersection of different legal orders, that is, by interlegality. . . . Interlegality is a highly dynamic process because the different legal spaces are non-synchronic and thus result in uneven and unstable mixings of legal codes.[21]

---

[17] Cotterell, *op. cit.*, p. 291.
[18] Teubner, "Juridification — Concepts, aspects, limits, solutions" in G. Teubner (ed.) *Juridification of Social Spheres* (1987), pp. 3—48.
[19] Galligan "Judicial Review and the Textbook writers", *Oxford Journal of Legal Studies* Vol. 2, No. 2, pp. 257–76.
[20] *ibid.*
[21] De Sousa Santos, *op. cit.*, pp. 297–298.

Evaluation of the developments differ. Hayek, who considers that law has no purpose except to provide the abstract rules through which individual citizens carry out their purposes, sees the supplanting of "autonomous law" by increasingly bureaucratic regulation.[22] Habermas speaks of the excessive colonisation of the life world by law and argues that the proliferation of law and regulation threatens the production of moral meaning in everyday life.[23] "Others have adopted a less pessimistic response and have seen positive potential in the diversification of the forms of legal regulation."[24]

I want now to turn to a consideration of my approach to housing law. The development of a sociological approach to law over the last 25 years has challenged orthodox legal thinking by using the methods and knowledges of the social sciences to illuminate legal issues.[25] Our understanding of landlord and tenant relationships is increased by the use of statistics on the number of tenancies covered by the Rent Acts or by observing possession procedures in the county court. Sociology of law has provided impact studies of homelessness laws. Both urban sociologists and economists have made extensive studies of all aspects of housing provision, some of whom have at times included consideration of the law.[26] All of these take an "external view of law": ultimately the concern is with the impact of law on the wider society rather than with legal doctrine. The latter has been the domain of the orthodoxy and is reflected in traditional jurisprudence. We have seen challenges presented to this approach by the development of myriad forms of regulation. The critical legal studies movement has also been undertaking guerilla warfare from "within". Its slogan is to take doctrine seriously,[27] while debunking the positivists and deliberately creating uncertainty about law's claims to validity.

---

[22] Hunt, *Explorations in Law and Society : Towards a Constitute Theory of Law* (1993).

[23] Habermas, "Law as Medium and Law as Institution" in G. Teubner (ed.) *Dilemmas of Law in the Welfare State* (1986).

[24] Luhmann, "The Self Reproduction of Law and its Limits" in G. Teubner *op. cit.*, pp. 111–127. Hunt, *op. cit.*, p. 307.

[25] Cotterell, *op. cit.*

[26] An example of each would be P. Saunders *A Nation of Home Owners* (1990) in which the author discuss the significance of tenure and M. Ball *Housing Policy and Economic Power* (1983) in which the author discusses the impact of the land development process on the form of owner-occupied housing.

[27] Hunt; "Critique of Law: What is Critical about Critical Legal Theory?" *Journal of Law and Society*, Vol. 14, No. 1, p. 12 at p. 19.

Nevertheless the critical movement does grant law a degree of autonomy. Some of the theorists concerned with the legitimacy of law discussed above are also keen to establish a degree of autonomy for law. Luhmann (1986) and Teubner (1986 and 1987) have developed the theory of autopoiesis which argues that law must be seen as a self-referential system of communication. The claims of many of the "externalists" and "internalists" to know about law have been influenced by postmodernist thought. Nelken (1991) provides an excellent and comprehensive study of the clash between science and law which these ideas have stimulated. He inevitably concludes that we need to take elements from both sides. Hunt is also keen to avoid the creation of these boundaries and argues in favour of a relational theory of law which attempts to straddle them:

"Its project is one which takes 'law' as its object of inquiry but which pursues it by means of the exploration of the interaction between legal relations and other forms of social relations rather than treating law as an autonomous field of inquiry linked only by external relations to the rest of society."[28]

It differs from the more conventional sociology of law because it explores the internal interconnections between different forms of legal relations and is concerned with the diversity of legal phenomena:

"It . . . embraces the idea that the 'presence of law' within social relations is not just to be gauged by institutional intervention but also by the presence of legal concepts and ideas within types of social relations that appear to be free of law . . . [it] draws attention to the differential combination of legal and non-legal relations present within particular types of relations which leads to the suggestion that this affects and possibly determines different forms of legal relations depending on the social practices and institutions to which they relate."[29]

Conversely, the field of legal relations is open to extra-legal relations thus making it important to consider the interactions between them.

[28] Hunt, *op. cit.*, p. 16.
[29] Hunt, *op. cit.*, p. 17.

However, it would be only too simple to pursue this approach in a mechanistic way seeking out relationships of a legal and extra-legal manner and finding different forms which "fit" different relationships.

I want to avoid wherever possible boundaries constructed around dichotomies: external and internal analysis of law; policy and practice; public and private worlds; and public and private law because my object of study straddles all of these. Because my study is socially and economically located the tendency might be to take an external view of law and develop an instrumental approach which might fail to recognise the role of legal doctrine. Nevertheless, the study is not defined by its location. It is defined legally: my interest is in the changing forms of legal relationships within this area of activity. It is not, however, a study which develops an analysis from orthodox legal categories such as occupational status. Arden and Partington (1984) (now Arden et al, 1994) developed this approach. They explain the classes of occupation known to the common law and then the classes of protection created by statute which are based on the common law classification. Their starting point is the individual legal form. The broader relationships constructing that legal status, such as the economic, social and legal position of the landlord, are treated as being outside the field of analysis. This is not to deny the significance of the individual classification, of great importance to a legal adviser needing a route map, but to suggest that what is needed is "a critical distance from the self-conception of legal professionals".[30]

I intend to use tenure, a concept with disparate meanings which emerge from different discourses, as a starting point. Law constructs a strong meaning for this term which is almost unrecognisable to others interested in the social and economic significance of housing provision. Their focus is generally broader and collective (generally, see the journal, Housing Studies). They are concerned with the economic effects of owner-occupation on the macro-economy, with the creation of market forms within the local authority sector and the economic viability of the private rented sector. There is a heated debate on the significance of owner-occupation on social and political habits. Can class be based on consumption as well as production

---

[30] *ibid.* p. 13.

relationships? Are consumption relationships more important than production relationships in understanding housing provision? Law is hardly mentioned, presumed to provide the technology. Lawyers would recognise few of these conceptualisations which sweep aside so many legally significant distinctions. However, pondering the different meanings given to concepts such as tenure allows other ways of seeing to emerge, such as the construction of legal and non-legal relationships and the degree of correspondence between them.

The law relating to housing has been loaded with a variety of values and is a prime example of interlegality, the mixing of uneven and unstable codes. In what follows, I limit my discussion to a general outline of the framework which is developed in more detail in the chapters which follow. I want to distinguish three spheres of relationships which are relevant to the provision of housing. The first is the individual relationship which the occupier has with the provider. I intend to discuss two main forms, the mortgage for consumption of freehold or long-leasehold dwellings,[31] (which is a charge on the legal estate) and the lease, in the case of the consumption of rented property. I will call these the **individual property relations**. They are embodied in legal forms which represent classical models of liberal legality. Individuals are deemed to possess the capacity for autonomous action and each is thereby the same as everyone else. Within this model, law provides for the co-existence of individual liberties while the state acts impersonally through law in the form of general rules which define, clearly and publicly, the individual rights of formally equivalent legal subjects. The laws are abstract and impersonal, embodying a formal rationality. The mortgage and the lease are rooted in the private law assumptions of freedom of contract and equal bargaining power. As Cotterell points out:

"Through the use of the concept of property . . . it becomes possible to banish almost entirely from the discourse of private law recognition of one of the most dominant features of life in a society of material

---

[31] Not all dwellings are purchased with a mortgage. Where no mortgage is required then the purchaser has a temporary relationship with the seller before becoming an outright owner in the case of freehold property. In the case of long leasehold, there is a continuing relationship with the freeholder.

inequalities – that of **private power**. . . . however much more one
person may own than another, the general freedom of transactions and
the equal security of property which the law affords to all subjects
makes it possible for legal ideology to affirm that the equality of legal
subjects is in no way compromised by the inequalities in the nature and
amount of assets which they are said (in legal doctrine) to own."[32]

The evolution and subsequent ossification of the common law of
mortgages in the early twentieth century provides a particularly
apposite example of liberal legality as we shall see in chapter three.

The second sphere consists of the statutory interventions which
purport to protect the weaker party, thus embodying some of the
values of the welfare state. These would be characterised by Ewald as
"social law." We can see these as superimposed on and interacting
with the individual property relationships. These statutory interventions construct divisions based on the identity of the parties. So,
protection for mortgagors under statute depends upon the nature of
the mortgagee; one Act covers all residential mortgagors but not
those with bank loans, while another covers non-building-society
lenders. Other statutes have constructed the meaning of the local
authority landlord and distinguished it from the private landlord. The
housing association landlord has been the subject of a number of
constructions based on differences from the other two types of
landlord. Establishing why these distinctions have emerged and the
meaning of the different forms of protection on offer is important. I
will call these relationships the **individual statutory relationships**.

My third sphere looks outward rather than to the individual and
attempts to encompass a wider understanding of the meaning of
regulation. These relationships regulate or place the providers within
a wider set of power relations. The most obvious of which in the area
of housing are, perhaps, those between central and local government;
but housing associations are heavily embroiled with the Housing
Corporation and their financiers and building societies operate not
only in the context of national regulation but also within the
disciplines of the international financial markets. I intend to call this
the **sphere of regulatory relations**.

As suggested earlier, the development of "social law" undermines
the core premise of classical liberalism. The anonymous legal subject

---

[32] Cotterell, *op. cit.*, p. 82.

gives way to the wage earner, the consumer, the professional as the laws become goal oriented. These developments have necessitated the expansion of the state's administrative apparatus to balance and regulate. Loughlin contends that there is an implicit belief among lawyers in the superiority of common law principles. This leads to a tendency "to construe narrowly any legislation which is not entirely compatible with the symmetrical structure of the common law."

"while it may be going too far to say that there is a definite affinity between the common law and the philosophy of laissez-faire it might not be entirely surprising if common lawyers engaged in strict scrutiny of legislation based on the principle of state intervention and collective action. These two factors, the belief in the superiority of the common law and its roots in an earlier era, may well combine to produce an outlook of scepticism towards administrative schemes for the collective provision of services or regulatory controls provided for by social legislation."[33]

Which of course brings us back to Jennings.

These three spheres of relationships represent the interlegality. They are connected in sometimes complex ways, not necessarily through correspondence, and they are not static. Tensions seem to emerge in one sphere but are resolved in another. Power relations shift within the spheres. Issues will emerge at different points so, for instance, struggles over rent levels in both the public and private sector were framed within the individual statutory framework in the seventies. The 1972 Housing Finance Act provided for a fair rent in the public sector, the 1977 Rent Act imposed rent restriction in the private sector. In the eighties, this issue emerged in the regulatory sphere as a struggle over housing benefit claims between two institutions of the state.

I intend to explore these concepts through a discussion of four major occupational relationships: home ownership funded by a mortgage, renting from a local authority, housing association and a private landlord. I construct a matrix of four occupational groupings

---

[33] Laughlin; "Beyond Complacency", A Review of Wade, Administrative Law 1982, (1983), *Modern Law Review*, Vol. 46, p. 666 at 670.

which has three different but interconnected spheres of relationships. Tracking the changing relationships and power balances facilitates comparison across the occupational divides. It also enables me to unpick a fixed idea of tenure and to replace it with layered meanings. The three spheres are artificially separated for ease of description and analysis. Chapters two to five explore the three spheres of relationships within specific occupational groupings, as it were vertically. Chapter six considers what can be learned by considering the spheres of relationships horizontally. I conclude by considering whether the discussion of housing law offers any insights into a broader discussion of the nature of law in contemporary society.

# Chapter 2

# Owner-Occupation

## Introduction

The twentieth century has witnessed the development of a mass market in owner-occupation although the legal foundation for this expansion emerged from the property law reforms of 1882–1925, at a time when the overwhelming majority of the population rented their dwellings from landlords. Over the century the availability of funds from building societies has provided an increasingly important source of finance for potential purchasers (Merrett, 1982, Forrest *et al*. 1990) while the structure and powers of building societies which were established in the Building Societies Act of 1874 remained almost unchanged until 1986. Nonetheless these continuities of form mask very considerable changes in relationships.

This chapter explores the particular spheres of power relationships which constitute the world of owner-occupation using the matrix set out in the preceding chapter. The discussion will focus primarily on those owners who are purchasing their property with money borrowed on a mortgage. These form a majority of the sector at any one time (over 70 per cent in 1993) but by no means all of it. A small number of dwellings are bought outright both at the top and the bottom of the market and increasing numbers of dwellings are occupied by owners who have paid off their mortgages.

In this introduction we will consider some of the key issues in the development of owner-occupation before turning specifically to the relationships within the sector. While general economic conditions

17

have stimulated and facilitated the growth in home ownership, in particular substantial increases in ownership have occurred at times when real wages have risen in relation to house prices, governments have encouraged and supported this expansion. The concept of the property-owning democracy emerged in the 1960s. In particular it is associated with the newly elected Labour government in 1964:

"[I]n a clear convergence with Tory thinking, owner-occupation was presented [by the newly elected Labour government in 1964] as the supreme goal in a nation of individual households. This became quite explicit in the government's first housing white paper, The Housing Programme 1965 to 1970".[1]

The white paper argued that the expansion of building for owner-occupation was "normal" and reflected "a long term social advance which should gradually pervade every region".[2]

Since 1979 the increase in owner-occupation has been a central feature of the Conservative government's housing policy. The Thatcher government had a very strong ideological belief in the value of home ownership and the property-owning democracy. Throughout the eighties the government was stressing not only the social benefits of owning but also the economic:

"Home ownership gives people independence; it gives them a sense of greater personal responsibility; and it helps to spread the Nation's wealth more widely. These are important factors in the creation of a more stable and prosperous society, . . .".[3]

Thus one of the justifications for policies providing support for the growth in home ownership was that they gave more people access to wealth creating capacity.[4] Despite the problems caused to home owners by recession and government policy in the 1980s, the 1995

---

[1] Merrett, *Owner Occupation in Britain* (1982), p. 35.
[2] MHLG (Ministry of Housing and Local Government), *The Housing Programme 1965 to 1970*, Cmnd. 2838 (1965), p. 8.
[3] DoE, *Finance for Housing Associations: The Government's Proposals* (1987), p. 2.
[4] Murie and Forrest, "Wealth, inheritance and housing policy" in *Policy and Politics*, Vol. 8, pp. 1–19.

white paper continues to promote "sustainable" home ownership as good for the country and good for the individual.[5]

One product of this commitment to home ownership over the last 30 years has been a wide range of specific schemes designed to broaden the social and economic base of the sector, to bring in groups who might be described as more marginal. The first scheme was the long leaseholder's right to enfranchise under the Leasehold Reform Act 1967 (Stewart, 1981). (These rights have been extended under the Leasehold Reform, Housing and Urban Development Act 1993). During the seventies and eighties governments tried to reduce the cost of entry through savings schemes and tax incentives for low-income purchasers and to reduce the cost of the dwelling itself through the provision of grants to improve older and cheaper properties and by offsetting the price of the land. Most of these schemes were administered by local authorities who had powers themselves to lend money to potential purchasers thought to be too risky for building societies. Many of the schemes proved unattractive economically or just too complicated and did not lead to a significant increase in the number of owners (see Booth and Crook, 1986).

The real success proved to be the right to buy provisions under the 1980, and subsequent, Housing Acts. In total since 1979, 1.5 million local authority and housing association tenants have bought their homes, 1.25 million under the right to buy.[6] The 1993 Leasehold Reform, Housing and Urban Development Act continued the programme by introducing a scheme whereby public sector rents could be converted into mortgages.[7] There are also schemes which provide cash grants to allow certain local authority and housing association tenants to move out and purchase houses in the private sector and schemes which provide shared ownership although both schemes involve small numbers.

In 1995 the government announced its intention of extending home ownership to housing association tenants who presently are unable to buy (because their landlord is a registered charity or they have become tenants since 1988). The proposal is to introduce a

[5] DoE, *Our Future Homes. Opportunity, Choice, Responsibility: The Government's Housing Policies for England and Wales*, Cm 2901 (1995), p. 2.

[6] DoE, *Private Renting in England 1993/94. Housing Research Summary*, No. 36.

[7] Hughes and Lowe, *Social Housing Law and Policy* (1995), pp. 75–80.

voluntary purchase grant to assist tenants to buy their existing dwellings at market value.[8]

These legislative moves have been accompanied by financial support for owner-occupiers. The most significant measure has been mortgage interest tax relief (MITR).

"The abolition of the schedule 'A' taxation of owner occupiers in 1963 (which was the tax on the imputed rental income enjoyed by owner-occupiers) in the context of the continuation of mortgage interest tax relief effectively created an incentive to home owners to use their house as an investment. Owners receive what is in effect a subsidy on the access payments but pay no tax on the imputed rental income *nor* on the capital gains made when they sell."[9] (original emphasis).

MITR assisted 8.5 million home owners with mortgages and cost £3 billion in 1994/95 (a fall from £5.2 billion in 1992/93). The cost of income support for mortgage interest, payable to almost 500,000 unemployed, elderly, sick or disabled owners, cost £0.9 billion in 1994/5 (£1.1 billion in 1992/93).[10]

"The cost of Mortgage Interest Tax Relief has, since the beginning of the 1980s, exceeded the cost of general subsidies to council housing, both globally and per household. By 1991/92 even the level of Income Support help with home buyers mortgage costs exceeded general council housing subsidies."[11]

There have been attempts since the late eighties to reduce not only the regressive nature of this tax relief but also its overall cost.[12] In the

---

[8] DoE, *The Legislative Framework for Private Renting*. Consultation Document. (1995).

[9] Lowe, "The social and economic consequences of the growth of home ownership" in Birchall, *Housing Policy in the Nineties* (1992), p. 73.

[10] Means tested benefits as distinct from general "brick and mortar" subsidies are also available to enable tenants to meet their rents. In 1994/5 housing benefits payable to all tenants (as distinct from general subsidies) amounted to £8.6 billion (£4.3 billion to council tenants, £4.3 to tenants renting in the private rented sector and from housing associations) DoE, *Private Renting in England 1993/94*. Housing Research Summary. No. 36. (1995), p. 8.

[11] Wilcox, *Housing Finance Review 1993* (1993), p. 162.

[12] First, the relief is restricted to the first £30,000 of borrowed money, secondly relief is payable to the property rather than to individuals thereby preventing multiple tax relief in relation to one property, thirdly, relief is payable only at the basic rate of taxation rather than the higher rate and finally the rate at which it is payable has been gradually reduced so that from April 1995 it is at 15 per cent.

nineties measures to restrict the availability of income support for home owners are emerging. These changes increase the cost and the uncertainty of owning, matters to which we will return in a later section.

Nevertheless, the property-owning democracy, as it has emerged, has offered not only the security of a home of one's own choice in which to live but also access to wealth accumulation. In the 1960s property prices increased between 5 per cent and 10 per cent per annum. The stability of the sixties market was replaced by great volatility in the seventies but prices did not fall in money terms. Buying a house at the limit of one's resources was considered sound financial advice: a sure winner in the medium term. Thus as Doling and Ford suggest:

> "Any belief at the start of the 1980s that there would be high returns from investing in home ownership had a strong empirical basis. House prices had outstripped the performance of inflation in retail prices as well as of average increases in popular investments such as shares and savings bonds."[13]

However, in the eighties the volatility continued and prices fell although this reduction was not obvious to many. The home as a sure financial asset had become established as a very powerful idea, particularly when constructed in opposition to the perceived disadvantages of renting. The renter does not enjoy the status of a part-owner of housing stock (which is the legal construction of the renting relationship: see next chapter) but is the subject of unfavourable comparison between owner and tenant.[14]

It can be argued that capital accumulation in a home has only "paper" value because it cannot be realised. However, considerable equity withdrawal, replacing some or all of the value of the dwelling by new lending, occurred in the 1980s (Lowe, 1992). Astute home owners could improve their financial position markedly by selling and buying at the right moment and also by increasing the gearing on their asset. The higher the gearing the greater the return on the

---

[13] Doling and Fords, "The changing face of home ownership," *Policy and Politics*, (1991), Vol. 19(2), p. 13.
[14] Gray, *Element of Land Law* (2nd ed., 1993), p. 936.

owner's capital. The number of owner-occupiers who moved house increased by over 60 per cent between 1982 and 1987 and the amount of equity withdrawal associated with moving trebled.[15] This is reflected in the increase in building societies' advances from less than £10 billion in 1980 to more than £35 billion in 1987.[16] Another major and significant source of equity withdrawal occurs through housing based inheritance (when the house of a dead owner is sold by relatives) (see Lowe, 1992 for a discussion of the research in this area).

Equity "leakage" had a major impact on the economy as a whole in the eighties, contributing to a boom in consumption. Lowe and Watson estimate that £14.4 billion of equity was withdrawn from the housing market and entered the personal sector in 1984.[17] These levels caused considerable anxiety to the Bank of England and to the government in their attempts to predict expenditure and regulate an overheating economy.

Another aspect of the relationship between the housing market and the wider economy can be seen in the fate of small businesses. The very rapid development of self-employment and small businesses in the eighties, particularly in the south of England, was supported by the appreciation of residential properties. There is evidence to suggest a strong dependence of new business creation on house price increases. The consequences of the slump from the late eighties has had a marked effect on these activities leading to bankrupt businesses and repossessed homes.[18]

The deregulation of the financial sector by the Financial Services Act 1985 and the impact of the 1986 Building Societies Act on building society activity sparked off an inflationary house price spiral. There was an explosion in borrowing, and mortgage debt rose steeply throughout the early to mid-1980s. Then in the late 1980s "an overheated, over-indebted, hypermobile housing market rapidly

---

[15] Lowe, "The social and economic consequences of the growth of home ownership," in Birchall's *Housing Policy in the Nineties* (1992), pp. 75, 79.

[16] Smallwood, "Building Societies: Builders or Financiers?" in Birchall's *Housing Policy in the 1990s* (1992), p. 61.

[17] Lowe, *op. cit.*, p. 76.

[18] Forrest and Murie, "Home Ownership in Recession," *Housing Studies* (1994), Vol. 9, No. 1, p. 71.

degenerated towards a gridlock of immobile households adjusting to very different expectations of home ownership".[19]

The construction of ownership was buffeted in the early 1990s. The prolonged recession with government policy focused on the desire to control inflation in a period of high real interest rates has led to regular headlines about a million home owners being "trapped" by their mortgaged property and suffering considerable financial difficulty including repossession of a depreciating asset. A new term, "negative equity", has entered the language. Since 1990 mortgage interest rates have exceeded that of inflation and swallowed up the debate about equity leakage.

Another aspect of the property-owning democracy emphasises its perceived social and political advantages, in particular the greater freedom from regulation and independence that property ownership is seen to provide. Home owners are seen by sociologists and politicians as forming a specific interest group. There has been considerable academic debate on whether home owners form a distinct social class based on their consumption of a commodity rather than their productive relationships, described by some authors as a consumption cleavage, (Saunders, 1990; Lowe, 1992) or whether tenure is merely a contingent factor (Forrest et al, 1990; Forrest and Murie, 1994).

At one level politicians consider the relationship between owning and voting, at another increasing home ownership has been at the heart of Conservative policy of transferring social responsibilities to the market. Their response to the crisis of legitimacy described in the preceeding chapter has been to limit welfare provision because of the demands that it raises. The expectation of social rights to housing puts pressure on governments to provide them. If the responsibility for provision is relocated in the market, the issues become ones between the individual consumers and individual suppliers, in the present case between mortgagors and mortgagees not between voters and government.[20] We will see in the subsequent sections the way in which the general social problems of the housing market are translated into individual rights of mortgagors and the tensions which

---

[19] *ibid.* p. 55.
[20] Doling and Ford, "The changing face of home ownership," *Policy and Politics* (1991) Vol. 19(2), p. 109.

result. However, the paradox is that the majority of the population are now individually affected by government economic policy through the housing market. "In so far as home ownership individualises the impact of government economic policy it may be that political implications are greater under home ownership than under council housing".[21]

While government confidently supported the development of owner-occupation as a wealth creating process and a way of shifting social responsibilities to the market, it has had greater difficulty dealing with the considerable annoyance of owners at the collapse of that ideal.

The perceived universal benefits of ownership were never available to specific groups such as those who were obliged to buy homes in many of the inner city areas (see Karn et al, 1985, Stewart, 1981). Now owner-occupation houses over two-thirds of the population and the segmentation in the market is far greater. It houses a wide variety of households with very different economic circumstances in very different types of dwellings.[22] Changes in the wider economy mean that many economically vulnerable households, some traditionally unaccustomed to the burdens of ownership, have produced a tension in the way that property owners are perceived by the legal system. It is worth stressing that at the time when the great nineteenth-century reforms were being mooted and instituted only 10 per cent of households were owner-occupied compared to the present 68 per cent. Property transactions form the backbone of the private legal system with a range of measures developed to facilitate the easy transfer necessary in an industrial market economy. Property law mediates this process on the assumption that there are two equal parties to the transaction who know what they are doing. The concept

---

[21] *ibid.* p. 117.

[22] For example, many council tenants who bought flats on long leaseholds are in considerable difficulty. They have been affected not only by the general drop in market value but also specifically by the policy of many building societies of not lending on these types of flats. They can also face the prospect of substantial costs for any repair undertaken to the block as a whole by the local authority. The 1995 government white paper recognising these difficulties proposes to introduce measures to enable local authorities to assist them and to encourage the growth of a "healthy local market for resale" DoE, *Our Future Homes. Opportunity, Choice, Responsibility: The Government's Housing Policies for England and Wales.* Cm 2901 (1995), p 14.

of a vulnerable occupier, which brings with it some sense of a need to protect against the excesses in the market, is not one that merges easily with a property-owning democracy with its connotations of self sufficiency, market forms of insurance against risk and release from the shackles of the state. The mismatch between legal form and application will appear in a number of ways in what follows.

This chapter considers three sets of relationships: the individual property relationships created in the world of mass purchase and ownership of property; the individual statutory relationships which not only provide some protection to mortgagors but also construct the different categories of lenders; and finally the overarching regulatory framework for owner-occupation in particular that of the building societies which dominate the structure of this sector. I will argue that the interactions between these different spheres are creating considerable tensions which lead to a reassessment of the power of the owner.

## Individual Property Relations

A. CHANGING HOUSEHOLDS INTERESTS.

The property law reforms which culminated in the 1925 Law of Property Act, as all first-year law students are taught, were designed to facilitate the alienation of property, to emphasise the exchange rather than the use value of the property, by reducing the number of legal interests which could exist in land. Co-ownership of land is still possible but now necessitates a trust for sale. This device enables the trustees to deal freely with the property as a commodity and satisfy the beneficial interests of others from the proceeds of sale. Purchasers need only be concerned that they pay the proceeds of any sale to two trustees. The emphasis is clearly on sale, the exchange value, yet it is this legal form which underpins contemporary home ownership.

As Cotterell states:

> "Property law in capitalist society has been concerned, above all, with identifying and protecting assets which are economically valuable as objects of commerce."[23]

---

[23] Cotterell, "The Law of Property and Legal Theory" in Twining's *Legal Theory and Common Law* (1986), p. 92.

25

There is a tendency, he argues, towards "the agglomeration in a single legal person of the exclusive right to possess, privilege to use, and power to convey the object of property".[24] The law has come to recognise an ever increasing number of assets as objects of property, but has a preference for making absolute rights in them. There are limitations to this process. The pressure to recognise entitlements as property rights leads in the other direction to the proliferation of limited property rights, such as to use and enjoy assets held by others, or in English law to fragmentation of the concept of property right.

> "But the circle of problems is completed . . . because any such rationalization and. entrenchment in doctrine of this diversity of property forms further prevents the clarity of property right which capitalist economic activity requires."[25]

The property law reforms of the early twentieth century show a tendency towards this agglomeration although the common law system displays a considerable flexibility to accommodate changing forms of wealth through its concept of fragmentation of ownership – many kinds of property held by different people in relation to a single material source of wealth. The conceptual developments in the law of property which have accompanied the growth in mass home ownership show both the strengths and limitations of the common law and illustrate the power relations which dominate this sector.

In the legal text books there is an owner who holds a specific legal interest in land, either a freehold or leasehold estate. If the owner has a mortgage, the estate is encumbered with a legal interest which usually takes the form of a charge by way of legal mortgage. The social and economic practice of home ownership followed this legal model for many years. Dwellings were bought by husbands who were the sole breadwinners to provide for homemaking wives who would not make a direct monetary contribution to the purchase of the home. Those involved in owner-occupation tended to be those with stable professional incomes.

Changed economic and social circumstances have transformed this picture. At least three trends can be discerned. First has been the

---

[24] *ibid.* p. 92.
[25] *ibid.* p. 93.

change in women's economic and social circumstances. Women now have direct access to money acquired through working which they can use as a contribution towards the purchase of the property. In many cases, the combined resources of both partners to a relationship are essential to enable the home to be bought at all. Joint legal ownership of the matrimonial home is now the norm rather than the exception. This change in women's economic position has also contributed to a re-evalution of the nature of marriage which is now seen more as an equal partnership. In practice, as the case law in this area demonstrates, this equality is often illusory.

Secondly, marriage might be a more egalitarian institution but it is far less stable. One in three marriages end in divorce. Subsequent remarriage is common. Many choose not to marry at all but to cohabit. Young people leave home and establish households either on their own or with other single people. Generally, living arrangements are more flexible and transitory than a generation ago. Mobility is greater: it is estimated that households move on average every seven years.

Thirdly, coupled with these social and economic changes in households, has been the spread of owner-occupation to lower income groups. These households are more vulnerable to unemployment and the general vagaries of the economy, although the effects of the recent recession has created widespread financial difficulties. Households can be very exposed to debt, with 90 per cent or even 100 per cent of the purchase price being met by mortgage. The income of a number of household members might be necessary in practice to meet the costs of purchase. This need for collective incomes to finance purchase is specifically recognised in the public sector right to buy provisions whereby up to three family members of the secure tenant are entitled to share in the purchase (Housing Act 1985, section 123).

These developments have placed severe pressures on the legal structure of home ownership. There are two interacting sets of relationships at the core of these changes. The first involves the relationships between the parties owning and occupying the property. Whose interests in the property are recognised and on what basis? The second involves the relationship between this often amorphous grouping and the interests of the financiers. The individuals involved in these arrangements have their own interests to protect against each other but they also have to establish their relationship with the financiers. As we shall see it has involved considerable adaptation of legal concepts to cover these rapidly changing contexts. I do not intend to provide a detailed account of the case law (what follows assumes some knowledge of the law in this area), rather I wish to show the interaction between doctrine and these relationships.[26] To make this task somewhat easier in the midst of complexity I will use five examples:

1. The property is owned legally by one person (A) who pays the mortgage and is the sole occupant.
2. The property has one legal owner but two people occupy the premises. The legal owner (B) pays the mortgage, the other occupier (C) does not make any "contribution" to the purchase of the property.
3. The property is owned legally by two people both of whom occupy the premises. One (D) pays the mortgage, the other (E) does not make any "contribution" to the purchase of the property.
4. The property is owned legally by two people both of whom occupy the premises. Both (F and G) contribute equally to the purchase of the premises.
5. The property is owned legally by one person but is occupied by two. The legal owner (H) pays the mortgage but the other (J) contributes towards the purchase of the premises.

There are an astonishing array of legal difficulties posed by these seemingly straightforward situations. The first is posed by the meaning and legal significance of occupation. Can living in a house confer rights? The answer varies: all the legal owners have a right to occupy. C will have an inherent common law right to occupy if she is a wife but not otherwise. This matrimonial right to occupy has been reinforced and extended by The Matrimonial Homes Act 1967

---

[26] Gray (1987) provides a good discussion of the law in this area: see in particular chaps. 10–13 and chaps. 22–26. The later edition (1993) while updating the material also narrows the discussion somewhat.

(now consolidated as the Matrimonial Homes Act 1983)[27] to cover both spouses. Otherwise, the non-married, non-owning occupiers in the examples will occupy as tenants or more likely in a "family" arrangement as licensees of the owner.

However, if the parties are not married then the right to occupy will depend also on the nature of their interest in the property. Here we have to enter the world of trusts both for sale and implied/ constructive. If there is more than one legal owner then automatically there will be a trust for sale: the legal owners act as trustees for the beneficial owners. In practice, if two people buy a house together they will be both trustees and beneficiaries. There can be an unequal split in the assets, with one entitled to more than the other. There will be a trust for sale in examples 3 and 4 although the beneficial shares might vary between them. The beneficial arrangements will depend on the nature of the agreement between the parties, essentially their intention at the outset as set out in a trust document. If there is no such trust document, then the initial common intention will have to be deduced from the available evidence including subsequent actions.

It is when we turn to example 5 that we start to see some of the difficulties. Can J claim any interest in the property, if so is this interest a property or a personal right? The claims by women and, to a lesser extent, other vulnerable adults based broadly on some concept of expectation raised by contributions of some sort have led to considerable stretching of the doctrines of property law. In particular the courts have developed the concepts of the implied and constructive trust and the doctrine of proprietary estoppel to deal with situations where expectations have been raised and are considered legitimate by a predominately male judiciary. The rules applying to these concepts often seem esoteric and confused. A trust whether implied or constructive is used where it is possible for the judges to deduce an initial common intention, which can be established by subsequent actions, to share the assets.

---

[27] The 1995 Family Homes and Domestic Violence Bill replaces the Matrimonial Homes Act 1985 and consolidates the legislation in this area. (See Gray 1993, pp. 153–165 for further discussion.)

The problem for many women has been to establish this intention through actions. Such intention can be evidenced by contributions to the acquisition of the property. There seems to be a continuum — the more the contribution resembles the type of activity carried out by men the more likely it is to be recognised. Thus direct contributions to the mortgage or the deposit are recognised. It has been argued successfully that the use of a woman's income to support the family so that the entire male income can be used for the mortgage is a recognisable contribution. The difficulty comes on the contribution of servicing. Devoting 30 years of your life to servicing and supporting a partner which allows him or her to sustain a career as well as maintaining the house on a day to day basis does not of itself constitute a contribution. Equally the more intimate the relationship between the parties the more difficult it is for the property lawyers to find the basis for a trust relationship.

Proprietary estoppel steps into the same area. As Gray says:

> "By identifying the circumstances in which certain claims may or may not be asserted in relation to titles in land, the doctrine has itself helped to reformulate the concept of a 'property right' — a consequence which of course has generated its own difficulties."[28]

The doctrine is not clearly defined but has been used and developed by judges grappling with very varied situations. Gray describes it thus:

> "If the owner . . . has expressly or impliedly given some assurance respecting present or future rights in his land, he cannot conscionably withdraw that assurance if the person to whom it was given has meanwhile relied upon it to his own detriment."[29]

The property lawyers try to distinguish between the application of the constructive trust and proprietary estoppel: some argue that the remedies available through proprietary estoppel are thought to offer less substantial property interests. In practice, they are argued in the alternative (see Gardner, 1991).

---

[28] Gray, *Elements of Land Law* (2nd ed., 1993), p. 312.
[29] *ibid.* p. 314.

This may seem a long way from the difficulties of example 5, but the "contributors" claim to a property interest will be based on these two concepts. The outcome will depend very much on the specific circumstances including the degree of intimacy between the parties, the nature of the contribution and the interpretation that the particular judge will put on the circumstances surrounding the case. The general point to be made is that with the changing social and economic circumstances the courts are attempting to adapt concepts which allow for the development of new property rights. The degree to which these are recognised seems to depend on the relative power of the parties involved in the situation and relies very considerably on the exercise of judicial discretion.

The case of *Burrows and Burrows v. Sharp* (1991) 23 H.L.R. 82 illustrates these developments very clearly. The appellant, Mrs Sharp was a 77 year old widow who had lived in her two bedroomed council house in Bromley since 1931. She lived with the youngest of her ten children, Gillian Sharp (46) who was physically disabled. Mrs Sharp obtained housing benefit to pay the rent. Mrs Burrows was Mrs Sharp's granddaughter. She lived with her husband and two children in another council property. In 1985 Bromley Council told Mrs Sharp that she could buy the house, which was valued at £38,500, with a 60 per cent discount. The price to be found therefore was £15,400. A deal was struck between Mrs Sharp and the Burrows. Mrs Sharp would exercise her right to buy, the purchase would be financed by a mortgage guaranteed and paid off by the Burrows who would inherit the house on condition that they would look after Gillian for the rest of her life. The Burrows could not afford the mortgage and endowment repayments and their own rent so they decided to give up their own flat and move into the house with the Sharps. They would then obtain a mortgage to finance an extension to the property. Solicitors drew up a will for Mrs Sharp leaving the property to the Burrows on condition that they look after Gillian. A trust deed was executed. This proved not to reflect the intentions of the parties because it assumed a bare trustee holding property as nominee for an absolute beneficial owner and who bound to transfer the property on demand. In other words it assumed that the Burrows were entitled immediately to the entire interest in the property. The Burrows sub-let their flat to a friend illegally so that

31

they ceased to be secure tenants under the 1985 Housing Act even if they could subsequently recover possession from the sub-tenants. Almost inevitably the arrangement, which involved four generations attempting to live in a two bedroomed house, broke down almost immediately. Great acrimony ensued which meant that Mrs Sharp and her daughter were obliged to spend their days away from the house. The Burrows wanted the property vested in them absolutely in line with the trust deed but not the intention of the parties. No settlement proved possible. How was this mess over the interests of four generations living in a very small council house to be resolved? The Court of Appeal tackled the problem as follows. First, they considered it unconscionable for Mrs Sharp to evict the Burrows and deny them succession to the property and yet hold on to the benefit which would accrue from the mortgage and from their financial support towards the cost of the purchase. An equity had arisen out of their expectations which would have to be satisfied. The question was how. Should the Burrows be given the right to live in and subsequently own the property? The court thought this unworkable. Should the Burrows move out but continue to pay the mortgage? This was also thought unworkable because it involved the assumption that they would look after Gillian but, was no longer tenable. The court decided to order a refund of the Burrows expenditure. What did this amount to, given that they had lost their secure status and lost the expectation of owning the property? The court took a "robust" view of these losses. It ordered the Burrows to leave once they had been released from the endowment mortgage arrangements, that the trust deed be set aside and Mrs Sharp be required to repay to the Burrows the expenditure they had incurred.

Doctrinally the Court of Appeal made no distinction between the equity raised by proprietary estoppel and a constructive trust. It exercised very considerable discretion to try to achieve a workable solution to the difficulties caused by this very ordinary transaction between a group of people with very minimal financial resources. That it required the Court of Appeal to sort out reflects the difficulties encountered in dealing with competing claims to property interests among non-traditional groups. The irony of this saga is that the cost of the legal proceedings would fall as a statutory charge on the property because both parties obtained full legal aid. As Dillon

L.J. pointed out whatever the outcome of the appeal both parties will be the losers. Mrs Sharp had lived securely in her property for sixty years, Gillian Sharp would have succeeded to the tenancy on her death, the Burrows had a secure tenancy of a flat. All three interest groups had access to modest but secure use values. One can only assume that the exchange value created by the right to buy at a discount provided the incentive to join the property-owning democracy.

So far we have only considered the relationships between the various parties wishing to establish an interest in property. We turn now to a consideration of the relationship between these interest seekers and their financiers. To what extent are the rights to occupy and to have some form of interest in the property personal, and to what extent are they defensible against third parties in particular the mortgagee of the property? How powerful are they?

In order to discuss these issues we need to return to the five examples set out above. Financiers need have no anxieties about the first case. If A cannot repay the mortgage, the mortgagee will be able to repossess the property unhindered by any other claims to the proceeds which might take priority. In case two the presumption is that there is no co-ownership (one legal owner, two occupants, no contribution by the non-owner) and therefore, no trust for sale. The question is whether there are any occupational rights which can be protected in priority to the mortgagee. This will depend on the status of the occupants, if the non-owner is a spouse then she will be able to register a statutory right to occupy under the Matrimonial Homes Act 1983 and any dealings with the property will be subject to her interest. However, this right is often totally illusory: it requires a hostile act of registration against the title held by the other party and it requires knowledge of the existence of the right. If the occupants are not married then there is no protection against the rights of the mortgagee. Cases 3 and 4, where there is co-ownership of the legal title, requires the mortgagee to deal with both parties and to pay any proceeds of repossession to them as trustees. Distribution of these proceeds will depend on the equitable shares in each case.

The problem comes once again with case 5 which technically can be described as undisclosed equitable co-ownership on the assumption that J has an equitable interest resulting from her contributions.

33

What happens if H decides to mortgage or indeed sell the property with or without her knowledge? Will she be evicted because the purchaser or the mortgagee, if there is a failure to repay, have a greater or prior claim? The answer to these questions provide an interesting account of the courts attitude to women, particularly those who are wives, and to the relative claims of institutional financiers and vulnerable individuals. The issue can also be seen to an extent as a tension between "private" occupational rights and "public" commercial transactions. It would be impossible here to provide a comprehensive account of the complex legal issues which have arisen in this area in the last fifteen years and I refer the reader to accounts in the standard texts (Gray, 1993).

A single trustee for sale such as H in our example can legally sell or mortgage the property although the 1925 legislation was designed to prevent such a situation arising.

> "As Murray J. said in *Northern Bank Ltd v. Beattie* [1982] 18 NIJB, p 1, the phrase 'the eternal triangle' has nowadays taken on a new meaning for the judge in the Chancery Division. A typical dispute involves 'a husband-mortgagor of his matrimonial home' a bank mortgagee of that home, and an estranged wife still living in the home."[30]

Broadly speaking the interests of wives were not recognised until the 1970s. Where the title to the property was unregistered, priority between a wife and a mortgagee depended on the equitable doctrine of notice: the mortgagee of a single trustee for sale took free of the wife's equitable interest unless the mortgagee had actual or constructive notice of the interest. The mortgagee was not deemed to have notice of the interests of a wife through her joint occupation of the family home (*Caunce v. Caunce* [1969] 1 W.L.R. 286).

In registered land areas the wife's interest did not take priority because her interest was not overriding by reason of section 70(1)(g) of the Land Registration Act 1925 which concerns "the rights of a person in actual occupation". Essentially the presumption was that wives occupied houses through their husbands and therefore their presence did not bother the mortgagee.

The recognition of these rights to occupy in conjunction with an equitable interest came with the House of Lords judgement in

---

[30] Gray, *Elements of Land Law* (2nd ed., 1993), p. 559, fn. 10.

*Williams & Glyn's Bank Ltd v. Boland* [1980] 2 All E.R. 408. A sole trustee husband had subsequently mortgaged the property to the bank as security for his business loan. The wife had contributed to the purchase of the property but had no knowledge of the mortgage transaction. The Bank had made no inquiries about the wife's interest. The case concerned registered land and therefore the issue concerned whether the wife was in actual occupation of the land. If so, she had an overriding interest which took priority over the bank's charge. The House of Lords decided that she did have such an interest and, therefore, the bank was unable to exercise the mortgagee's right to recover possession of the property to recover its security.

This decision has been heralded as the triumph of social justice over commercial interests. Family security was considered more important. Women's changed position within households was recognised. Lord Wilberforce considered that it was quite appropriate to depart from "an easy-going practice of dispensing with enquiries as to occupation beyond that of the vendor and accepting the risks of doing so" [1980] 2 All E.R. 408 at p. 415. He recognised that this obligation was the consequence of the widespread development of shared interests in ownership. The decision affected the entire class of beneficial co-owners, not only wives, who could be described as being in actual occupation of land and understandably it was not a popular decision with either financiers or conveyancers. It raised questions about how far the obligation to make inquiries extended? It would seem to cover co-habitees, adult relatives and what are described as "unorthodox" domestic relationships such as gay couples or platonic relationships. Also, what constitutes occupation? Social habits have changed, making it impossible to assume a standard constant sharing of one living space particularly in an era of high job mobility and fragmented domestic arrangements.

Building Society practice soon adapted to deal with some of these issues. Mortgagors are required to declare all occupants living in the premises on their application forms. Wherever appropriate societies require mortgages to be taken out in joint names; elsewhere they ask other occupants to consent to the mortgagee taking priority, leading in part to the development of the law in relation to undue influence. Nonetheless, the courts seemed to retreat from this high ground of

35

individual justice. This retreat takes a number of forms. First, is the general implication that this advantage will be exploited by women who will collude with indebted husbands to foil the financiers.

> "It remains exceedingly questionable whether the wives in *Boland* should have been allowed to enjoy the prospects of their husbands' business prosperity, while retaining an immunity from the shared misfortune of their adversity".[31]

One might add perhaps that the wives might have been able to decide whether they wished their home to form part of the adversity if they had been party to the decision.

Secondly, there is general concern for the position of the financiers and various attempts to safeguard their position. The Law Commission argue that "it is not satisfactory in principle that the present state of the law . . . should expose lenders, whether institutional or not, to additional financial risks".[32] While these risks represent a constraint on the commercial exchange value of the property, one might argue that they give priority to the use value of the home in an era of homelessness. It is also somewhat difficult to picture the plight of massive institutional lenders with surpluses or, in the case of banks, profits running into billions of pounds when seen in comparison to a woman left in the home to pay off a mortgage about which she had no idea, often dependent on limited income or state welfare.

Finally the House of Lords in *City of London Building Society v. Fregg* firmly resisted an extension of the *Boland* approach to protect the equitable interests of occupiers where a mortgage transaction had been executed by two trustees for sale. Instead the courts have started to whittle away at the consequences of the *Boland* decision. Some decisions have tended to tackle technicalities in the law but have had the effect of restricting its application. *Abbey National Building Society v. Cann* in which the House of Lords established that there was no scintilla temporis between the completion of the purchase and the mortgage of a property if they were transacted contemporaneously. A purchaser who relies on a building society or bank loan never acquires anything but an equity of redemption. There is, therefore,

---

[31] Gray, *Elements of Land Law* (1st ed., 1987), p. 850.

[32] Law Commission, *Transfer of Land—Land Mortgages* (1991), Report No. 204, para. 64.

no possibility of an equitable interest coming into existence in this moment.

Two others ways can be detected. In the face of the full frontal attack on the existence of the claimed equitable entitlement[33] the judges seemed to have taken a very restrictive approach to the question of recognition. Without an interest, there is no question of priority.

It is precisely in circumstances of women's contribution to the purchase of the property that the courts have developed rules which make any interest very hard to establish as we have seen before. The leading case is *Gissing v. Gissing* [1971] A.C. 886 which insisted on a strict test of "referability" for the contribution made by the woman. The contributions had to be clearly referable to the common intention which the parties had at the outset over the distribution of the assets. In practice couples do not sit down and construct a common intention which they act on clearly and precisely over 30 years of partnership. More importantly women who are the losers in this situation are often reluctant to negotiate these matters in a context where they have less access to financial resources. While there have been indications that a more liberal interpretation might emerge (*Grant v. Edwards* [1986] Ch. 638) *Lloyds Bank Plc v. Rossett* [1990] 2 W.L.R. 867 once again establishes a hard line (see Gardner, 1991).

The other way that the courts have readjusted the balance in favour of the financiers is through the concept of estoppel. Its use can be seen in the case of *Equity and Law Home Loans Ltd v. Prestidge and another* [1992] 1 All E.R. 909. Mrs Brown sold her former council house for a net sum of £10,340. The man with whom she cohabited purchased a new house costing £39,950. Mrs Brown contributed around £10,000 from the proceeds of her sale. The rest was raised by a mortgage of £30,000 from the Britannia Building Society. The house was conveyed into the sole name of Mr Prestidge (P) who was also the sole mortgagor. Mrs Brown had been advised by her solicitor that the building society would be unwilling to lend to her as she had an outstanding county court judgment. Mrs Brown was not happy with this arrangement but concurred in order to achieve the

---

[33] Gray, *Elements of Land Law* (2nd ed., 1993), p. 576.

purchase. The suggestion was that the house would eventually be transferred into joint names but this did not happen. Subsequently, P remortgaged the property with the plaintiffs for £42,835. This was used to redeem the Britannia mortgage but the rest was pocketed by P. Mrs Brown only found out about the remortgage later, shortly before P left having paid no repayments. The arrears due on the instalments were such that Mrs Brown, now living on social security, was not able to take over the mortgage. The plaintiffs sought possession of the property. Mrs Brown argued that she had a beneficial interest in the house, not disputed by P, and that her interest could not be incumbered by a mortgage about which she knew nothing.

What had the plaintiffs done to establish whether there were any equitable interests in this property in the post-*Boland* world? They had asked P to confirm whether there was any other person residing in the property. He had replied that the only other person was Mrs Brown "who is my common law wife". He had repeated this information in a subsequent form. When asked whether Mrs B had executed a Deed of Consent to the mortgage he replied "no but will". Based on this information the plaintiffs made the offer.

Relying on the judgment in *Boland* one would be tempted to think that the plaintiffs would take second place to Mrs B. However, there is a difference in circumstances. Mrs B agreed to the first mortgage. The courts have been very reluctant to allow a beneficial co-owner to remain silent about their rights at the time when a transaction with a third party takes place and then assert them later as having priority over the third party. *Bristol and West Building Society v. Henning* [1985] 1 W.L.R. 778 considered this unconscionable and Mrs Henning was estopped from claiming priority for her interest.

It has been argued that wilful non disclosure of the interest leaves the owner of the interest open to the charge of coming to the court with hands that are not clean, the phraseology of Murray J. in *Ulster Bank Ltd v. Shanks* [1982] N.I. 143. The question for the Court of Appeal in this case, given the *Henning* judgment, was did the remortgage make a difference? The answer was yes and no. The Court followed *Henning* in establishing that this house could not have been bought without the first mortgage and consequently it could not have been bought without the remortgage. Therefore, Mrs

Brown would have consented to this transaction if she had been consulted. She cannot take priority simply because of the remortgage. But only £30,000 was necessary to purchase the house. The Court of Appeal agreed with the lower court that the plaintiffs should be entitled to enforce their security only to such extent as would represent an advance of £30,000 plus interest. Unlike *Boland*, possession was granted but Mrs Brown could receive some of the proceeds once the mortgagor's interest and costs had been satisfied.

This case illustrates some general points. The first is the appallingly poor advice available to people involved with property claims but with limited means. (This was equally obvious in the *Sharp* case.) The second is the mismatch between behaviour and the doctrine as evolved through the courts. In what sense did Mrs Brown wilfully not disclose her equitable interest? Mustill L.J. was "quite unable to see how Equity and Law could be regarded as owing her any duty of care which could alter the consequences of her initial imputed consent to the incumbering of the property" (1992: 916c). Why is she the one with unclean hands, such a vivid phrase, compared to the financiers who by any standard were alerted to the potential for difficulty here? Thirdly, the case although illustrative of the general issues in this area is doctrinally uncertain relying for its authority on the Henning case but extending it to a remortgage arrangement and ignoring other authorities which would have allowed the court to come to a different decision (see Lunney, 1993). Finally, it illustrates once again the allure of the asset value of the property. This house within six months was worth £12,800 more, a sum which P managed to withdraw without any problems at all.

This "eternal triangle" of wives, husbands and creditors has also generated much controversy in another area of law associated with mortgaging the family home. We have seen in an earlier section the increasing use of the family home as security for loans to small businesses and we have also seen the impact of the recession in the late eighties. We have also noted the increasing trend for spouses to hold jointly the legal title to the family home. Where this is not the case after the *Boland* case, a wife will be required to sign a consent form for any mortgage arrangement. This combination of factors results in situations where a wife, under pressure or misunderstanding caused by her husband, signs a charge over the family home in order to secure a loan to a business which, although conducted by the husband, often provides the family income (Fehlberg, 1994). The consequences of this action has led to a very substantial volume of litigation in which wives have attempted to avoid liability on the grounds of undue influence and misrepresentation. There have been 13 Court of Appeal and two House of Lords decisions in the last nine years[34] in which the courts have considered the uneasy balance between "private" spousal relationships and "public" third party security transactions (Fehlberg, 1994).

Gray points to a similar shift in the courts to that seen earlier:

> "During the mid-1970s the English courts developed a broad approach which placed a heavy reliance on the fashionably continental concept of 'abuse of a dominant position' in the context of an 'inequality of bargaining power' between the parties. During the 1980s the balance of judicial concern moved significantly away from solicitude on behalf of borrowers, only to threaten to return during the 1990s towards a more protectionist stance."[35]

The gradual recognition of fragmented interests in property brought about by the changed social and economic circumstances of owner-occupation has created tensions within the law. The attempt to satisfy both increased occupational rights and beneficial interests has led to the development of discretionary powers exercisable by the courts. To some extent this has led to the potential for readjusting power relationships between the various members of households. This fragmentation has caused considerable confusion doctrinally as to what constitutes a property right and has raised alarm within the commercial sector. It is perhaps not surprising that these emerging entitlements have not proved to be very substantial when matched against the interests of financiers.

---

[34] The House of Lords judgements are *Barclays Bank plc v. O'Brien* [1993] 4 All E.R. 417 and *CIBC Mortgages plc v. Pitt* [1993] 4 All E.R. 433. See Gray, 1993: 968–973 and Fehlberg, B. "The husband, the wife, the bank and her signature", *Modern Law Review*, Vol. 3, pp. 467–475. 1994 for discussion of the law in relation to undue influence and misrepresentation.

[35] Gray, *Elements of Land Law* (2nd ed., 1993), p. 968.

B. EVOLUTION OF THE MORTGAGE RELATIONSHIPS.

In this section I wish to look more specifically at the evolution of the mortgage relationship. The vast majority of purchasers obtain their finance from building societies. They accounted for 60 per cent of total outstanding mortgages at the end of 1990, the banks 29 per cent and the centralised lenders, 7.7 per cent.[36]

Thousands of transactions each year between individual mortgagors and institutional mortgagees are based on the legal form of the mortgage. (There are presently almost 10 million "domestic" mortgagors). Yet the form of the mortgage is based on the social and economic circumstances of the eighteenth century when there was no mass market in homes. It evolved at a time when the shining principles of freedom of contract and the sanctity of property were in the ascendency.

In the twentieth century, the huge increase in the use of the mortgage has had negligible impact on the law. This might be considered surprising given the development of property concepts described in the last section. There could be a number of explanations for this seeming inactivity. On the one hand, it could be that the principles and form of the mortgage provide an adequate foundation. On the other, it could be that there is a legislative framework which relegates the importance of the mortgage agreement. Neither offers the answer. Rather it is that the relationships between the parties to the mortgage have not been regulated legally but administratively by the institutional lenders. The mortgagor's position and potential for protection has been far more related to the nature of the lender than it has been to the contract of mortgage. However, because of the changing relationships of the financiers, in particular the exposure of the building societies to market forces, the basis of the relationship is crumbling and leaving mortgagors exposed to the vagaries of the mortgage form and very limited, piecemeal statutory protection.

This section will consider the history of the law of mortgages and its application to the contemporary context before moving, in the

---

[36] Pryke and Whiteheads, "An Overview of Mortgage-Backed Securitisation in the UK", *Housing Studies* (1994), Vol. 9, No. 1, p. 77.

next section, to consider the statutory interventions which have constructed the mortgagor's relationship to particular lenders.

Mortgage law is very much a product of equity. In the seventeenth century, a legal mortgage of freehold land was created by the conveyance of the fee simple estate to the mortgagee with a covenant for re-conveyance on redemption of the mortgage. A legal mortgage of leasehold land involved the assignment of the residue of the mortgagor's term of years to the mortgagee with the proviso that it would be reassigned on repayment of the loan. The mortgagee's security was the legal title. If the mortgagor did not pay the capital sum on the date specified for repayment, the mortgagee kept the property. Over the next two centuries the Court of Chancery whittled away at the common law form of the mortgage in order to make it a security instrument not one of appropriation. The Court enabled the mortgagor to redeem the mortgage on repayment at any time even after the date fixed. The rights of the mortgagor during the period until repayment came to be known as the equity of redemption. While in law the mortgagee appeared to own the property, equity regarded the mortgagor as an owner whose title was subject to a mortgage. The mortgagor's "equity" came to be seen as constituting a proprietary interest in the land which could itself be bought, sold and mortgaged (Gray, 1993).

Historically, this equitable intervention has been seen as an attempt by the courts to prevent exploitation of the mortgagor by the mortgagee, the assumption being that "necessitous men are not, truly speaking, free men, but, to answer a present exigency, will submit to any terms that the crafty may impose upon them." (Lord Henley L.C. in *Vernon v. Bethell* (1792) 2 Eden 110). The judges were keen to find these oppressive and unconscionable terms in a world where usury was officially outlawed. The balance of legal protection tended to be in favour of the borrower, quite contrary to the legal form. These developments cannot be divorced from their social and economic circumstances. The borrowers were landowners, in need of cash at a time when they could not use their land as capital. Essentially the courts were protecting landowners against the moneylenders. Equity developed the doctrine that no "clogs or fetters" should be imposed on the exercise of the equity of redemption. Thus any condition which tended to impede the possibility of redeeming the property unincumbered by any collateral obligation could be struck out of the contract.

But as the legal historians have demonstrated the rise of capitalism and its flowering needed an appropriate legal system, one in which commercial principles dominated (Atiyah, 1979; Stevens, 1978). Equitable principles designed to protect landed estates fitted uncomfortably with the laissez-faire principles of freedom of contract and *caveat emptor*. The equitable approach to mortgages seemed to be immune to these developments. With the merging of the common law and equitable jurisdictions as a result of the 1880s Judicature Acts, the tensions became obvious in the cases considered by the House of Lords. The Edwardian law lords through "the most elegant judicial legislation" attempted to balance the:

> "old equitable doctrine, which allowed no "clogs" on the equity of redemption in mortgages, and the need to allow modern companies to transact their businesses by raising money through the new form of floating charge, the debenture."[37]


CONTEMPORARY MORTGAGE RELATIONSHIPS.

In this section I intend to discuss the contemporary mortgage context by concentrating on the individual mortgagor's relationship with the mortgagee building society. While the Law of Property Act 1925 introduced general reforms to this legal relationship, more recent statutory intervention has been concerned primarily with occupancy rights. The latter will be discussed in a subsequent section where I will also consider mortgage relationships with lenders other than building societies.

What sort of relationship is created between the home buyer and the building society during the purchase? The dominant approach is administrative: a standard mortgage application form will be filled in which the buyer or buyers provide details of earnings and liabilities. The building society will probably offer the buyer the possibility of

---

[37] Stevens, *Law and Politics: The House of Lords as a Judicial Body 1800–1976* (1978), pp. 146–147.

either an endowment or an instalment mortgage. There has been a very considerable growth of endowment mortgages from the mid eighties: a rise from 56 per cent of all mortgages to 75 per cent in 1990. Repayment mortgages have fallen from 42 per cent to 20 per cent of the market over the same period (Ford and Bull, 1992). It is also possible that a mortgagor will be offered one of a number of mortgage arrangements which are designed to reduce costs over the initial period of the mortgage. These take the form of a reduced interest rate for an initial period. A mortgagor might also be offered a fixed interest rate for a period.

There has been considerable unease at the lending practices of building societies in the late eighties including their enthusiasm for endowment mortgages which provide for the repayment of the capital sum through an insurance policy. While interest is payable on the outstanding loan, the insurance premiums are designed to cover the capital sum to be repaid at the end of the mortgage term. Some policies offer the possibility of an additional capital sum at redemption. They also provide building societies with a commission, unlike the instalment form. The suspicion is that societies are motivated not only by the interests of the home buyer but also by the commission which they obtain from the insurance company. There is little evidence that societies offer a comprehensive assessment of the disadvantages as well as the advantages which include the possibility that the insured sum will be insufficient to cover the outstanding debt. In the difficult economic context of the early nineties this once remote possibility has become a reality for some.[38] In any case, it is by no means always the case that the endowment form offers the best arrangement financially for all home buyers, particularly if the mortgagor experiences financial difficulties with repayment.[39]

I will use as an example the form used for a repayment mortgage by one of the largest societies. The mortgagor might be surprised to find that the "total debt becomes due on the payment day" which is defined in the covering standard terms as the first Monday of the month starting in the month next after the date of the charge. The mortgagor might wonder why s/he has to pay many thousands of

[38] Scott, "Endowments take another bonus hit", *The Observer*, December 11, 1994, p. 16.

[39] Ford and Bull, *Mortgage Arrears: Services to Borrowers in Debt* (1992), p. 22.

pounds back shortly after arranging to pay in instalments over the next 25 years but this form accommodates the legal arrangement necessary to bring the equity of redemption into action. The key terms of the mortgage as far as the mortgagor is concerned are contained in the incorporated provisions and rules (Building Societies Act 1986, s. 10(1)). The mortgagor is also liable to insure the property. In practice, the society usually arranges this with their own favoured insurer. Because of the possibility of restrictive practice the mortgagor is usually offered a choice and can, if s/he insists, use an alternative as long as the society approves.

When a borrower requires a mortgage for over 75 per cent of the value of the property, the lender will usually require that an indemnity insurance policy be taken out (Council of Mortgage Lenders, 1992). This involves a one-off payment by the borrower when the mortgage is entered into. There have been considerable difficulties with these policies over recent years. The key problem is that borrowers are not always aware that the policy insures the lender not the borrower against any potential loss. Borrowers cannot take out such cover as insurance companies will only deal with lenders on a bulk purchase basis.[40] The insurer is entitled to attempt to recover any sum used to reimburse the lender from the borrower. Until recently, insurance companies have not often used this remedy but the increase in claims has led to a change in policy (Birch, 1994).[41] The lack of awareness of the implications of these policies is surprising given that the Building Societies Act 1986 requires the borrower to be informed at the outset that s/he is liable for any shortfall should the property be repossessed and that the lender is insuring against this possibility. The Council of Mortgage Lender's statement of practice in relation to mortgage arrears first issued in 1991 also requires the lender to make the borrower aware of the nature of this policy (Council of Mortgage Lenders, 1992).

The mortgagor agrees "not to create any tenancy or lease or part with or share occupation or possession of the property or any part of it". This term is frequently breached with dire consequences for the

---

[40] NACAB, *Dispossessed: Citizens Advice Bureau evidence on mortgage arrears and repossessions* (1993), p. 39.
[41] *ibid.* p. 39.

unsuspecting tenant faced with possession proceedings initiated by the mortgagee (Council of Mortgage Lenders, 1992).

The mortgagor also agrees "not without the written consent of the Society to make any disposition of the property". Section 91(2) of the Law of Property Act 1925 gives the court power to order the sale of a mortgaged property, but until recently the court has only exercised this power when the mortgagee consents to the sale.

Under another term of the mortgage agreement the mortgagor agrees to repay the accumulated interest, however calculated, and the capital outstanding in regular instalments. Interest payments are satisfied first, so in the early years a very high proportion of the monthly instalment will consists of interest. If "on realisation of its security by the Society the net proceeds shall be insufficient to discharge the Total Debt the Borrower will immediately pay the amount of the deficiency with interest until payment." In other words there is a personal covenant to repay any outstanding debt. One month's default on repayment renders the whole sum due. Thus the borrower is immediately responsible for the whole sum as soon as one repayment is missed. It also activates the mortgagee's right to possession. The mortgagee's entitlement to possession of the mortgaged property is not dependent on the default of the mortgagor and arises at the outset of the mortgage even before the fixed date for redemption. However, usual building society practice is to grant possession to the mortgagor until default occurs. We will return to a discussion of possession proceedings in the next section.

These terms are to be expected in a security document which allows a mortgagor a very long term, often 25 years, in which to repay the loan. Noticeably absent from the document is any reference to the mortgagor's rights although the mortgagee's rights are set out in some detail. There is no reference to the statutory rights in relation to possession proceedings or the duties of the mortgagee if it exercises the power of sale. There is no information or advice on any procedure for dealing with difficulty over repayment, although there is now a code of good practice issued by the Building Societies Association and Council of Mortgage Lenders on this matter (BSA/ CML, 1994). In other words this is a contract on the mortgagee's standard terms which is reminiscent of local authority's one-sided tenancies of the sixties (see chapter 4 for further discussion).

46

This document contains another very significant term. "The Society may from time to time when its Board of Directors considers it necessary or advisable increase or reduce the Interest Rate." In order to increase the rate the society must give notice in writing to the borrower at the last-known address. The increase operates from the first day of the next month after the month in which the notice is given. Thus the borrower agrees to any interest rate which the society might charge over a potential 25 year period. What other commercial contract would give one party such an advantage? It raises the question of uncertainty although:

"A legal argument based on uncertainty has, however, been dismissed in the context of unilaterally variable interest rates in a debenture (*ANZ Banking Group (NZ) Ltd v. Gibson* 1981: 525)".[42]

Is such an unqualified power "harsh and unconscionable" under the general equitable jurisdiction? There has to date been no successful legal challenge to the right of mortgagees to adjust interest rates at their discretion. The writers of the standard reference book on building society law have tended to think until recently that it was open to doubt whether such a power was legally valid particularly if the mortgagee were an individual.[43] However, with this unlimited unilateral power forming the basis of modern institutional lending practice they now suggest that there is little likelihood of a successful challenge.[44]

One justification for this acceptance of the variable interest rate mortgage lies in the financial structure of building societies which borrow short and lend long in a context where they obtain the bulk of their assets from the retail saving sector. Long-term fixed-rate mortgages would expose them to potential liquidity problems. The other reason for acceptance of this mortgagor vulnerability is drawn again from the nature of the mortgagee. Building societies have enjoyed a very special place within the financial markets. Their history as mutual friendly societies concentrating on the provision of finance almost exclusively for the purchase of residential property has

---

[42] Gray, *Elements of Land Law* (2nd ed., 1993), p. 959, fn. 15.
[43] Wurtzburg and Mills, *Building Society Law* (14th ed., 1976), p. 166.
[44] Gray, *op. cit.*, p. 959; Wurtzburg and Mills, *Building Society Law* (15th ed., 1989).

created a reputation for socially responsible practices. Their interest rates, although variable, have reflected and been legitimised by government policy. The social and economic position of building societies has protected mortgagors from exploitation. Deregulation of the financial markets and the severe recession in the economy and the housing market have put significant strains on this relationship as we shall see shortly.

The borrower is given one legal and usually one administrative way of dealing with an unwanted increase in the interest rate. First, the contract allows the borrower to redeem the mortgage within three months of notification with no penalty for early redemption. Secondly, societies, wherever possible, offer some arrangement to ameliorate the increase such as lengthening the term of the loan.

Is it possible for building societies to protect further their security against inflationary pressures and recover their outlay in real terms? In the 1970s interest rates on mortgages were negative in real terms because the rate of inflation was higher than the rate of interest charged to mortgagors. This was made possible by the societies' sheltered market position but also because the same inflation was producing rapid increases in house prices so that the security was rarely jeopardised. The economics of the eighties produced a different situation. The interest rates now charged were very real with inflation at say 5 per cent and interest rates at 11 per cent.

The validity of index-linked building society mortgages did not arise, however, until 1983. The ground had been prepared by *Multiservice Bookbinding Ltd v. Marden* [1979] Ch. 84 which had established that index-linking capital and interest payments was neither contrary to public policy nor necessarily harsh or unconscionable. The case had involved two independently advised companies, who had agreed to what turned out to be a very bad deal for the mortgagor: indexing the pound to the Swiss franc. It might have been an unreasonable term but it was not one which would trigger equitable relief. In any case the loan related to commercial premises which had trebled in value during the loan period. The Nationwide then tested the legality of index-linking for building societies and won in *Nationwide Building Society v. Registry of Friendly Societies* [1983] 1 W.L.R. 1226. So in theory a building society could insist on a variable interest rate and index-link the loan to offset any potential loss. In practice, the use of index-linking would undermine the basic tenet of the property-owning democracy of the asset value of the home.

In summary, the standard building society mortgage agreement constructs a relationship in which the mortgagor is potentially at a severe legal disadvantage. Legally, the building societies seem to be at liberty to act with great freedom (subject to the terms of the Law of Property Act 1925). There has been very little consideration by the courts of this arrangement because the relationship between the mortgagor and the building society is a product of the position which the societies have held in the wider financial world. Commercialism and sanctity of contractual rights won in the key case of *G. and C. Kreglinger v. New Patagonia Meat and Cold Storage Company* [1914] A.C. 25. Lord Parker of Waddington declared that:

> "there is now no rule in equity which precludes a mortgagee . . . from stipulating for any collateral advantage, provided such collateral advantage is not either (1) unfair and unconscionable, or (2) in the nature of a penalty clogging the equity of redemption, or (3) inconsistent with or repugnant to the contractual and equitable right to redeem." (1914: 61).

It is possible to argue that the social and economic circumstances which had given rise to the flowering of the equitable doctrine had changed. The landed estates by this time were now able to raise money through sale and in any case there had been considerable fusion between industrial and landed capital which made special treatment for the latter less pressing. Stevens sees the development of the common law during this period in terms of the different traditions of the judges:

> "Had the ascendancy of the law lords trained in the old school of Equity been maintained, it is arguable that much of the formalistic and legalistic tone of the later part of the [Victorian] period might not have developed. Slowly, however, during the 1880s, the influence of the common lawyers grew and . . . the reliance on widely stated equitable principles diminished."[45]

So the flexible and interventionist approach to the mortgagor's position came to an end, never to be regained. The legal assumption

---

[45] Stevens, *Law and Politics: The House of Lords as a Judicial Body 1800–1976* (1978), pp. 138–139.

now was that this was a commercial transaction negotiated between knowledgeable and equal parties on the terms which should be enforced. Meanwhile, the building societies were evolving through the growth of the permanent rather than terminating variety. Despite the collapse of the Liberator and the Birkbeck in 1892 and 1911 respectively there were 1723 societies in 1910 with total assets of £76 million, lending £25 million per year. Institutionally, they were preparing to fund the development of home ownership through the mortgage at the same time as the courts were ceasing to exercise flexibility in the area. The 1874 Building Societies Act provided the legal framework within which they were broadly to operate until 1986.

The 1925 property reforms recast the form of the mortgage to better reflect reality. The mortgagee now obtains an interest in the property which secures the loan while the mortgagor retains ownership.[46] However, the equitable construct still remains. The mortgagor's rights in the mortgaged property are known as the equity of redemption. The redundant contractual date of redemption remains but is fixed at a date very soon after the commencement of the mortgage. Thereafter, the equitable right to redeem takes over.

The need for radical reform of the law of mortgages to meet contemporary needs has been recognised by the Law Commission in its report in 1991. They argue that the artificiality and complexity of the law impedes understanding, making "it difficult to ensure that the parties to a mortgage fully understand their rights and obligations and the consequences of default in repayments".[47] The complexity also has impeded the development of standardised mortgage documents which would be more easily intelligible to the parties. The effects of the archaic law on mortgages when coupled with the substantial inequality in bargaining power between the institutional lenders and the individual home owner will be seen in the next section.

---

[46] The methods for the creation of a legal mortgage of freehold land are set out in section 85(1) of the Law of Property Act 1925, for leasehold land in section 86(1). There are two ways: by demise (or in the case of leasehold land a sub-demise) for a term of years absolute, subject to a provision for cesser on redemption, or by a charge by deed expressed to be by way of legal mortgage. The latter method is by far the most common.

[47] Law Commission, *Transfer of Land—Land Mortgages* (1991), Report No. 204, p. 3.

The societies are very dependent on their public image of social responsibility and, until recently, they have been able to avoid unwanted exposure in the courts. However, the consequences of these agreements, particularly the power to levy variable interest rates, are now reaching the courts although as the societies join other lenders in exercising the mortgagees right to possess and to sell the judges are overseeing repossessions not scrutinising agreements. The relationship between the mortgagor and mortgagee remains an administrative one until the borrower experiences difficulties. Once the borrower has fallen into arrears, mortgagees rely on their legal rights and the balance and responsibilities under the mortgage shifts firmly in favour of the lender (NACAB, 1993).

The number of mortgages has increased in the eighties as home ownership has increased (from 6 million in 1980 to over 9 million in 1991). The numbers of borrowers in arrears has also increased substantially over recent years. At the end of 1991 there was a peak of 275,350 loans in arrears of six or more months compared with 32,920 in June 1982 (Ford and Bull, 1993). By the end of 1994 this figure has dropped again to 133,700. The top 30 building societies had a total of 98,370 borrowers with over 12 months arrears (overall there were 117,110) at the end of 1994.[48] Repossessions (by members of the Council of Mortgage Lenders) have also risen substantially, from 4,520 in 1983 to a peak of nearly 70,000 in 1992 to 49,210 in 1994.[49] The numbers started to rise again in the first half of 1995 to 25,200 as building societies took a tougher line on long-term arrears.[50] It is however important to recognise that these figures represent under 1 per cent of all loans.

The difficulties of indebted mortgagors has been made worse by the collapse of the housing market, so that quickly selling the property, trading down and using the capital gained to pay-off debts is presently not an option to many mortgagors. It is estimated that in addition to the 1.27 million households with negative equity (*i.e.* the

---

[48] Dwelly, "Top 30 building societies' long term arrears cases", in Fast Facts, *Roof*, July/August (1995), p. 23.

[49] McConnell, "Owner-occupiers: recent developments", Legal Actions, May (1995), p. 10.

[50] Hughes, "Home Loan Evictions Increase as Prices Drop and Lenders Run Out of Patience", *The Guardian*, July 27, 1995, p. 2.

dwelling is mortgaged for more than it is now worth), there are another 1.7 million households with insufficient equity (less than £5,000) to move. This lack of equity is currently affecting a total of one in five households.[51]

The aim of the mortgagor in arrears is usually to limit as far as possible the extent of their indebtedness but also to retain possession of their home. However, the relationship between the parties does not necessarily make these two objectives compatible. There is evidence that lenders are imposing the costs of arrears management on the individual borrower. Thus, societies are charging for letters written to the borrower, home visits and debt counselling. They are commencing possession proceedings (to safeguard their position rather than with the intention to repossess) and adding the legal charges to the borrower's debt. (NACAB, 1993).

One way that the mortgagor can use to try to limit liabilities is to sell the property. The mortgagee's refusal takes on a new significance with falling house prices. If the mortgagor sells the mortgagee will not be able to recover the whole of their security and any outstanding sum becomes an unsecured debt. Thus the lender has nothing to lose by refusing. The borrower continues to be responsible for the debt which will increase with falling prices yet does not have the power to limit the damage by selling. In *Palk and Palk v. Mortgage Services Funding plc* (1992) 25 H.L.R. 56 the mortgagee had obtained an order for possession which was suspended but the company intended to let the property until such time as it decided to sell it. The rental income would not cover the sum due under the mortgage. The mortgagor sought to sell the property but the lender refused. The Court of Appeal exercised its discretion under section 92 (1) of the Law of Property Act 1935 to order a sale against the wishes of the mortgagee thereby overriding the contractual rights of the mortgagee. The Vice-Chancellor recognised that the "interests of the mortgagor and the mortgagee do not march hand in hand in all respects" *Palk and Palk* (1992) H.L.R. 60. He went on "Although the mortgagee is plainly entitled to protect his own interest, he is not entitled to conduct himself in a way which unfairly prejudices the mortgagor" *Palk and*

---

[51] Roof, "Home owners unable to move in 1994" Fast Facts, *Roof*, May/June 1995, p. 16.

*Palk* (1992) H.L.R. 61. The mortgagee must recognise that the mortgagor has an interest in the property and is also under a personal liability for the shortfall. L.J. Kerr made it clear, however, that the court's discretion will only be exercised against the mortgagee's wishes when a substantial part of the mortgage debt is outstanding in exceptional circumstances.

One of the features of the recent increase in repossessions has been the number of "voluntary" surrenders taking place without a court order. In the early 1990s around 40 per cent of borrowers abandoned their homes or returned their doorkeys. This is a response to the lack of equity in these dwellings but also a wish in some cases to avoid continuing liability for any outstanding debt.

Borrowers whose homes are repossessed voluntarily or through a court order are sometimes under the misapprehension that this process ends any further responsibility for outstanding debt (Birch, 1994).

> "Although deprived of the use of the asset . . . and with no control over how quickly or for how much the property is sold, the borrower remains responsible for continuing interest payments, for maintenance and repair costs, for the costs of the sale as well as for any capital shortfall once the property is eventually sold."[52]

We have seen that the lender might recover some of these losses from the insurer but that insurers are increasingly pursuing borrowers to recover these sums (Colbey and Hunter, 1994).[53] In these circumstances it is not surprising that some borrowers try to "do a moonlight flit".

Building society mortgagees pursue possession proceedings in order to realise their security through sale of the property in most cases. The power of sale is contained in the Law of Property Act 1925 (sections 101 and 103). The effect of these powers is to vest the legal estate in the mortgagee:

> "it may perhaps reflect the latent capitalist emphasis of the 1925 legislation that, except in relation to the application of the proceeds of

---

[52] NACAB, Dispossessed: *Citizens Advice Bureau evidence on mortgage arrears and repossessions* (1993), p. 35.

[53] Colbey and Hunter, "Long shadow which haunts the repossessed", *The Guardian*, September 17 (1994).

sale, this statute does not expressly impose any specific ethical standard or code of conduct on the selling mortgagee."[54]

Gray however argues that the courts have gradually imposed a standard akin to that of trustee on the mortgagee in these circumstances.[55] The Law Commission has suggested that the courts have discretion to impose a time limit over the period after repossession during which interest may be charged.[56]

However, the translation of this standard into the practice of institutional mortgagees faced with substantial arrears and the inability to sell the properties in a housing market in slump is not always easy.[57] Societies have found themselves in possession of dwellings which if released on to the market would not sell but would also further impede the chances of recovery.

We return to the issue of the accountability and regulation of institutional mortgagees in a later section after we have considered the statutory interventions in relation to occupation.

## Individual statutory relationships

The statutory intervention in the area of mortgages is piecemeal and adds to the unsatisfactory levels of complexity in the law of mortgages. The key provisions are contained in the Administration of Justice Acts 1970 and 1973 and the Consumer Credit Act 1974. They have different origins: the former is concerned with the occupancy rights of residential mortgagors, the latter with regulating credit transactions and extortionate credit bargains, involving in the present context, second mortgages and the "fringe" finance sector. However, in practice the provisions are used to tackle similar difficulties with different mortgagees.

Generally, building societies and local authorities are exempted from the provisions in the 1974 Consumer Credit Act which relate

---

[54] Gray, *Elements of Land Law* (2nd ed., 1993), p. 1008.
[55] *ibid.* p. 1009.
[56] Law Commission, *Transfer of Land—Land Mortgages*, Cmnd. 145 (1991), pp. 57–58.
[57] The National Association of Estate Agents (1994) has published guidance for lenders and their advisers on how properly to sell repossessed homes.

both to extortionate credit bargains (section 137) and consumer credit secured loans (section 16). The latter provisions only relate to loans of under £15,000 which, in present circumstances, practically rules out almost all loans on first mortgage. There is no limit on the extortionate credit provision. Thus statutory intervention has helped to construct different categories of lender: those who attract greater potential interference with the agreement in the name of consumer protection and those who do not warrant it. The evolution of the protection of possessory rights also reveals assumptions on the subject for protection. While mortgagees of residential property are subject to the provisions of section 36 of the Administration of Justice Act 1970, which offers some protection to mortgagors in difficulty, these provisions do not apply to a mortgage securing a regulated agreement within the Consumer Credit Act.

We have seen that a legal mortgage grants the mortgagee a legal estate in the mortgaged property which under the law of mortgages thereby grants the mortgagee an unqualified right to possession of the mortgaged property. The mortgagee is entitled to possession from the outset unless, as in the building society example earlier, the mortgagee contracts differently. The right does not depend on default.[58] Historically the High Court had exercised its inherent jurisdiction to grant a stay of possession proceedings to enable the mortgagor to repay overdue mortgage sums. The Chancery Masters tended to be liberal in the exercise of their powers. However, *Birmingham Citizens Permanent Building Society v. Caunt* [1962] Ch. 883 established that a court could only adjourn a hearing for about 28 days to allow the mortgagor in arrears to pay off the mortgage. This judgment firmly readjusted the balance of power back to the mortgagee at a time when governments were encouraging the development of the property-owning democracy. The Payne Committee on the Enforcement of Judgment Debts (1969) recognised the need to provide mortgagors with a similar level of assistance to that

---

[58] In *Quennell v. Maltby* [1979] 1 W.L.R. 318 Lord Denning in the Court of Appeal suggested that a mortgagee could be restrained by the court from obtaining possession "except where it is sought bona fide and reasonably for the purpose of enforcing the security and then only subject to such conditions as the court thinks fit to impose" [1979] 1 W.L.R. 318 at p. 322. This view did not prevail past the obvious merits of the individual case.

offered to tenants leading to the provisions in the Administration of Justice Act 1970.

The 1970 Act contains a badly drafted section aimed at giving the court the ability to grant relief to residential mortgagors in possession proceedings. Section 36 gives the court the power to adjourn possession actions or to postpone the grant of possession of "dwelling houses" in certain circumstances. This section does not oblige the mortgagee to undertake proceedings in order to secure possession but in practice most reputable mortgagees do proceed in this way, not least to avoid the possibility of committing an offence under the Criminal Law Act 1977. There are at least four problems with the section. First, the section was initially drafted in such a way that the court had to be satisfied that the mortgagor is likely to be able, within a reasonable period, to pay *any sums due* under the mortgage. In the first case under the statutory provisions, the mortgage contained a clause rendering the whole sum outstanding due on default of an instalment. The court considered the reasonableness of repaying the entire sum rather than the arrears (*Halifax Building Society v. Clark* [1973] Ch. 307). The defect was remedied by section 8(1) of the 1973 Administration Act which defines sums due as those which the mortgagor would have expected to be required to pay if there had been no default clause.

The second issue related to the ambit of the section 36 of the 1970 Act. It was eventually established that the sections covered endowment mortgages where, for instance, the default might relate to the collateral premium or in relation to the interest payments although it took a somewhat tortuous reasoning to achieve the result (see *Governor and Company of the Bank of Scotland v. Grimes* [1985] Q.B. 1179). The protection does not extend to bank overdrafts secured against the property (*Habib Bank Ltd v. Taylor* [1982] 1 W.L.R. 1218).

Thirdly, who is entitled to benefit from this legislation? We have seen that a number of people can be contributing informally to the mortgage but also that a number of other occupiers might be in need of protection against possession proceedings. A mortgagor's spouse is entitled to tender mortgage payments (Matrimonial Homes Act 1983, section 1 (5)). However, she cannot do this unless she knows that there are difficulties. At common law she has no right to be informed of the mortgagor's default by the mortgagee on the assumption that it would be impracticable for a building society to undertake such a task (*Hastings and Thanet Building Society v. Goddard* [1970] 1 W.L.R. 1544). The position is ameliorated by the Matrimonial Homes Act 1983, section 8 (2), which grants a spouse the right to be joined as a party to any possession proceedings. If she has registered her statutory right to occupation under the Matrimonial Homes Act, section 8 (3), then she has a right to be served with the notice of possession proceedings. It does not cover the position of the wife who knows nothing about the action.

While rights of spouses might look somewhat illusory in practice, other contributors and occupants fare worse. There are no such rights for non-married sharers. In the case where the mortgagor has rented out the property, albeit contrary to the agreement, can the tenants satisfy the requirements under the Administration of Justice Act 1970 as persons deriving title under the mortgagor? The Court of Appeal was not willing to adopt this interpretation, leaving many tenants who knew nothing of the original mortgage, with means, but no right to pay (*Britannia Building Society v. Earl*, [1989] E.G.C.S. 154). Thus, the property rights which we witnessed emerging in the earlier section fail to achieve much recognition in these circumstances.

Finally, the courts have to decide whether the mortgagor is going to be able to pay off the arrears *within a reasonable period* and maintain the original payments. How long is a reasonable period in which to pay off the outstanding arrears? There is some judicial opinion to suggest that in some circumstances a reasonable period would extend to the outstanding term of the mortgage (*First Middlesborough Trading and Mortgage Company v. Cunningham* (1974) 28 P. & C.R. 69; *Western Bank Ltd v. Schindler* [1976] 2 All E.R. 393). In many cases the security would not be jeopardised in the longer term (see McConnell, 1985). In the absence of a realistic ability to pay the arrears the court cannot exercise its discretion in favour of the mortgagor. The mortgagor, however, may be able to persuade the court that it is in the best interests of both parties that s/he should be given some opportunity to sell the property to satisfy the debts (*Target Home Loans Ltd v. Clothier* [1994] 1 All E.R. 439; although see also *Cheltenham and Gloucester Building Society v. Ensor* (1992), unreported).

The usefulness of these statutory provisions depends entirely on the practical context of their exercise. The administrative arrangement which assumes a sturdily independent and economically capable property owner has not been conducive to an era of mass arrears which require quick intervention to prevent disaster. If the mortgagor approaches a building society with financial problems at an early enough stage, the policy is usually to try to assist and prevent further problems. However, research has shown that borrowers do not find it easy to contact their mortgagees.

> "Defaulters regard their situation as an intensely private one, as an individual responsibility and burden, and as personally shaming. . . . These influences in turn affect the way households manage debt by sometimes making it difficult for them to seek help, to activate social networks and tap into an additional range of resources, or to challenge the demands of creditors, however problematic or damaging for them."[59]

While mortgage default is perceived by the mortgagor as a personal failure, the rapid rise in the level of default is strongly related to the economic recession in the late 1980s. It is also a consequence of the longer-term changes in the labour market in the 1980s and 1990s in which full-time permanent jobs have been replaced by part-time, temporary and nominal self-employment. Ford's detailed case studies of mortgagors in debt reveals clearly that the restructuring of employment leading in many cases to lower and more irregular incomes as well as outright loss of employment is a main cause of mortgage difficulties. Matrimonial breakdown is also associated with default although it is often preceded by debt (Ford, 1988). In their recent work for the Department of the Environment, Ford et al. conclude that the current problems of mortgage arrears and possessions are far from over and that it is unlikely that arrears will fall back to the levels seen in the mid-1980s given the current trends in the labour market:

> "towards a further decline in full-time, male skilled employment, an increase in service sector employment, much of it part-time, low paid work, as well as an increase in temporary working and self employment and sub-contracting."[60]

---

[59] Ford, *The Indebted Society: Credit and Default in the 1980s* (1988), p. 68.
[60] Ford, Kempson and Wilson, *Mortgage Arrears and Possessions; Perspectives from Borrowers, Lenders and the Courts* (1995), pp. 109–110.

Building societies have also found it difficult to respond to significant number of borrowers in arrears whose difficulties are a result of individual fecklessness. Historically, they have been lenders of money, not housing advisers or debt councillors. Because their administrative systems have not been geared to debt management, they have been relatively slow to put in place the procedures necessary to deal with these difficulties. Ford and Bull in their survey of mortgage lenders concluded that even in early 1990s "lenders continue to give a low priority to dealing effectively with customers in arrears and the services provided for them".[61] They point to the absence of what could be described as a customer oriented approach to their services in this area.

> ". . . building societies persist with what can be characterised as 'underdeveloped' arrears management structures and practices that actively (but not necessarily intentionally) propel a proportion of borrowers towards the courts and possession and in the process probably raise the organisation's costs."[62]

Even after the development of more comprehensive arrears policies, there generally seems to be a gap between the stated policy and practice. Lenders continued to rely heavily on a narrow range of forbearance arrangements with short time horizons particularly relying on a recovery strategy of current monthly payments plus a sum for arrears even in an era of rising interest rates.[63]

By the end of 1991, the political outcry about the level of arrears and, in particular, possessions prompted the government to give the lenders 48 hours in which to come up with some initiatives to tackle the problem. Consequently, lenders have developed more systematic and proactive practices on arrears management including contacting borrowers as soon as there is default rather than waiting for up to three months. These measures have contributed to a drop in the level of possession although Ford *et al.* (1995) point to continuing gaps between a policy of securing effective recovery agreements and the practice and to different levels of commitment by lenders. Some still

---

[61] Ford and Bull, *Mortgage Arrears: Services to borrowers in debt* (1992), p. 57.

[62] Ford, *The Indebted Society: Credit and Default in the 1980s* (1988), p. 171.

[63] Ford, Kempson and Wilson, *Mortgage Arrears and Possessions, Perspectives from Borrowers, Lenders and the Courts* (1995), p. 42.

rely on their contracts, their lawyers and the district judges in the county court to obtain possession (see Birch, 1994 on the practices of one leading building society).

We turn now to the role of the county court in mortgage possession and in particular the way in which the district judges have interpreted their discretion under the Administration of Justice Act 1970. Whether or not a borrower ends up in the court depends on a combination of their circumstances and their lenders' policy and practice with regard to litigation (Ford *et al.*, 1995). It is not necessarily the culmination of the coherent recovery strategy. For example, research for the Civil Justice Review found that a third of banks and building societies had not enquired about a defendant's circumstances before the hearing (SAUS, 1987). New County Court Rules have improved this position somewhat by requiring many more details about the borrower's circumstances.[64]

Research in the early 1980s on possession actions in Coventry County Court had also suggested that a large proportion of the actions were taken where the mortgagees' security was not substantially at risk and that there was scope for solutions which did not involve court proceedings. It also suggested that even in the early 1980s the actions were not confined to any one sector of the housing market (Doling *et al.* 1984a).[64a] Research in Birmingham County Court during the same period revealed that a key determinant in the outcome of possession proceedings (whether the order was suspended or not) was the presence of or written representation by the defendant. However, only a minority of defendants, around 40 per cent, did appear in court or made representations.[65] More recent studies have found the same relationship between attendance and suspended orders but that over 50 per cent of defendants are now attending court.[66]

---

[64] County Court (Amendment No. 3) Rules 1993, S.I. 1993 No. 2176; County Court (Forms) (Amendment No. 2) Rules 1993, S.I. 1993 No. 2174.
[64a] Doling, Karn and Stafford, *A Study of Mortgage Actions in Coventry County Court. Centre for Urban and Regional Studies*, Working Paper No. 96 (1984a).
[65] Doling, Karn and Stafford, *Mortgage Arrears and the Variability in County Court Decisions: A Survey of Cases at Birmingham County Court*. Centre for Urban and Regional Studies, Working Paper No. 95 (1984).
[66] Ford, Kempson and Wilson, *Mortgage Arrears and Possessions: Perspectives from Borrowers, Lenders and the Courts* (1995).

There has been some empirical work on the exercise of the judges' discretion with respect to suspended orders under the Administration of Justice Act 1970. The district judge must decide what is a reasonable period in which the arrears can be repaid in addition to the normal monthly payment. Doling *et al.* found a wide variation in the reasonable periods used, with an average period of 10 months (1994a; 1994b). Later studies have found that district judges allow a maximum time of 18 months to two years as a reasonable period to clear arrears (Ford and Bull, 1992; NACAB, 1993). The most recent study, in mid-1993, found that the average period had lengthened to exceed four years.

> "Based on courts records from two courts, research showed that in 1991, the arrears payment required was almost half the average current monthly payment. By 1993 it had fallen to a third.[67]

The most recent survey of 15 county courts by Ford *et al.* for the Department of the Environment confirms that

> "once the case comes to court the outcome depends as much on the approach taken by the district judge as it does on the borrowers' circumstances, the current position with regard to their mortgage payments, or the stance of the lender.[68]

All the judges have lengthened the period over which they would allow borrowers to pay although not in any uniform way. The exercise of their discretion was a mix of objective calculation and subjective judgments and experience. In this context it is not surprising to find that the number of suspended orders had increased. The researchers also found that some district judges had started to grant new types of suspended possession orders.

> "Instead of calculating a reasonable period and then fixing the amount to be paid off the arrears, they made formal orders for possession 'suspended on payment of the whole of the arrears in twelve months in addition to all future payments due under the mortgage'."[69]

---

[67] *ibid.* p. 80.
[68] *ibid.* p. 79.
[69] Ford, Kempson and Wilson, *op. cit.*, p. 87.

The borrower under this arrangement was expected to meet the regular monthly payments only. At the end of a year, the position was reviewed to see whether the borrower could start to pay off any of the arrears.

Generally, the studies stress that there are few predictable outcomes to the processes involved in the management of mortgage arrears. Only a minority of those borrowers who made administrative agreements to pay off arrears are able to comply with them. Less than a quarter of borrowers in arrears are summonsed by the court. Of those summonsed, two-thirds are granted a suspended order although a quarter of those with suspended orders were unable to comply with the requirements. However, those people who lose their homes following court action are generally in a worse position financially than those who have not been taken to court (Ford *et al.*, 1995).

Ford *et al.* (1995) argue that the increased presence of defendants in the county court and the extension of the judges discretion has slightly shifted the power relations between the borrower and the lender but it must be remembered that once the mortgagor is in default the balance of the relationship has moved sharply in favour of the rights of the mortgagee.

Building societies are very much at the responsible end of the market in borrowed money. What is the position of those who obtain loans from credit companies and fringe financiers? Money is being lent to those who usually cannot obtain it elsewhere by organisations which are not dependent on a reputation of social responsibility. They are often lending to high risk borrowers and their terms reflect this. Here mortgagors are not only exposed to variable interest rates but also extremely high rates of interest and sometimes draconian terms.

We need to pause for a moment in the discussion of statutory relationships and reconsider the individual mortgage agreement in these circumstances. Can the general equitable discretion of the courts be used to temper harsh or unconscionable terms which might "clog and fetter" the mortgagor's equity of redemption? In *Cityland and Property (Holdings) Ltd v. Dabrah* [1968] Ch. 166, the defendant purchased the house in which he had been the tenant with the benefit of a loan provided by the plaintiff landlord. The defendant paid monthly instalments which included a premium over and above the purchase price. This premium substituted for a rate of interest but translated into a rate of 19 per cent over three years. A default clause transformed this into a capitalised interest rate of 57 per cent. Goff J. considered these rates of interest to be unconscionable and substituted a rate of 7 per cent. The Dabrah case illustrates not only the courts willingness to intervene to rewrite unfair and unconscionable terms but also its uniqueness. It remains the only well-known instance in recent years in which the court has exercised its inherent equitable power.

The Consumer Credit Act 1974 also contains provisions which may assist certain vulnerable borrowers.[69a] Loans by both building societies and local authorities are excluded. A court which finds a credit bargain "extortionate" is authorised by section 137 (1) to "reopen the credit agreement so as to do justice between the parties". Extortionate is defined as grossly exorbitant or otherwise grossly contravenes ordinary principles of fair dealing (section 138 (1)). The courts however have hardly ever found an interest rate to be extortionate even when confronted with rates of 48 per cent (*Ketley Ltd v. Scott*, [1980] C.C.L.R. 37). The courts stress that they are mindful of the risks involved in this type of lending for which the lender must be compensated.

The Consumer Credit Act also offers statutory protection to borrowers with secured loans of less than £15,000 (regulated agreements). The provisions are therefore clearly directed at the second mortgage and fringe finance market (section 36 of the Administration of Justice Act does not apply to mortgages secured under a regulated agreement within the Consumer Credit Act). Under a regulated agreement the borrower can apply to the court for a time order to reschedule the payment of arrears (section 129) and to amend the agreement (section 136). The interpretation of these sections have only recently been subject to review by the Court of Appeal. The court must consider what is just to both the lender and the borrower before it makes a time order. If the borrower is unlikely to be able to resume payment of the total indebtedness with extra time then the

---

[69a] These Consumer Credit Act 1974 provisions apply to any person (creditor) who lends money to an individual (debtor) and to whatever money is lent.

order should not be made. The court can, however, vary the contractual interest rate and extend the original contractual term (*Southern and District Finance plc v. Barnes; J & J Securities Ltd v. Ewart; Equity Home Loans Ltd v. Lewis Legal Action*, May 1995) (see Stephenson, 1987).

A case which illustrates the vulnerabities of borrowers is *First National Bank plc v. Syed* [1991] 2 All E.R. 250. The Court of Appeal was concerned with a second mortgage (not the first which was with a building society). In 1986 defendants took out a loan with the plaintiffs of £5,000 plus a protected payment premium of £415. The agreement stipulated a monthly rate of interest of 1.45 per cent, but there was a power to vary. The annual percentage rate was stated to be 18.8 per cent. All payments were to be credited first to outstanding interest. If any repayment was unpaid for more than 14 days the balance of the loan and interest outstanding became payable at compound interest rates. In addition the defendants agreed to pay all legal and other costs incurred by the plaintiffs in protecting and enforcing their charge with interest until paid off. Mr Syed was made redundant but he managed to pay the loan regularly for seven months during which time virtually the whole repayment was devoted to interest, but then faced difficulties. As a consequence of missing one instalment his total outstanding debt now stood at £5,610. Repayment after this time was sporadic. By August 1989 the outstanding sum was £2,065. Some payments were subsequently made but by October 1990 the sum was £2,137. The defendants had made a number of appearances before county registrars during this time and had been able to obtain a suspended possession order under section 36. Finally the registrar refused to suspend the order any longer and the defendants appealed. The court felt unable to use any of the powers discussed above. To quote Dillon L.J.:

> "Many . . . borrowers appear in person in the courts, without legal representation or legal advice, to plead for more time before they are evicted. On the other side mortgagees will appear with counsel, and in our experience in previous cases mortgagees' counsel have come to the court well equipped with arguments why time should not be granted, and very ready to refer to case law which has held that by virtue of his estate in the land a legal mortgagee has a right to possession of the mortgaged property but without having addressed their minds at all to

the basis, in statute or otherwise, of the court's power to suspend or stay a possession order." ([1991] 2 All E.R. 250 at 251–252.)

The defendants were in just such a position with the added element that they were also paying for the mortgagee's counsel. The judge instructed plaintiff's counsel to present all the relevant provisions. (He failed to notice the fact that the Administration of Justice Act provisions do not apply to regulated agreements.) However, the judge was clear that he had very little room to manoeuvre because the arrears were now so high as to make their repayment within a reasonable period impossible. It did not seem just to grant a time order which would "require the plaintiff to accept the instalments the defendants can afford, when those will be too little even to keep down the accruing interest on the defendants' account" ([1991] 2 All E.R. 250 at 256).

The case demonstrates the interaction between the terms of the agreement and the operation of the statutory provisions. They are almost in inverse relation. The harsher the terms, the less likely the borrower is able to demonstrate an ability to repay and thereby activate the provisions. The Syeds now face the loss of their home which will, one suspects, render very little equity once the debts are settled. These include the plaintiffs' costs which stood at £3,290 before the present action. They may also face the prospect of being deemed intentionally homeless if they apply for rehousing by the local authority. (See Hickman, 1994 for discussion of this case.)[70]

Generally, private law treats the owner-occupier as it would any property owner and expects him/her to conduct their affairs according to commercial principles. The pressures to recognise new proprietary interests has resulted in complex and discretionary developments in the law. Within households, there has been a struggle to gain individual access to property interests in the dwelling which historically has had considerable asset value. Use value, which

---

[70] From July 1995, the Unfair Terms in Consumer Contract Regulations 1994 (S.I. 1994 No. 3159), intended to supplement European Council Directive 93/13, may offer another opportunity for mortgagors to challenge oppressive mortgage terms. Unfair contract terms, apart from the "core" terms which define the main subject-matter of the contract or the adequacy of the price will be unenforceable by the supplier (mortgagee) against the consumer (see Holbrook, 1995; ELKS, 1995, for further discussion).

often involves maintaining rights to occupancy by those holding lesser or no property interests, conflicts with asset value. The latter is of prime concern to the external relationships which affect this group of individuals. The interests of occupiers particularly of those holding some form of proprietary right pose a considerable threat in the set of relationships which arise from the mortgage transaction. When these interests are viewed by the courts from the perspective of the mortgagees they seem to shrink or disappear in a cloud of technicalities.

While there has been considerable judicial activity in the ownership question, there has been virtually none in relation to the other security issue, the mortgage. We have seen that the equitable jurisdiction which was so creative in the earlier years of the development of the mortgage as a security instrument ossified at precisely the time when building societies were starting to develop their role as mass lenders. The extraordinary form of the building-society mortgage with its unilateral variable interest rate has been the contractual basis for millions of transactions. Protection from the one-sidedness of the mortgage contract had been provided by the delicate balance of interests between the individual mortgagor and the building societies.

In other circumstances, when the borrower is obliged to resort to fringe finance either to purchase the property or more often to finance another activity through a second mortgage, the borrower takes what is on offer and hopes that his or her economic ability will win through. The courts have been unable to mould their inherent equitable jurisdiction to fit these circumstances. Statutory protection has been piecemeal and based on protecting consumers using credit rather than directly at the problems of using the security of the home to achieve this credit. Perhaps the very dominance of the building society has stifled the development of the law of mortgages generally. The Law Commission has now recommended radical review of the law of mortgages.[71]

---

[71] The Commission recommends that there should be only two standardised forms of mortgage, the formal land mortgage and the informal. Almost all mortgages of property which includes a dwelling-house will be classified as a protected mortgage. Such mortgages will be subject to specific statutory requirements (Law Commission, 1991).

The fine administrative balance which has protected the majority of building society mortgagors is now under considerable pressure. The building societies are the subject of new sets of relations within the regulatory sphere which threaten this balance.

## Regulatory Sphere

The Regulation of Benefit Building Societies Act 1836 gave societies official recognition and established a "certifying barrister" (subsequently the Chief Registrar of Friendly Societies) to register societies' rules and offer advice.[72] Permanent societies, the modern form of society, which offered both savings and lending facilities, evolved in the mid-nineteenth century. A Royal Commission in 1872 recommended that societies should retain their mutual status rather than adopt the structure of banks, companies incorporated under the 1844 Joint Stock Companies Act:

> "The two forms of undertaking . . . have an equal right to subsist, the one for the use of those who seek to make capital, the other for those who seek, having made it, to use it."[73]

The report of the Royal Commission led to the Building Societies Act in 1874. The Act granted societies corporate status alongside banks while limiting the activities of societies to building and owning land for the purposes of conducting their business. Loans could only be made in the form of mortgages. Societies were able to issue short-term shares and borrow from depositors up to two-thirds of the sum secured by mortgages. The ability of societies to invest assets was restricted to a narrow range of securities. Members gained limited liability. The powers of the Chief Registrar to oversee the activities of the societies were strengthened in the Act and again in 1894. This legal structure persisted without great modification until the introduction of the 1986 Building Societies Act.

---

[72] Boleat, *The Building Society Industry* (1986), p. 31.
[73] Royal Commission on Friendly and Benefit Building Societies, *Second Report*, Parliamentary Papers, Vol. XXVI (1872), p. 21 quote in Boddy, *The Building Societies*, (1980), p. 9.

The impact of building societies grew rapidly in the inter-war years while their numbers declined sharply from 1,336 at the end of 1918 to 960 at the end of 1939 by which time they were lending to an estimated 1.5 million borrowers.[74] The next surge in development came in the 1950s when many more houses were built for owner-occupation. The societies were beginning to be incorporated into housing policy, for instance, the government lent the building societies £100 million to channel into the purchase of pre-1919 houses under the House Purchase and Housing Act 1959. The number of building societies continued to fall, from 835 societies at the beginning of 1950 to 273 at the end of 1980, while assets rose.[75] Throughout the period of expansion regulation was exercised by the Chief Registrar of Friendly Societies, whose powers to oversee prudent management of assets and to prescribe cautious liquidity ratios were also strengthened.

We saw in the last section that societies manage their inherently unstable financial arrangement of borrowing short and lending long, through the variable interest rate mortgage. As Boleat states:

> "The variable rate mortgage means, in effect, that building societies are lending short-term in that the rate of interest on their loans can be varied at very short notice. Equally important is the fact that because rates of interest can be changed simultaneously on both sides of the balance sheet, the margin between the borrowing and lending rate can be kept very small because societies have the knowledge that it will always be adequate."[76]

This situation can be contrasted with the American savings and loan associations which operate with fixed rates. They must allow sufficient margin in their lending rate to cover changes in the borrowing rate. This led to very serious difficulties in an era of very high interest rates requiring them to offer high investment rates to stay competitive.

By the seventies, relatively stable interest rates had become a thing of the past. House prices soared and then collapsed in 1973.

---

[74] Boleat, *op. cit.*, p. 42.
[75] Boleat, *op. cit.*, p. 53.
[76] *ibid.* p. 66.

Throughout the seventies and early eighties the building societies maintained an official cartel on the rates of interest to be recommended for both borrowing and investing. The result was that their interest rates were fixed collectively rather than competitively and were often substantially below the prevailing market rates. This system came under increasing strain in the seventies. The Labour Government, however, did not want to see rapidly rising interest rates translated into more expensive home loans and was obliged to provide societies with an interest subsidy in 1973 and a £500 million loan in 1974 to keep interest rates to borrowers down.

The outcome of this system was cheaper mortgages but at the cost of availability. For most of the seventies there was a mortgage famine because the societies were not offering competitive interest rates to investors. This was translated into considerable criticism of building society lending practices which denied mortgages to all but the most secure. Societies required often substantial savings by applicants and applied strict rules on multiples of income and percentages of property value lent. Those living in inner city areas found it almost impossible to obtain a loan as did those with non-traditional dwellings or non-traditional earning patterns (Stewart, 1981; Karn *et al*, 1985; and Forrest *et al*, 1990). Legally there could be no challenge to the operation of this discretion over access unless it could be found to discriminate under sex or race discrimination legislation. For many inner city dwellers the only alternative was fringe finance and credit institutions offering the terms demonstrated in the previous section.

While the Labour Government's housing policy review (DOE: 1977) was in favour of retaining the recommended rate the Governor of the Bank of England was not. His view was indorsed by the Wilson Committee in 1980, which reviewed the operation of the financial institutions and recommended greater competition, and also by the incoming Conservative Government.

The societies were able to operate satisfactorily in the savings market in the 1960s and 1970s because of the constraints on competitors such as the banks. However, in the late 1970s and early 1980s the banks were able, in a more deregulated market, to compete for personal savings and in the early 1980s the building societies were buffeted by the substantial intervention of the clearing banks into the lending market. Banks increased their share of lending from 8 per cent in 1980 to 36 per cent in 1982. The trend continued so that by 1987 banks and other lenders accounted for nearly 50 per cent of the market.[77]

The general deregulation of the financial markets in the eighties and the increased competition on both sides of the business of building societies finally ended the interest rate cartel in 1983. The days of mortgage famine were over, as societies became less conservative in their lending in order to maintain their market share. The loans to income ratios widened to 3 or 3.5. The percentage of loan to dwelling value increased. In 1980 the average first time buyer borrowed approximately 74 per cent of the value of the property. By 1988 this had risen to 85 per cent. "In each year of the second half of the decade more than half of all first time buyers had loans exceeding 95 per cent of their property value".[78]

The Building Societies Act 1986 is the product of this changed climate (see Boddy, 1989 for background to the Act). The basic equation of societies lending long to homeowners and borrowing short from investors has been compromised. Societies are now able to diversify. They can attract non-retail deposits: the large societies can retain up to 40 per cent of their assets in non-retail deposits. (Many of the wider activities are only possible if the building society has a total commercial asset base of not less that £100 million.) They can establish and invest in subsidiaries in the United Kingdom and Europe; they can offer a wide range of financial services and services in relation to land (which includes such activities as estate agency); and they can offer unsecured loans. The Act also established a maximum liquidity ratio now that risk taking is possible within prescribed limits.

Deregulation in the financial sector and changes in the practices of building societies are widely seen as responsible for the inflationary house-price spiral which characterised the later eighties. We have already noted the explosion in lending which ensued. Societies are

---

[77] Boddy, "Financial Deregulation and UK Housing Finance: Government Building Society Relations and the Building Societies Act, 1986" in *Housing Studies* (1989), Vol. 4, No. 2, p. 94.

[78] Doling and Ford, "The changing face of home ownership", in *Policy and Politics* (1991), Vol. 19(2), p. 111.

also seen as making over-enthusiastic use of their new freedoms, such as aggressive marketing of insurance and endowment mortgages and the ill-fated move into estate agencies. In mid-1988 the housing market faltered, interest rates rose from about 9.5 per cent in May 1988 to 15.4 per cent in February 1990, the economy moved into recession, and the housing market collapsed leading to a sustained slump from which it has yet to recover.[79]

Building societies in the 1990s have been obliged to deal with default by mortgagors caused by loss of income and increases in interest payments. They have reconsidered their strategies, adopting more conservative lending policies but also developing schemes designed to keep borrowers within the sector not only to enter it (*e.g.* low start/deferred payment mortgages). They have also been obliged to set aside substantial sums to cover losses for the first time in their history and have developed arrears management practices. We have seen that these have not necessarily been very well developed or successful but Doling and Ford argue that services introduced to tackle the consequences of recession will give rise to increased consumer expectations which will be sustained in a better economic climate.[80]

We have argued that the Conservative Government's support for home ownership in the 1980s is part of a wider ideological view about the role of the state. Home owners are expected to be less reliant on the state, pursuing, as consumers, any complaints they may have against the providers not against the government. Building societies and other lenders have faced considerable public criticism for their policies in the eighties which are seen by many as irresponsible and contributing to the present misery of many thousands of homeowners. Nonetheless, this criticism has also been levelled at the government for its policies of supporting the wealth creating concept of the property-owning democracy and translates into pressure for policies now to assist mortgagors in difficulties and to revive the housing market.

Building societies were put under considerable pressure by government to develop policies which limited the number of repossessions.

---

[79] Forrest and Murie, "Home Ownership in Recession", in *Housing Studies* (1994), Vol. 9, No. 1.
[80] Doling and Ford, *op. cit.*, p. 113.

At Christmas 1991 they were obliged to come up with some specific rescue packages in partnership with housing associations. These involved funds being made available from lenders to enable housing associations or others to purchase repossessed properties and relet them through mortgage-to-rent and shared ownership schemes. In exchange, the government undertook to pay directly to the lenders (rather than via the borrowers) the £750 million of mortgage interest due from mortgages on income support in exchange for an informal agreement that lenders would not pursue repossession against those in receipt of income support (The Social Security (Mortgage Interest Payments) Act 1992). The government subsequently also suspended stamp duty on house purchases as an incentive to the market. These initiatives have not had the impact hoped for, demonstrating that individual financial difficulties are complex and not easily converted into standard schemes (Ford and Wilcox, 1992; Foster, 1992; Foster *et al.*, 1995). In a further initiative at the end of 1992, the government provided an extra £750 million for housing associations to buy 20,000 empty repossessed properties which has been more successful. While the overall number of repossessions dropped between 1991 and 1994 from 75,540 to 49,210, they have started to increase in 1995. 25,200 properties were repossessed in the first six months of 1995, an increase of 4 per cent over the previous six months. This drop is attributable to the lenders' improved mortgage arrears management policies described earlier and to the district judges' increased use of suspended possession orders on more generous time scales than to the specific mortgage rescue packages (Ford *et al.* 1995). There is evidence that the informal agreement not to repossess those on income support is being breached by building societies who are concerned about the level of arrears for some mortgagors who have now been given a substantial period in which to recover (Ford *et al.*, 1995).

A wider tension has developed between government policies which encourage the spread of home ownership to lower income groups and the desire to limit state responsibility to this sector. The insecurity of owning has become very obvious for those who are on low incomes or in financial difficulty. Although almost all domestic mortgagors are eligible for mortgage interest tax relief on first mortgages, home owners are not eligible for housing benefit, the means-tested form of housing support available to tenants. Those who are unemployed, sick, disabled or elderly do have some access to the income support system. Although the numbers are small, the numbers have risen from 281,000 in 1989 to 556,000 in 1993 and with it the cost to the Exchequer (£1.2 billion in 1993). The minister responsible for social security, however, considers that this is an area where the social security system is patently not giving value for money.[81] From April 1995 there has been a ceiling of £100,000 up to which the mortgage interest is paid by the Department of Social Security. Existing borrowers receive no help on a new claim for the first two months. Half of their mortgage interest is paid direct to the lender for the next four months and thereafter the full amount of interest is paid. After October 1995, new mortgagors lose the right to have their interest covered for the first nine months of any period of unemployment. Lenders will probably require mortgagors to insure against the risk of sickness and unemployment.[82] The aim is to encourage mortgagors to be responsible for their own risks and to insure against financial difficulties. The insurance industry has started to develop mortgage protection policies but there are reports of considerable difficulties with the present terms of these policies and their effectiveness.[83] Only 10 per cent of existing mortgagors and 20 per cent of new mortgagors have such policies. Birch considers that little more than half of existing mortgage interest income support claimants would be considered for private insurance.[84] For many more the cost will be prohibitive. Ford *et al.* argue that in their current form "they take borrowers' resources that might otherwise be put towards mortgage payments, while offering little in return".[85]

If private insurance becomes a prerequisite to lending by mortgagees, in the absence of a state welfare safety net, it act as a brake on the expansion of owner-occupation. This has led some to argue for

---

[81] Griffith, "The benefits of housing", in *Legal Action*, July (1995), p. 9.

[82] Luba and Madge, "Recent developments in housing law", in *Legal Action* (1995), p. 10; Griffith, "Income Support and Mortgage Interest: The New Rule" in *Legal Action* (1995), pp. 17–19.

[83] NACAB, Dispossessed: *Citizens Advice Bureau evidence on mortgage arrears and repossessions* (1993), pp. 17–20.

[84] Birch, "There may be trouble ahead", *Roof*, March/April, pp. 26–29.

[85] Ford, Kempson and Wilson, *Mortgage Arrears and Possessions: Perspectives from Borrowers, Lenders and the Courts* (1995), p. 62.

an increase in mortgage interest tax relief and others to argue for the development of a means-tested mortgage benefit, possibly by withdrawing tax relief from the better-off mortgagors (Ford and Wilcox, 1992; Foster, 1992). The former benefits all owners and is costly, the second targets state expenditure on those in need but also recognises state responsibility to support some, which the present Government is not keen to encourage.

Building societies are faced with falling house prices, potential losses and difficulties in further expansion in the home ownership market coupled with continued pressure from competitors. One response is to diversify their activities perhaps to become more involved with funding the development of social housing particularly the expansion of a newly constituted private rented sector (see chapter 3); or the housing companies resulting from the large scale transfer of local authority stock (see chapter 4); or the future development of housing associations (see chapter 5). However, there seems little evidence presently that they would wish to become involved in new forms of housing funding (Smallwood, 1992).

The Government has announced proposals in 1995 to extend the existing powers of societies permitting them greater opportunities to diversify their activities but also increasing their duties to account to their members (Treasury, 1995). Some of these proposals will require primary legislation, although the Government is discussing with the building societies the extent to which they can incorporate the proposals to improve accountability into a voluntary code of practice or members' charter. Changes to the powers of the societies will be introduced as far as possible through existing powers to make secondary legislation under the 1986 Act.

The focus for societies is presently on the restructuring of their businesses. The Building Societies Act 1986 introduced mechanisms whereby societies can merge and/or convert themselves into banks. The biggest society, the Abbey National, was the first to convert into a public limited company in the later eighties (*Abbey National Building Society v. Building Societies Commission* [1989] 5 B.C.C. 259). In the 1990s the emphasis has been on mergers between societies or, in some cases, mergers between banks and building societies, leading to increased concentration within the sector. Much is rumoured but the proposed terms of two schemes have been considered by the

Building Societies Commission and by the courts (*Cheltenham and Gloucester Building Society v. Building Societies Commission* [1994] 4 All E.R. 65; *Building Societies Commission v. Halifax Building Society* [1995] 3 All E.R. 193). One of the arguments in favour of these moves to company status is that it will improve performance and increase accountability (see chapter 6).

Although increasingly the activities and to an extent, the legal framework of building societies mirror those of banks, the Building Societies Act 1986 established a specific regulatory system and body, the Building Societies Commission, which has wide-ranging supervisory powers, particularly to ensure prudent financial management. Parliamentary attempts to widen the membership of this body to include those representing housing interests were resisted.

The performance and practice of lenders over the last 15 years have, however, led some to argue that there is a need for greater regulation of their activities than at present (NACAB, 1993). While investor protection is overseen by the industry regulator, borrower protection tends to be embodied in voluntary codes of practice (CML/BSA, 1994) backed up by the somewhat underdeveloped statutory protections discussed in the previous section. Shareholders and borrowers with complaints also have access to the statutorily required industry-wide ombudsman scheme established under the Building Societies Act 1986 which is discussed in more detail in chapter 6.

## Conclusion

Changes in market relations have interacted with the mortgage form to affect the balance of power between the individual mortgagor and the societies. The borrower in the nineties is far more financially vulnerable as a result of the shift to the market allocation of mortgages although s/he is not so dependent on the consequences of rationing by administrative systems. Fewer need resort to the fringe lenders for initial loans although many use this sector for second loans. Relationships are now based on the private legal form of the mortgage while the lenders increasingly move into the world of the international money markets.

The owner-occupier as a consumer in need of protection is a relatively new phenomenon and as yet the mechanisms associated with consumerism have not developed to any great extent within the sector. Whether market based mechanisms will provide adequate means of protection in an increasingly diverse sector remains to be seen.

# The World of Renting Relations: An Introduction

The next three chapters discuss a variety of occupational groupings based on rented relationships, provision by private landlords, local housing authorities and housing associations respectively. I adopt a similar framework to that used in the discussion of owner-occupation. This involves splitting the concept of tenure into three spheres of relationships. The first sphere is the individual property relationship between the landlord and the tenant which is based on the legal concept of the lease, one of the cornerstones of property law. However, the conceptual framework of the common law form of the lease is also contractual: there are two equal parties entering into a contract (of tenancy) which embodies their agreement. Tensions between proprietary and contractual approaches to the concept of the lease emerge in the case law. In recent years there has been a tendency to emphasise the contractual nature of the property relationship.

The residential property relationship represented in the lease embodies both economic and social relations which are translated into a variety of co-existing property related claims. Allen and McDowell argue that, in addition to the economic form of the rent relation which is represented by the monetary payment, there are distinctive social aspects to the rent relation between the landlord and tenant (1989). The first arises from the fact that the commodity, residential space, is sold over time. The letting relationship is therefore one of hire:

> "[W]hen a landlord sells the use of a particular space for a certain period of time the property rights of control and benefit attached to the space are uneasily divided between landlord and tenant. Both landlord and tenant represent conflicting claims to possession, one based on ownership and the other based on the hire of a commodity, residential space. . . . On the one hand, the tenant has purchased the right of use

of a property. On the other hand, the tenant has purchased the right of use of a property. The rights of control and benefit are unclear . . .[1]

They also stress that residential space possesses its own intrinsic ideological markings. Landlords sell "homes" which are associated with deep-seated emotions of security and enjoyment.[2] The different positionings of the landlords leads to different interpretations of these property-related claims.

Not surprisingly, most of the discussion of the legal basis of the lease has taken place in relation to the private landlord and tenant relationship (both residential and commercial). As we shall see there has been far less discussion of the property relations of the social landlords (local housing authority and housing association landlords) and their tenants. The relationship between local authority tenants and their landlords has been very much an administrative and political arrangement, a product of the development of public sector housing provision. Consequently, local authority tenants have hardly been perceived as holding a proprietary interest and have not relied on this property relation with their landlord. Housing association landlordism is a product of private philanthropy and more recently of public social housing policies, neither of these traditions has emphasised tenants' proprietory interests, although housing associations are private landlords.

The second sphere involves a discussion of the various statutory interventions which have occurred over the twentieth century which recognise the limitations of relations based on common law. These statutory interventions have been wide ranging, seeking generally to restrict the landlord's ability to remove tenants and also to determine a rent. They have imposed additional obligations on landlords such as duties to keep certain dwellings in structural and external repair and set procedural requirements such as the provision of a rent book. These rights and duties are superimposed on and modify the existing tenancy, adjusting the relationship between the parties.

The statutory interventions also construct types of landlord. Within this second sphere, distinctions emerge between local author-

---

[1] Allen and McDowell, *Landlords and Property. Social Relations in the Private Rented Sector* (1989), p. 46.
[2] *ibid.* pp. 46, 47.

ity landlords which since 1980 are obliged to offer secure tenancies to the vast majority of their occupiers and private landlords whose tenants either hold assured or more commonly assured shorthold tenancies. Housing association landlords have been constructed by legislation in a variety of ways, between 1980 and 1988, as public landlords offering secure tenancies, since 1989, as private landlords offering assured tenancies although not assured shorthold tenancies. The outcome is a complex and bewildering array of statutory provisions constructing numerous categories of occupation.[3]

This extensive regulation of tenancies challenges assumptions associated with the ownership of property: it represents a restriction on the landlord's rights of ownership.[4] Within some sections of the private landlord sector this strong sense of property leads to a resistance to housing reforms which offer tenants increased involvement in the management of or rights over their homes as we shall see in our discussion of the leasehold enfranchisement legislation in the next chapter.

These statutory interventions are described in the subsequent chapters as the sphere of individual statutory relations. The ways in which they interact with the individual property relations varies between the rented sectors and depends to a considerable extent on the positioning of the landlord. So, for instance, the security of tenure provided to a private tenant under the Rent Act 1977 is a personal right. Similarly, the public sector security is personal under the Housing Act 1985. However, the Housing Act 1988 security for private and housing association tenants is proprietary in nature.[5]

This leads to the third sphere of relationships which are affected by the nature of the landlord and their positioning within wider regulatory frameworks. Local authority landlords are statutory bodies. While the property relations of council tenants have not formed the basis for their relations with landlords and individual statutory status was only granted in 1980, the relationship of council tenants with their landlords has developed within a public law framework:

---

[3] These are described very clearly and extensively in Arden and Partington's *Housing Law* (1994) which provides generally a comprehensive legal coverage of the area of housing law under discussion within this book and is recommended to those wishing to explore the issues in more depth than is possible here.

[4] Bright and Gilbert, *Landlord and Tenant Law. The Nature of Tenancies* (1995).

[5] Bright and Gilbert, *op. cit.*, p. 119.

"While landlords and tenants in the private residential . . . sector rely on property and contract rights, local authority tenants have to fit many of their similar claims into public law actions."[6]

However, as we shall see in chapter 4 the dominance of this sphere of relations potentially enables them to challenge different aspects of the renting relation to those associated with the private lease. For instance, tenants (and potential tenants) have used the public positioning of their landlords to challenge collective allocation and rent policies. The non-public nature of housing association landlords which presently seems to deny tenants access to public law has equally restricted the development of these types of challenges as we shall see in chapter 5.

The relations of both local authority and housing association landlords with their tenants are deeply affected by their complex relationships with their own financiers and regulators. Local housing authorities have been subject to increased intervention from central government. The Housing Corporation has had a growing regulatory role in relation to housing associations. The form in which this regulation occurs has also been changing. Private landlords have been less enmeshed in broader regulatory relations although there is growing pressure to incorporate some of them.

Not only does the significance of the different spheres vary according to type of landlord, for instance statutory regulation has been far more extensive in the private rented sector than in the local authority sector while private landlords have been subject to little general regulation as landlords, but each rented sector has felt the impact of general economic changes and substantial government intervention in recent years. These changes have transformed the balance of power within these spheres of relationships.

It will be that changes in the individual statutory relations between landlord and tenant have led to a reduction in the significance of this sphere. Developments within the general regulatory sphere have led to a greater reliance on contractual and consumerist forms of regulation across the sectors. Tenants are still constructed differently as secure, assured or shorthold but their landlords are increasingly been described as "social" irrespective of their public or private law

---

[6] *ibid.* p. 111.

form. Tenants themselves are increasingly becoming citizens consuming housing services, their relationship with landlords enshrined in good practice guides, charters and guarantees.

The next chapter will chart these developments in relation to the private landlord and tenant relationships. The following two chapters will consider developments within the local authority and housing association sectors.

# Chapter 3

# Private Landlordism

## Introduction

It is perhaps paradoxical that the market sector of residential letting is the one which has been the subject of the most direct legal intervention in the relations between landlord and tenant. These statutory interventions have taken a variety of forms, including requirements in relation to housing standards, rent regulation and security of tenure. They are blamed by some for the decline of the sector, while others consider them a product of the failure of the sector to meet basic housing needs. There is, however, no disagreement over the scale of the decline in this sector. Before the First World War over 90 per cent of the population was housed in the private rented sector. By 1990, the sector housed just over 7 per cent of households (London Research Centre, 1993) although there is some evidence to suggest that this decline has ceased.

By the mid-nineteenth century, the appalling conditions in the urban slums had become a public issue. Early intervention took the form of public health measures instigated by the state to alleviate some of the consequences of urban squalor. This was achieved first through local bye laws designed to check poor and insanitary construction, then under the 1875 Public Health Act through the general powers granted to sanitary authorities to make bye laws that provided detailed control over building standards and layout.[7] Inter-

---

[7] See M. Daunton (1987) *A Property-Owning Democracy*, Chap. 2 for a short but highly informative account of the historical debates about the decline of the private landlord sector.

vention in relation to the existing stock took the form of slum clearance powers under the Torrens and Cross Acts[8] subsequently consolidated in the Housing of the Working Classes Act of 1890.[9] The last of these permitted local councils to build dwellings without the necessity of prior clearance action. (See Ormandy and Burridge, 1988; Arden *et al*, 1994, for further discussion of environmental health standards.)

While some have argued that the use of these powers precipitated the decline of the private landlord, Daunton (1987) argues that a more likely explanation is to be found in the legal and fiscal relationships of the landlords in both Scotland and England. Landlords were disproportionately liable for local taxation which was made even more burdensome by the First World War. This, coupled with the form of tenancy prevalent in Scotland (the tenancies were yearly rather than weekly which was the more common form in England), had caused considerable political tension in that country prior to the war. In addition, a cyclical downturn in property was rendered permanent by the war time imposition of rent and mortgage controls. The 1915 Rent and Mortgage Restriction Act, prompted by riots on the Clyde, prohibited the raising of rents above a standard rent. It also prohibited the recall of mortgages and the raising of interest rates.

Once again, some argue that landlords never recovered from this period although even in 1946 over 50 per cent of the population still rented their properties privately.

Coleman however suggests:

> "Despite the imposition of rent controls in 1915, never totally lifted from the sector, new properties were later made exempt. Although rates and finance were increasingly a problem for landlords, many houses in the 1930s were built indifferently to sell or to rent: about 900,000 new rented dwellings, almost half the total built by private enterprise."[10]

---

[8] The Artisans' and Labourers' Dwellings Act 1968 (Torrens Act) permitted a council to order the owner of an insanitary house to demolish or repair it at his own expense. The Artisans' and Labourers' Dwellings Improvement Act 1875 (Cross Act) gave power to demolish whole areas.

[9] This Act had three parts: Pt. 1 covered area demolition; Pt. 2 demolition or repair of individual houses; Pt. 3 permitted councils to construct and own working-class lodging houses.

[10] Coleman, "Private rented housing: the next steps" in Best, R. et al. (eds.) *The Future of Private Renting: Consensus and Action* (1992) p. 26.

He sees the reimposition of rent controls in 1939 on the outbreak of the Second World War as the spur for the "more rapid marginalisation of the the private landlord" private landlord", even though in 1946 over 50 per cent of the population still rented their properties privately.

Hamnett and Randolph (1988) see the development of owner occupation as the main reason for the decline of the private rented market. They argue that the private investment which funded landlordism in return for interest payments was increasingly channelled into the building societies from the late nineteenth century onwards. Building societies gradually deprived landlords of their traditional sources of private capital but then lent funds to them in a form which greatly increased the costs of borrowing to landlords.[11] Landlords were not able to defray these costs through subsidies because they were excluded from the housing subsidies structure which emerged in the 1920s.

Daunton (1987) suggests that this exclusion from the public subsidy system was partly due to the landlords' economic and political marginality. Landlords in the nineteenth and early twentieth century were generally small, local, middle-class entrepreneurs, rather than industrial capitalists or landed aristocracy, who found themselves isolated and unable to defend their interests within the emerging national political context. This exclusion from public subsidy has continued although, as we shall see, there is presently some reconsideration of the issue.

The disadvantages of landlordism have accumulated as Hamnett and Randolph argue:

"investor landlords have . . . suffered long term and cumulative disadvantage in comparison to home owners in relation to the costs of the finance required for the purchase of housing, the costs which are included in the calculations on which purchase is based, and by the long-term tendency for fiscal policies to favour owner occupation in terms of both taxes on rents (or imputed rents) and capital gains and through the building Societies' tax compositing arrangements."[12]

---

[11] Hamnett and Randolph, *Cities, Housing and Profits: flat break-up and the decline of private renting* (1988), p. 53.
[12] *ibid.* p. 75.

85

Each sector, private renting and owner occupation, becomes characterised by a particular fiscal and financial structure. Different values therefore accrue to a dwelling depending upon which sector it is in. This dual value system is not a product of rent control but of the emergence of owner occupation in its particular form. Landlords sold their properties rather than continued to rent them because they made capital gains by appropriating the difference between the capital values of properties in the rented and owner-occupied markets. They argue that the dual value system has distorted property valuation methods so that most landlords attempt to calculate rental yield in relation to the notional vacant possession value of their property:

> "Rather than rental income providing the basis of capital values, vacant possession values now form the basis for the determination of adequate return. . . . This . . . creates tremendous pressure to increase rents well above their level under the traditional valuation system. Rent controls and security of tenure . . . have helped to deflect this pressure and, in effect, acted to preserve the TI (tenant investment) value of any rented property under control."[13]

We will return to this point in the subsequent discussion of rent regulation. The consequence has been that the "traditional" investment form of landlordism has been to a large degree displaced by the speculative residential property trader for whom rents are secondary:

> "Profits could only be made by buying at values depressed by low rent, selling properties made vacant by evicting the tenants, skimping maintenance or by avoiding the rent acts by precarious deals involving the license, holiday , lets and company lets . . ."[14]

The sector gradually acquired some of the characteristics of a black market (epitomised by the activities of Rachman in 1960s in London).

---

[13] *ibid.* pp. 78–79.
[14] Coleman, "Private rented housing: the next steps" in Best, R, et al. (eds) *The Future of Private Renting: Consenus and Action* (1990), p. 26.

Calls for deregulation of the sector are often based on this assumption that a revived rental sector will result from decontrol. Kemp (1990) argues that both the anti- and pro-market lobbies tend to adopt an idealised view of the market which takes little account of the realities of renting in late twentieth-century Britain. As Kemp points out support for deregulation is based on three assumptions: that regulated rents are below free market levels; that the majority of private lettings have a regulated rent; and that rent regulation is the main reason for the continuing decline in the supply of private rental housing.[15] The first of these assumptions seems to be correct, the second is not, as we shall see later. In the light of Hamnett and Randolph's argument, the third is also very much open to doubt. We shall see that the 1988 Housing Act is a product of the ascendancy of the pro-market lobby.

While Conservative governments have had ideological sympathy with private landlordism and have generally favoured measures to reduce regulation of the sector, it has been difficult electorally to offer positive financial support to a sector which has continued to be seen as the unacceptable face of capitalism. The Labour Party has historically been clear in its opposition to private landlordism. Hence, since 1919 there have been eras of partial decontrol and eras of recontrol roughly equating with the terms of office of Conservative and Labour Governments. This uncertainty has simply added to the continuing decline of the sector.

It now seems likely that the private-rented sector is not going to fade away. The decline in the sector seems to have stopped or at least slowed down. The number of households renting from private landlords in England has increased by 17 per cent from 1.7 million in 1988 to 2.0 million in 1994 (DOE, 1995). There are a number of reasons for this. First, the Housing Act 1988 has ensured that there is an unregulated market for new lettings. Secondly, there is a greater supply of dwellings to rent of properties which cannot presently be sold because of the collapse of the housing market. A number of dwellings are being rented out by mortgagors unable to sell but also by those acting for mortgagees who have repossessed

---

[15] Kemp, "Deregulation, markets and the 1988 Housing Act", *Social Policy and Administration* (1990), Vol. 24, p. 149.

and are unwilling to release more properties on to a saturated market. Thirdly, the availability of specific financial incentives through the Business Expansion Scheme for those investing in the sector to which we will return. Fourthly, there is some confidence in the sector created by a growing consensus between the major political parties and housing specialists that there is a useful and socially acceptable place for private renting (See Best *et al*, 1992).

Policy development in relation to the private-rented sector is focused on stimulating investment by a new range of corporate commercial landlords not on resuscitating and expanding the existing types of landlord. The new breed of landlords are to be profit making, professionally responsible and managerially competent. The aim will be to encourage such acceptable, mainstream providers to ensure a seamless continuum between the social landlords and these newcomers in the independent rented sector. The problem remains how to attract them into the market. In exchange for new forms of investment, there is a shift in the forms of regulation away from individual statutory protection of tenants to a greater emphasis on contractual agreements There is a likelihood that landlords will be made to account publicly for their activities in exchange for subsidies rather than, as now, be policed in the courts. Thus landlords possibly might be on the verge of political rescue through an economic restructuring of landlordism.

However, if the new world has arrived, the old, embattled relationships engendered by decline still provide the experience for the majority of tenants. I turn now to a discussion of the different spheres of relationships beginning with the individual property relationships. This discussion does not attempt to be a comprehensive coverage of landlord and tenant relationships. Instead my aim is to capture the changing relationships within the sector generally and then to concentrate particularly on issues concerning rent and the consequences of the repositioning of the other rental groupings for this sector. There are, however, a number of excellent texts which provide such detail (Arden *et al.*, 1994, Partington and Hill, 1991, Bright and Gilbert, 1995). Finally I provide a brief case study of a specific issue within the private rented sector, the demand for leasehold enfranchisement, to illustrate some of the wider points made in the chapter.

# Individual property relations

In chapter 2 we saw that the growth in owner-occupation had led to social and economic diversity within the sector. All the empirical research on the private rented sector reveals the diversity produced by decline. A national survey of private landlords in 1994 found that:

> "Unlike other sectors of the economy, residential housing to let is not dominated by companies. . . . More than half of privately rented dwellings were owned by private individuals and couples. Little more than a quarter was owned by partnerships and private or public companies. The remainder were owned by a range of other types of landlord, such as churches, the Crown Commissioners, government departments and educational institutions.[16]

Landlords are generally not professional property managers. Crook et al. found that for the majority of landlords who were private individuals, letting accommodation was not a full-time activity. Three out of five were owned by landlords in paid work and the majority of those not in work were retired. Only one eight were owned by individuals who were full-time landlords (1995: 6):

> "For the landlords of nearly two thirds of addresses owned by private individuals, rent from residential lettings accounted for a quarter or less of their total income."[17]

This same survey found that for the majority of corporate landlords letting accommodation was not their core business.[18] The management of this stock was undertaken by the landlord alone in 63 per cent of the addresses with only a quarter being managed solely by agents.[19]

A similar diversity is found among those who live within the sector:

> "Many private tenants are elderly, have low incomes, rent unfurnished houses or flats and have lived at their current address for many years.

---

[16] Crook et al., The Supply of Privately Rented Homes: Today and Tomorrow (1995), p. 6.
[17] ibid. p. 6.
[18] ibid. p. 6.
[19] ibid. p. 7.

By contrast, a high proportion of private tenants, particularly in the furnished subsector where new lettings are concentrated, are young, often single, usually without children. rent rooms or flats and have lived at their present address for at most a year or two."[20]

Generally, households living within the sector have low incomes. Less than 50 per cent of private tenants are economically active. Since 1990 the proportion of tenants who are unemployed has increased from 5 per cent to 13 per cent. Thirty-six per cent of tenancies (excluding those in rent-free accommodation) were receiving housing benefit in 1993/4 (DoE, 1995).

As we have seen, residential property letting is not only an economic but also a social relation. Both aspects give rise to a range of expectations: landlords' claims are broadly based on property ownership, while those of tenants are based on hiring a commodity. Allen and McDowell argue that the particular mix of economic and social concern varies according to the type of landlord and leads to different strategies in relation to the sector. They therefore present empirical material on size and forms of landlords in terms of social and economic relations.

For traditional landlords such as the Church and charitable trusts, commercial activity is modified by a service ideology. "Their economic needs and the constituted meaning attached to their property are in opposition to one another".[21] Employers who also offer accommodation to their employees are not motivated by profit on their properties and therefore are not susceptible to the financial pressures for disinvestment.

The third category, informal landlords, "embody the contradiction between the economic and social roles of rented housing in its sharpest form".[22] Many are resident landlords, a by product of the increase in owner occupation. For this group:

"Property is considered as a series of social rights over personal possessions and not, in any clear sense as a form of capital. This

[20] Kemp, "Deregulation, markets and the 1988 Housing Act" in *Social Policy and Administration*, Vol. 24, pp. 145–155.
[21] Allen and McDowell, *Landlords and Property. Social Relations in the Private Rented Sector* (1989), p. 49.
[22] *ibid.* p. 51.

property relation is 'lived' as a form of authority; that is, as an individual's right to the unfettered power over their personal possessions."[23]

These landlords generally lend their homes in exchange for an informal rather than commercial rent. These three types of landlords are more enmeshed in the social relations of renting than the next three to be discussed who to varying degrees emphasise economic relations.

Investor landlords are the residue of the earlier private rented market. These private property companies, private trusts or individuals own properties which are a legacy from a more profitable era. They are particularly affected by the changed image of landlordism from a profit making service to one of Rachman exploitation. Having lost a legitimate social role along with a sufficient return from their investment, they leave the sector at the earliest reasonable chance.

For the fifth category, commercial landlords, "rented housing is considered solely as a commodity, unsullied by the ideology of the home."[24] Within this group are the trading landlords "for whom the letting of property is simply a moment in the process of realisation of their capital, a phase of the disposal process".[25] The final group, the financial landlords (public property companies, insurance companies and pension trust funds), share a capitalist orientation towards housing with the commercial landlords. However, they are distinguished by the size of their available capital, their different source of finance, the minimal role that rented housing holds in their investment portfolios and their vulnerability to the negative stigma of private landlordism.[26] Unlike the commercial landlords, they generally seek to withdraw from the sector.

While the studies demonstrate the disparate nature of landlords and the variety of their social and economic relations with their tenants, there is no overt recognition of this diversity in the individual property relations organised through the lease. The lease has been described as embodying the very potent symbols of the

---

[23] ibid. p. 52.
[24] Allen and McDowell, op. cit. p. 54.
[25] ibid. p. 54,
[26] ibid. p. 55.

common law of a right based on property ownership and the freedom to contract as an equal (Cotterell, 1986). Historically, the leasehold relationship was founded on contract. Gradually it became accepted that the lessee had a right to possession which could be protected against third parties and passed over a conceptual line between a personal right and a proprietory one. Its proprietory status was confirmed by section 1(1) of the Law of Property Act 1925 in which it is recognised as one of the two estates in land along with the fee simple which can exist at law. This dual nature gives rise to some conceptual difficulty:

> "Viewed from the perspective of property, the lease represents a conveyance of a proprietary estate in land . . . Viewed from the perspective of contract, however, the lease is manifestly different from a conveyance of a fee simple in that a conveyance of a leasehold interest does not represent a fully executed contract. . . . There remains today a significant tension between these competing proprietary and contract-based perspectives."[27]

One of the consequences of the proprietary perspective is that some of the remedies available for breach of leasehold obligations are peculiar to the landlord and tenant relationship.[28] These include distress for rent which allows landlords who are owed rent to take goods from the premises and sell them in order to satisfy the arrears and relief against forfeiture which restricts the landlord's ability to regain possession for breach of the terms of the contract.

Another consequence of the fact that the tenant is granted a legal estate upon entering into the contract is, as Gray pointed out, that the courts have tended to view the contract as completed at the time of grant. This approach suggests that the grant of the lease is similar to a contract of sale and not, as suggested by Allen and McDowell, one of hire. The landlord provides the land but not services during the relationship. It follows from this that:

> "normal contractual remedies were frequently not allowed following breach. Once the lease had been executed the tenant was seen to have

---

[27] Gray, *Elements of land law* (2nd ed. 1993), pp. 673–674.
[28] I am indebted in this section to Bright and Gilbert's discussion of the nature of tenancies in their book *Landlord and Tenant Law* (1995).

received what was bargained for, the law would protect the tenant's possession of the land to ensure that the grant was not denied but beyond this the law did little to recognise that the tenant might lose other aspects of the bargain."[29]

The proprietary perspective therefore stresses the possession-rent relationship; that is, the economic relation. The tenant covenants to pay rent while the landlord covenants to keep the tenant in quiet enjoyment.[30] In this perspective the landlord is expected to keep away.

The dominance of the proprietary approach to the relationship between landlord and tenant developed in relation to agricultural land. The tensions begin to emerge once the lease is used for residential and industrial lettings where:

"the detailed covenants in the lease form an important part of the bargain and the ongoing obligations of the landlord to supply services and amenities to the tenant are often as important as the possession of the land.[31]"

A failure to perform these service level agreements generate their own remedy but do not affect the other level (possession-rent). Thus a tenant has no right to take part in a rent strike or withhold a service charge if the landlord is in breach of a covenant such as damages for breach of the implied repairing covenants in section 11 of the Landlord and Tenant Act 1985 (*Di Palma v. Victoria Square Property Co. Ltd* [1985] 3 W.L.R. 207). This legal level more closely reflects the social aspect of the rent relation described by Allen and McDowell and the lease facilitating hiring rather than selling residential space.

There seems to be, however, a growing tendency to expose the law of leases to a much more comprehensive application of ordinary contract principles although tensions continue. American authorities are now seeing the modern residential letting as representing a commercial transaction which results in the sale of a package of consumer utilities of shelter and convenience (Gray, 1993; Bright and

---

[29] Bright and Gilbert, *Landlord and Tenant Law. The Nature of Tenancies* (1995), p. 78.
[30] Quinn and Phillips (1969), quoted in Bright and Gilbert, *ibid.* p. 78.
[31] Bright and Gilbert, *ibid.* pp. 80–81.

Gilbert, 1995). From this standpoint "the urban tenant is frequently a purchaser of goods and services under a specialised form of consumer contract".[32] Two recent cases demonstrate the developments in England. In the county court judgment, *Hussein v. Mehlman* [1992] 2 E.G.L.R. 87, Stephen Sedley Q.C. held that the doctrine of repudiation applied to leases. This enabled tenants living in appalling conditions which were clearly in breach of the implied covenant to repair to end their three-year assured shorthold tenancy prematurely and to obtain damages. He held that the plaintiffs by vacating the house and returning the keys had accepted the repudiatory conduct of the defendant (the breach of the repairing covenent) as putting an end to the contract.

In *Hammersmith and Fulham London Borough Council v. Monk* [1992] 1 All E.R. 1 these competing perspectives were discussed in the context of whether a periodic joint tenancy could be determined at common law by a notice to quit given by one of the joint tenants without the concurrence of the other in a context where the tenancy did not specifically provide for this occurrence. In this case the joint tenancy was granted to Mr Monk and Mrs Powell who were cohabiting. They decided to separate and Mrs Powell moved out. She sought to determine the tenancy by serving the appropriate notice without the knowledge of Mr Monk. The council was willing to rehouse her if she followed this course of action.

Lord Browne–Wilkinson suggested that there were two instinctive reactions to these circumstances which led to diametrically opposite conclusions: first, that it cannot be right for occupancy of a joint home to be unilaterally terminated by one party thereby destroying the right of the other but, secondly, that it was impossible to require that the one who quits the home to continue indefinitely to be liable for the discharge of obligations to the landlord under the tenancy agreement. He recognised that these two reactions were mirrored in the legal analysis. The first reflects a property-based understanding of Mr Monk's rights, the latter is a contract-based understanding of Mrs Powell's position ([1992] 1 All E.R. 1 at 10). The House of Lords held that the contract perspective should prevail and in the absence of

---

[32] Gray, *Elements of Land Law* (2nd ed., 1993), p. 675.

express provision a joint tenancy could be terminated by one joint tenant.

We can now consider the implications of these legal, social and economic constructions of renting relations. The first point to make is that the legal proprietary perspective on the leasehold relation reflects the economic aspect of the relations of renting above and the contractual perspective, which places greater emphasis on the continuing relationship between landlord and tenant, reflects the social aspect of the rent relation. However, as pointed out earlier, occupiers tend to perceive the service elements of the relationship as a part of their rights to live in a decent, secure dwelling. For tenants these are included in their claim to property.

Secondly, the different types of landlords with their own social and economic priorities within the rent relation will have differing reactions to the construction of the leasehold form. The arrangements between informal landlords, predominately resident owner-occupiers, are far more likely to look like personal contracts rather than property transactions given that under English law there is no requirement in law for a lease for a term not exceeding three years to be in writing (sections 52 and 54(2) of the Law of Property Act 1925). In many ways the rights and duties associated with leasehold property relations are incidental. However, the informal nature of these arrangements does not necessarily mean that they are conflict free or equitable. Resident landlords, for instance, were found by one study to harass their tenants disproportionately (Nelken, 1983).

Allen and McDowell found in their study of London landlords that commercial/trading landlords were generally not interested in maintenance of their properties, and were keen to find ways around protective legislation by using residential licences, holiday and company lets and to maximise rent payments (1989). For this group clearly the service elements of the lease were not a priority.

Some landlords make full use of the distinction between a lease and a licence to occupy because the former confers property rights which can be transferred and the latter is simply a contract which limits enforceability to the parties. While a lease need not be created formally it must nevertheless meet certain legal prerequisites to be classified as a lease. These involve a right to exclusive possession for the tenant and be granted for a certain duration (or a duration which can be rendered certain by one of the parties) but not necessarily involve the payment of rent.[33]

In addition, statutory protection is based on the property relation: residential tenancies have attracted protection through statute while generally licences have not. Landlords wishing to avoid statutory regulation have sought to offer occupational licences which do not have the essential legal requisites for a lease. This has led to considerable litigation on the distinction between a lease and licence. Licences have been challenged as shams, as tenancies in all but name (*Street v. Mountford* [1985] A.C. 809; *A.G. Securities v. Vaughan; Antoniades v. Villiers* [1990] A.C. 417).

Partington and Hill suggest that until quite recently the courts have tended to adopt a sympathetic attitude towards attempts by landlords to avoid the impact of the statutory schemes of protection (*Somma v. Hazelhurst* [1978] 1 W.L.R. 1014 but that the higher courts in the 1980s started to take an interventionist approach striking down sham licences, showing, often implicitly, their awareness of the interaction of the private form with the statutory framework.[34] Nonetheless, the decisions have remained firmly couched in the private law. So, the courts have considered the meaning of exclusive occupation and the form in which the rent is required by the occupancy document rather than deciding the case on the basis that the landlord was trying to avoid statutory protection under the 1977 Rent Act.

A considerable and complex case law has developed which only has relevance because of the distinctions in the nature of the landlord created by the Rent and Housing Acts.[35] This is illustrated by the fact that the distinction between a lease and a licence is of little relevance to local-authority landlords because their statutory framework under the Housing Act 1985 includes licensees within the protective provisions.[36] Thus, while the courts seem to be laying down generalised principles for the distinction within private law, in fact, they

---

[33] See Partington and Hill, *Housing law: Cases, Materials and Commentary* (1991), pp. 49–84; Gray, *Elements of Land Law* (2nd ed. 1993), pp. 677-706 for more detailed discussion of these elements.

[34] Partington and Hill, *op. cit.,* pp. 3, 49.

[35] See Gray, *op. cit,* pp. 706–732.

[36] The distinction is relevant in relation to a local-authority run hostel for the homeless: See *Westminster City Council v. Clarke* [1992] 2 All E.R. 393.

are making principles for an already defined group. The intricate interaction between the spheres of individual property and statutory relations can also been seen in the developments described earlier in relation to the contractualisation of leases. One consequence of the *Hussein* case is that the tenant's failure to pay the rent will be a repudiatory act exposing the tenant to an action for possession. The tenant will be obliged to rely on statutory protection to resist such a claim. The result in *Hammersmith v. Monk* undermines the security provided by the Housing Act 1985. The local authority would not have been able to evict Mr Monk but his co-tenant can do so simply by serving notice.[37]

A greater emphasis on the contractual nature of urban residential tenancies will require the development of a more consumerist approach to this sector. However, there are a number of obstacles. As we have seen, the tenants are not a homogeneous group, nor do they form an obvious consumer lobby. Landlords do not hold, as a result of their activities, a shared philosophy in the manner of the social landlords. While there a number of standard form tenancies in existence generally the sector has not developed model tenancy agreements embodying good practice in the manner of the social landlords. There are a number of associations which represent landlords but they have not generated the self-regulatory mechanisms usually associated with trade bodies. We will return to the issue in a subsequent section.

## Individual statutory relations

I intend to discuss these statutory interventions around four headings: general tenant protection provisions; security of tenure; harassment and illegal eviction; and rent regulation.

*1. General Tenant Protection Provisions.* The statutory interventions over the twentieth-century have increasingly recognised the residual

---

[37] As Bright and Gilbert, *Landlord and Tenant Law. Nature of Tenancies* (1995) p. 92 point out, the property approach has its limitations — it binds the parties together with their contractual obligations indefinitely.

nature of this sector and the black-market characteristics described by Coleman above. The legislation constructs the landlord as potentially harmful to the tenants interests and in need of policing. Partington and Hill argue that the purpose of much of the legislation has been to create a "poor persons lease" defining the rights and obligations of landlords and overriding the express obligations agreed by the parties.[38] There are a number of pieces of legislation which attempt to address this lack of knowledge of rights. Where a tenant has a right to occupy premises paying a weekly rent, the landlord must provide a rent book or other similar document (Landlord and Tenant Act 1985, section 4). This rent book must provide the name and address of the landlord (section 5 (1)) and certain statutorily defined information (section 5 (1) (a) and (b)).[39] Despite the fact that failure to comply with any of these requirements is a criminal offence (section 7 (1)), there is wide spread non compliance. The scope of the provisions is also severely limited. While tenants must be told of their rights not to be harassed or unlawfully evicted and their right to claim help with the payment of rent, they are not told of the landlord's statutory obligations in relation to repair and maintenance.[40]

The Landlord and Tenant Act 1985 (as amended by the Landlord and Tenant Act 1987) obliges the landlord to supply tenants under certain circumstances with information about his/her identity (section 1; section 2 deals with corporate landlords) or about any assignment of the property (section 3). Part 6 of the Landlord and Tenant Act 1987 also requires the landlord to provide the tenant with an address in England and Wales at which notice may be served on him by the tenant. The tenant is not obliged to pay rent or service charges until this requirement is met (section 48 (2)).

Generally, there has been no overall attempt to provide a private-tenants charter similar to that introduced into the public sector by

---

[38] Partington and Hill, *Housing Law: Cases, Materials and Commentary* (1991), p. 95.

[39] See the Rent Book (Forms of Notice) Regulations 1982, S.I. 1982 No. 1474 (as amended by S.I. 1988 No. 2198 and S.I. 1990 No. 1067).

[40] These include obligations under the Landlord and Tenant Act 1985, s. 11 which obliges a landlord letting a dwelling for less than seven years to keep in repair the structure and exterior of the dwelling-house and the installations for the supply of utilities; the Defective Premises Act 1972, s. 4(1); the Health and Safety at Work etc. Act 1974, s. 4(2); the Housing Act 1985, s. 190 as amended by the Local Government and Housing Act 1989, Sched. 9, para. 2; the Environmental Protection Act 1990, s. 79(1). See Partington and Hill, 1991: chap. 6 for discussion of these provisions.

statute in 1980 and under the Citizens Charter initiative in the nineties (see the next chapter for discussion).

*2. Security of Tenure.*   The right to security of tenure was introduced by section 1 (3) of the 1915 Rent and Mortgage Interest (War Restrictions) Act as a necessary adjunct to rent control. The basic framework remained until the Housing Act 1988 which uncoupled security of tenure from rent regulation for some new tenancies and ended security of tenure and rent regulation for others. Currently there are two different statutory regimes for tenants in the private-rented sector: regulated tenancies under the Rent Act 1977 and assured tenancies under the Housing Act 1988. The form of the security is similar. Tenants have the right to remain in the premises as long as they meet the conditions of tenancy. If the landlord wishes to obtain possession, s/he must first obtain a court order which will not be granted until the court is satisfied that a statutorily specified ground for possession has been met.

The Rent Act 1977 grants protected status to a tenant whose dwelling-house is let as a separate dwelling (section 1) subject to a number of exceptions (sections 4–16), the most significant of which involves residence in another dwelling in the same building by the landlord (section 12). A protected tenancy continues as a statutory tenancy once the original contractual term has been terminated (section 2). (Protected and statutory tenancies are collectively known as "regulated tenancies".) The Act allows a maximum of two statutory successions (Schedule 1). This right to succeed has been reduced in relation to deaths occurring after January 15, 1989 as a result of the Housing Act 1988, Schedule 4, Part 1.[41] A court cannot order possession of a protected or statutory tenancy until it is satisfied that there is suitable alternative accommodation available or one of the discretionary grounds as specified in Part 1 of Schedule 15 are made out or alternatively one of the compulsory grounds in Part 2 of Schedule 15 of the Rent Act 1977 are met (section 98).

---

[41] Succession under the Rent Act 1977 (as amended by the Housing Act 1988) is complicated, see Partington and Hill, 1991: 305–313.

Since January 15, 1989 it has not been possible to create new regulated tenancies.[42] Part 1 of the Housing Act 1988 creates two new statutory constructs; the assured tenancy and the assured shorthold tenancy. The former offers a similar level of security to the tenant as that available to a regulated tenancy (section 1). Its scope is potentially wider than that under the Rent Act 1977, for instance under the 1988 Act the resident landlord exclusion is more tightly drawn (Schedule 1, paragraph 10). A periodic assured tenancy is not terminated by a notice to quit (as in the case of a protected contractual tenancy) but continues until such time as a court orders possession (section 5 (1)). A fixed term assured tenancy becomes a statutory periodic assured tenancy at the end of the term (section 5 (2) and (3)). A landlord seeking possession must proceed by way of a notice of intended proceedings for possession (section 8).

While the statutory grounds for possession under Schedule 2 to the Housing Act 1988 are similar to those under the Rent Act 1977 they are less generous to the tenant, for instance there is a compulsory ground based on rent arrears of 13 weeks at the date of the hearing (ground 8)[43] and a discretionary ground of persistant delay in the payment of rent (ground 11). The Housing Act 1988 offers little right to succeed: Schedule 2, ground 7, provides a ground for possession against a successor unless that successor is exempted by section 17. This latter section generally permits succession by a spouse in residence at the time of the tenant's death.

However, the assured shorthold tenancy breaks with the framework of protection in existence since 1915. It offers a fixed-term lease for a minimum of six months with no security beyond its duration (section 20(1)). At the end of the term the tenant can remain but only until such time as the landlord seeks possession. There is a

---

[42] The Housing Act 1980 had attempted to reduce rent regulation and security of tenure but in a somewhat half-hearted way. Under this Act the assured tenancy provided security of tenure but no regulation of rent. Its use was restricted to "approved" landlords letting new or substantially renovated dwellings. The Act also introduced the shorthold letting which offered the tenant no security of tenure at the end of the letting but provided for rent regulation. Neither of these measures proved popular.

[43] The Government intends to legislate to reduce the period of arrears from 13 to eight weeks. DoE, *Our Future Homes. Opportunity, Choice, Responsibility: The Government's Housing Policies for England and Wales.* Cm 2901, (1995).

mandatory ground for possession available to the landlord (section 21). Tenants must be notified in a prescribed way that they are entering an assured shorthold tenancy prior to its commencement (section 20(1)(c) and (2)).[44] The assured shorthold effectively releases landlords from the fear of tenants refusing to leave. Not surprisingly it has proved popular with landlords: over two-thirds of the lettings covered by the 1988 Act are shortholds.

The Housing Act 1988 introduces market rents for both assured and assured shorthold tenancies to which we will return after discussing unlawful attempts at removing tenants.

*3. Harassment and Illegal Eviction.* History suggests that deregulation encourages landlords to attempt to force existing tenants to leave illegally:

> "The political legacy of the last major attempt at decontrol — the 1957 Rent Act — is such that the Government is sensitive to this criticism and has incorporated a strengthening of the law on harassment in the 1988 Housing Act."[45]

However, harassment of tenants is not confined to moments of deregulation, rather it is a persistent problem seemingly endemic within this residualised sector in which understanding of the consequences of letting is often poor and respect for law limited. A survey by the GLC in 1986 found that one in twenty private tenants had suffered harassment from their landlord in the previous year.

The statutory measures introduced initially in the Protection from Eviction Act 1965 to tackle these problems to some extent recognise this context. The present provisions are contained in the 1977 Protection from Eviction Act as amended by the Housing Act 1988

---

[44] The Government intends to legislate to reduce the procedural requirements necessary to create a valid assured shorthold tenancy because these "can pose a trap for inexperienced landlords, and may deter owners of empty properties from putting them to use". *Our Future Homes. Opportunity, Choice, Responsibility: The Government's Housing Policies for England and Wales.* Cm 2901, (1995). It also proposes to withdraw the right of shorthold tenants to refer their rent to a Rent Assessment Committee during the initial fixed term of the tenancy (DoE, *The Legislative Framework for Private Renting.* Consultation Document (1995).

[45] Kemp, "Deregulation, markets and the 1988 Housing Act" in *Social Policy and Administration* (1990), Vol. 9, No. 4, p. 152.

which creates both civil and criminal liability for unlawfully evicting and harassing a residential occupier. Section 1 of the 1977 Act (as amended by section 29 of the Housing Act 1988) provides the criminal liability. The number of prosecutions, however, have been very low – about 100 a year for the years 1983–1988.[46] The Act empowers local authorities to institute proceedings for these offences (section 6) and usually the police leave the enforcement to them. Penalties for successful prosecutions are often derisory.[47]

*McCall v. Abelesz* [1976] Q.B. 385 held that civil liability could not be founded on breach of the criminal provision in the 1977 Act. Harassed tenants can seek injunctions and damages under a number of heads including breach of the covenant for quiet enjoyment. The Housing Act 1988, sections 27 and 28 have now provided, under certain circumstances, for civil liability based on the commission of such an offence and widened the scope of the offence by reducing the evidential burden and altering the remedies by including damages for unlawful eviction based on the difference in value of the dwelling with vacant possession and with the sitting tenant. This private law approach, which attaches monetary value to the tenants occupancy, seems to have persuaded the courts to award relatively high sums in recent cases (see *Shafer v. Yagambrun* (1994) 31 C.L.N. 94.

*4. Rent Regulation.*  The Housing Act 1988 introduced market rents for new tenancies created after January 15, 1989. At the present time there are both regulated and market rents within this sector although obviously the former are being replaced by the latter.

The regulated system of rents was introduced in the 1965 Rent Act and is now contained in the 1977 Rent Act. Contractual rents of qualifying tenancies can be referred by either party to a public official, the rent officer, who is empowered by the 1977 Act to determine and then register a fair rent, although there is no obligation to do so. The rent can be redetermined every two years. There is an appeal from the rent officer to a rent assessment committee. The rent officer's determination is based on the statutory requirements set out in section 70 of the Rent Act 1977. These

---

[46] Partington and Hill, *Housing Law: Cases, Materials and Commentary* (1991), p. 265.
[47] *ibid.* p. 265.

involve disregarding personal circumstances and those matters set out in subsection (3) such as tenant improvements. The rent officer must also assume that:

"the number of persons seeking to become tenants of similar dwelling houses in the locality on the terms (other than those relating to rent) of the regulated tenancy is not substantially greater than the number of such dwelling houses in the locality which are available for letting on such terms." (section 70(2)).

Rent officers may use any appropriate method to come to a determination of the rent, taking account of this "scarcity value" (*Mason v. Skilling* [1974] 1 W.L.R. 1437. Generally, landlords have preferred methods which involved fixing a market rent and then deducting any scarcity value. Tenants have favoured calculations based on comparable registered rents. The latter became increasingly feasible with the passage of time while the former more uncertain. Some commentators have argued that in addition to the considerations within section 70, the rent officer can consider the fairness of the rent (Davey, 1992).

However, the introduction of the Housing Act 1988 tenancies, has put pressure on the comparable registered rents methods. Not surprisingly, a substantial gap in the levels of rent between regulated and assured/assured shorthold rents have developed. Landlords keen to reduce this gap are now able to provide evidence of market rents and to argue before the rent officer that there is little evidence of scarcity. In these circumstances the regulated rent would be the market rent. Just such an argument was made in the case of *BTE Ltd v. The Merseyside and Cheshire Rent Assessment Panel* [1992] 16 E.G. 111 where the landlord sought to rely on assured rent comparable arguing that the fair rent was a market rent less if there was no evidence of scarcity. He contested that there was no evidence of scarcity in the present case. The Rent Assessment Committee disagreed but Hutchison J. in the High Court seemed to agree and referred the case back for redetermination. The Committee required evidence of the lack of scarcity and in any case preferred to rely on their knowledge of the local market which led them back to comparable registered rents.

The increasing significance of assured rents is again obvious from the subsequent case of *Spath Holme Ltd v. Greater Manchester and*

*Lancashire Rent Assessment Committee* [1995] E.G.C.S. 134, in which Harrison J. suggested that although the Rent Assessment Committee was not bound to use assured tenancy comparators and could use a range of methods, market comparators might be expected to be used increasingly in the future in the same way as registered fair rent comparators were used increasingly following the Rent Act 1977. He suggested that weighty reasons needed to be shown to depart substantially from market rents recently agreed on similar flats within the same block. The Committee was not entitled to consider reasonableness but to determine the rent by reference to section 70 of the 1977 Rent Act alone.

The 1988 Act prohibited the creation of any new regulated tenancies after January 15 1989 and introduced market rents for both assured and assured shorthold tenancies. There is a residual right of reference to a rent assessment committee for both forms of tenancy, although it is proposed to withdraw this right for assured shorthold tenants.[48]. There is no direct control over rent levels on the initial letting of an assured tenancy. A statutory scheme of reference to a rent assessment committee for a subsequent review exists under section 13 of the Housing Act but a rent review mechanism in the lease prevails (section 13(5)). The committee must fix a reasonable market rent subject to specific disregards contained in section 14. An assured shorthold tenant may apply once during the initial fixed term to a rent assessment committee for a determination of rent which might reasonably be expected under such a tenancy (section 22 of the Housing Act 1988). However, the committee can only undertake such an determination if there are sufficient assured shortholds in the locality and if the rent payable is significantly higher than the "going rate" for such tenancies in the area (section 22).

While this sector has been the subject of a very substantial amount of statutory intervention, it is important not to overestimate the impact of this regulation on relations within the sector. We have already seen that the legislation on rent books is widely ignored and that on harassment and unlawful eviction has had little impact on these abuses. The impact of regulation of the Rent Act 1977 is also limited:

---

[48] DoE, *The Legislative Framework for Private Renting*, Consultation Document (1995).

"In 1988 26 per cent of all privately renting households had regulated tenancies with a registered rent whilst 33 per cent were held on regulated tenancies without a registered rent. By 1990 the former had been reduced to 18 per cent and the latter to 15 per cent".[49]

Although it is important to recognise that the existence of rent regulation seems to have the effect of holding down the rents of regulated contractual rents:[50]

"[A]t £36 per week [in 1990] only 33 per cent higher than the average registered rent. In the light of the much higher average rent levels for 1988 Act tenancies it would seem that many non-registered regulated tenancy rents were not set at 'market levels' but in the 'shadow' of registered rent levels."[51]

The impact of deregulation can be seen not only in the sharpely increased rents but also in the number of new tenancies created:

"Regulated tenancies with a registered rent had declined to 313,000 in 1990 (a decline of 131,000 or 30 per cent) and without a registered rent to 258,000 (a decline of 310,000 or 55 per cent). . . . By late summer 1990, there were 136,000 assured shorthold tenancies and 347,000 assured: 483,000 in all. This more than compensates for the decline in regulated tenancies although it does not greatly exceed the previous approximate rate of creation of about 300,000 new tenancies per year."[52] (Coleman, 1992: 35).

The sharp decline in the number of register tenancies would suggest that this sector will have almost disappeared by the mid-nineties.

These findings are supported by the changed attitudes of landlords. Crook *et al* found that just over half of landlords believed that the situation had changed to the advantage of landlords since 1988 but just over a quarter said that it had not. The improvements were easier repossessions, the ability to charge market rents and the greater

---

[49] Davey, "A Farewell to Fair Rents?" *Journal of Social Welfare and Family Law* (1992), p. 499.
[50] See also the earlier discussion of the impact of rent regulation on page 141.
[51] Davey, *op. cit.*, p. 500.
[52] Coleman, "Private rented housing: the next Steps" in Best, R. et al. (eds.) *The Future of Private Renting: Consensus and Action* (1992) p. 35.

acceptability of private renting. Landlords were, however, also finding that the economic recession and changes in the market were making properties harder to let.[53]

To summarise, with the decline of this sector over the twentieth-century, a wide range of statutory intervention has constructed the landlord as a potential economic and social threat to the tenant and in need of considerable regulation. This intervention has had relatively limited practical impact, although there is evidence to suggest that rent regulation reduces the ability of landlords to relate rents to the higher vacant possession valuations created by the dominance of owner-occupation. Its significance has often been symbolic, representing a battle over the role of the sector as a whole and the appropriate degree of state intervention in the area of private property.

The Housing Act 1988 provisions seemed to have stemmed temporarily the decline in the market although they are aimed more at rehabilitating private landlordism rather than the existing landlords. Private landlordism is being rehabilitated at a policy level. Landlords perceive a shift in power to their advantage. Economically, rents have risen very substantially, although this increase is leading to new uncertainties for both landlords and tenants.

## General regulatory sphere

Landlords are policed by the courts rather than regulated either by themselves or in the manner of the social landlords. The cost of provision within the local authority and housing association sectors has been reduced by the availability of general subsidies but it is the mark of this sector's political marginality that it has been denied access to any such benefit.

We have seen that the government has attempted to stimulate the entry of new landlords by deregulation but Mugnaioni sees two obstacles to these developments:

> "The first is that market rents do not provide an adequate return to tempt the suppliers of equity or debt funding into what is seen as an

---

[53] Crook et al., *The Supply of Privately Rented Homes: Today and Tomorrow* (1995), p. 13.

unconventional, capital-hungry, high-risk, illiquid investment. The second is that it is virtually impossible to provide good accommodation at rents below £100 per week without some form of subsidy."[54]

The increase in rents associated with deregulation have in fact been funded to a significant degree by a state subsidy in the form of housing benefit to individual tenants. In 1992/3 two-fifths of private-rented sector tenants were in receipt of housing benefit. In 1986/7 public expenditure on benefits to this sector was £996 million but had jumped to £3.8 billion in 1993/4.[55]

One problem is that housing benefit dissolves individual responsibilities for rent levels. With deregulation there is no check on these, rent levels can simply reflect the amount of public subsidy available. However, rent officers have been empowered by the Housing Act 1988 to protect the public purse, rather than to set fair rents, by determining the level of rent for the purposes of providing benefit. When a tenant makes an application to the local authority for housing benefit, the application is referred to the rent officer for a determination. The rent officer is required to determine whether the rent payable is significantly higher than the rent prevailing in the locality for similar types of tenancies. If so, then the rent officer must state what that rent would be. S/he also can consider whether there is underoccupation (Social Security Contributions and Benefits Act 1992, sections 123, 130 and 134–137 and relevant regulations).[56]

The determination has no direct effect on the rent or benefit payable. Its effect is on the level of subsidy recoverable by the local authority from central government. In general, as no subsidy is payable on benefit above the determined level, the determination fixes the benefit payable to the tenant. The disparity between determined rent and proposed rent is substantial, about 40 per cent.[57] Tenants must pay the difference, negotiate a lower contractual rent or fall into arrears and be evicted.

From October 1995 there are further restrictions on benefits for rents that are above the average for the particular type of property in

---

[54] Mugnaioni, "Quality Control", *Roof*, July/August 1992, p. 12.
[55] Wilcox, *Housing Finance Review 1993* (1993).
[56] The provision and regulation of housing benefit is a complex and fast moving area, dominated by delegated legislation: see Arden et al. 1994: 319–365 for comprehensive coverage.
[57] See "Fast Facts", *Roof* July/August 1994, p. 17.

the area.[58] Rent officers will fix "local reference rents" calculated at "the mid-point of a range of rents for similar accommodation in the locality". The rent officer will also assess the "property specific rent" for each individual property. Where the latter is less than the former, housing benefit will pay the lower amount. Where it is more, benefit will meet half the difference. Neither of these figures need bear any relationship to the contractual rent.[59]

The policy objective of these measures clearly is to limit excessive rents by providing tenants with an economic incentive to negotiate rents. However, the fear is that tenants relying on benefits will not be in a sufficiently strong position in the market to negotiate and will be forced into below average properties. There is also a strong possibility that the local reference rent will act as the floor rather than the ceiling for rents, thereby reducing any relationship between quality and rent levels which a market aims to produce.[60]

Arguably, therefore, rent officers are continuing to regulate rents but by a different method. Benefit ceilings would also act as a "kind of rent regulation in the housing benefit submarket".[61]

> "To some extent, therefore, rent ceilings that are low enough to save significant amounts of money could undermine the revival of the private rented sector *and* provide a backdoor form of rent re-regulation. . . . This highlights the fact that, with some 45 per cent of private tenants receiving housing benefit, the Government plays a key role in determining the level of effective demand; and also that a 'free market' in a textbook sense does not exist within the sector." (original emphasis).[62]

It is therefore housing benefit regulations rather than Rent Acts which hold considerable significance for, and regulate the relations between, landlord and tenant.

The Government has also begun to consider the provision of more general financial incentives to the sector. The Business Expansion

---

[58] Walentowicz, "Rent control returns", *Roof*, January/February 1995, p. 10.
[59] Griffith, "The benefits of housing", *Legal Action*, July (1995), p. 9.
[60] *ibid.* p. 9.
[61] Kemp, "Housing Allowances and Fiscal Crisis of the Welfare State", *Housing Studies* (1994), Vol. 9, No. 4, p. 540.
[62] *ibid.* p. 540.

Scheme (BES) which was introduced in the tax year 1988/9, allowed shareholders in companies providing dwellings, rented on an assured tenancy basis for five years, to obtain tax relief at their marginal rates of taxation. This scheme has proven exceptionally costly to the Treasury. To increase the size of the sector by 1 per cent through this method is estimated to require capital expenditure of around £10bn.[63]

> "Only a few BES properties were new additions to the housing stock. Repossessed housing accounted for over 20,000 units. It is difficult to know exactly how many of the remainder were newly built but our estimate (based on company prospectuses) is that only 20 per cent were new, which means that the BES financed around 12,000 new units. The other 69,000 were simply transferred into private renting from other tenures (or from one segment of the private rented sector to another in the case of university accommodation)."[64]

Perhaps not surprisingly, BES has been phased out by the 1992 budget. Nonetheless, the BES initiative was seen as part of a process of encouraging new forms of professional private landlordism. These landlords want incentives for potential investors in the form of tax shelters, tax breaks or capital allowances for companies and lenders, and support, through some form of underwriting, to create liquidity in residential property investment.[65]

The Government is now proposing to encourage institutional investment through the introduction of Housing Investment Trusts. These institutions will invest in trusts which will own and manage the properties thereby relieving investors of management obligations. Trusts will be exempt from capital gains tax and subject to a reduced rate of corporation tax. Unlike the BES scheme the tax breaks to the trusts will not be limited in size or duration.[66] The Government does not propose to offer the sector any direct subsidy which many institutional investors consider necessary to attract them into the

---

[63] For a further discussion of the Business Expansion Scheme see Crook *et al.*, 1995.

[64] Crook *et al.*, *The Supply of Privately Rented Homes: Today and Tomorrow* (1995), p. 20.

[65] For an analysis of these possible options see Crook and Kemp, 1993, and for a discussion of commercially viable rates of return, Crook *et al.*, 1995.

[66] Department of the Environment, *Our Future Homes. Opportunity, Choice, Responsibility: The Government's Housing Policies for England and Wales* (1995), Cmnd. 2901, p. 22.

private-rented sector. However, the Government intends to allow profit-making companies to bid for grants to provide social housing. The dwellings will be built to rent at below market rents or on shared ownership terms to people in housing need.[67]

Paul Mugnaioni, the former director of housing for Glasgow Metropolitan District Council, now director of Quality Street, a new company specialising in private renting, argues:

> "Quality Street, using debt, as opposed to equity funding, primarily from Nationwide, has demonstrated that it is possible for a professional, private sector, corporate landlord to deliver consistently high service and product standards across a broad spectrum of the market."[68]

Rachman is replaced by Quality Street. The language of policing is replaced by that of consumerism.

Access to grant assistance brings with it the requirement to be regulated in a manner similar to the social landlords. So these privately owned "social landlords" will be obliged to meet the same level of service as existing housing associations.[69] No such vetting or approval of Housing Investment Trust landlords is proposed, although such approval might also be necessary to secure the sector's reputation and be a prerequisite to investment by the financial institutions.[70]

Before moving to a conclusion, I would like to take a short diversion to consider a specific issue within the private rented sector—the quest for enfranchisement.

## The Evolution of the Leaseholder's Right to Enfranchise

This chapter has been concerned with the dynamic relationships between landlord and tenant as they have evolved in a sector which

---

[67] *ibid.* p. 30.

[68] Mugnaioni, "Quality Control", *Roof*, July/August (1992), p. 12.

[69] Department of the Environment, *Our Future Homes. Opportunity, Choice, Responsibility: The Government's Housing Policies for England and Wales* (1995), Cmnd. 2901.

[70] Crook, "The revival of private rented housing: a comparison and commentary on recent proposals," in Best et al. (ed.) *The Future of Private Renting: Consensus and Action*, p. 72.

has been declining for almost a century. This decline is primarily attributable to problems on the supply side of the relationship. The business of residential letting in a market dominated by owner occupation has few attractions. As the rented market shrunk, taking on characteristics associated with a residual sector, the financial and social advantages of owner occupation became more obvious to potential and existing tenants. While there is still considerable demand for private rented dwellings, particularly among the young and mobile, it is seen by most as temporary accommodation on the way to home ownership or permanent rehousing by a social landlord.

However, in certain circumstances some leaseholders have sought to increase their interest in their existing dwelling, often against the wishes of their landlords. While the rest of the chapter has concentrated primarily on the relationships surrounding short-term tenancies, this section considers the position of those who hold longer-term interests in houses and flats.

The demand for enfranchisement is an example of the interaction between the three spheres of relationships described above. Changes within the individual property relations, in particular the sale of long leasehold interests to occupiers, have been stimulated by preferential treatment of owner occupation within the general regulatory sphere. Long leaseholders' perception of their status as home-owners has stimulated demands for the right to enfranchise. These demands have been recognised through legislation, although this legislation has constructed a range of new relationships between leaseholders and freeholders.

Many estates in the later part of the nineteenth century were developed using the building lease. The freeholder granted a long lease, typically 99 years, of a plot to a lessee-cum-builder who would build a small number of dwellings. The lessee would either rent these dwellings out or, more often, sublease to a landlord who would rent them out on a weekly basis. This system was used to develop large areas of urban land for residential occupation by the more affluent artisans working in the new industries (see Stewart, 1981 for a detailed account of these developments in Birmingham).

The leasehold system has also been used for the construction of flats, partly because of the weaknesses in the freehold system in relation to the enforcement of positive covenants (see Law Commission, 1984 for further discussion). The greatest concentration of privately-owned blocks of flats in England is in London and the south-east. This market in London flats boomed before the First World War, leading to the construction of over 1,000 blocks of 10 flats or more (over 40,000 in total), and again in the 1930s:[71]

> ". . . by the outbreak of war in 1939, a further 56,000 flats in 1,300 blocks of over 10 flats had been built in Greater London. Some 39,000 flats in 800 blocks were built in inner London and 17,000 flats in 500 blocks in outer London."[72]

The building of these mansion blocks continued until the 1950s but then stopped.

By 1950, the outstanding terms on the original nineteeth-century building leases were diminishing, giving rise to long leaseholders' demands for protection of their interests. Leaseholders began to claim recognition of their investment in the property. The freeholder's claim to the property based on sanctity of contract and freedom of property was challenged on grounds of injustice and abuse of responsibility towards the leaseholder. While this argument found favour with a minority on the Leasehold Committee in 1950, the majority report disagreed. The 1954 Landlord and Tenant Act, Part 1 constructed the problem as one of lack of security and therefore granted long leaseholders at a low rent a right to remain at the end of the lease. The Act also entitled them to security of tenure under the Rent Act.

Until the 1950s the vast majority of occupants in these leasehold houses and flats held short-term tenancies. However, from that period, the growing owner-occupied market began to be felt first in relation to houses. Throughout the 1950s and 1960s leaseholding landlords were selling their remaining terms to sitting tenants or to incoming occupants. The premium paid for these unexpired terms was often more related to the value of dwellings within the owner-occupied market than to the value of the shrinking assets. The financial insecurity of these interests was recognised by mainstream

---

[71] Hamnett and Randolph, Cities, Housing and Profits: flat break-up and the decline of private renting (1988), p. 20.

[72] ibid. p. 21.

financiers, making building society mortgages very difficult to obtain. Many leaseholding purchasers in inner city areas resorted to "fringe" financiers (see Stewart, 1981). Therefore, by the 1960s long leaseholders were occupiers of the dwelling, seeing themselves as home-owners. The claim to property, based on ownership of a home, was recognised by the 1966 White Paper on Leasehold Reform (MHLG, 1966). The Leasehold Reform Act 1967 was to be based on the assumption that the land belonged in equity to the landowner and the house belonged in equity to the occupying leaseholder. This split of "equitable ownership" involves a serious interference with the contractual and proprietary interests of the freeholder. The contract of lease requires the lessee to render up the land and thereby all that is attached to it at the end of the term. In property law, the freeholder is entitled to recover the reversion unencumbered.

The 1967 Act gave the tenant of a house on a long lease at a low rent the right to acquire the freehold or the right to an extended lease. The provisions of the Act construct the terms for recognition of the leaseholder's claim. The leaseholder must be resident and therefore an owner-occupier, in a house (the claims of flat dwellers had yet to develop), and be of modest means. This last requirement is achieved through rateable value limits. In these circumstances the freeholders' claims, based on private property law, are overridden by the public interest of extending home ownership.[73]

However, it is in the price to be paid where the increased interest of the leaseholder is most clearly evident. The Act deems it equitable that the freeholder be compensated only for the loss of the site and not for the loss of the marriage value (the increased value created by the merger of the leasehold and freehold interest). Freeholder obstruction to the implementation of the Act was focused on this element (see Stewart, 1981).

The rights under the 1967 Act were extended in 1974 to include some houses with higher rateable value. Here, however, we see the

---

[73] This public interest in owner occupation was recognised by the European Court in *James v. United Kingdom* (1986) 8 E.H.R.R. 123 when the Duke of Westminster challenged the legislation on the grounds that it violated the right to property guaranteed by the Convention on Human Rights (see Bright, "Enfranchisement—A Fair Deal for All or For None?" The Conveyancer's (1994), p. 217).

construction of a slightly less deserving owner-occupier and greater recognition of the property interest of the freeholder. The price payable is based on terms more generous to the freeholder and allows him/her access to some of the marriage value.

We have seen that until the 1950s the occupiers of mansion blocks were predominately renting on short-term lease from investor landlords. Hamnett and Randolph have charted the rapid transformation of this rental market in London during the 1960s and 1970s:

". . . the 1966 census revealed that out of a total of 51,090 private sector flats in central London only 4,350 or 8.5 per cent were owner occupied. The remaining 91.5 per cent were privately rented. The number of purpose built flats in central London which had currently registered rents in mid-1980 was only 12,757. . . . Thus it appears that up to 70 per cent of central London's privately rented, purpose-built flat sector had disappeared from the rent registers by mid-1980."[74]

The relationships between owners and occupiers have been transformed by the development of a market for the sale of flats. Once this market had emerged, there developed a dual market in flats in a manner similar to that described earlier in the chapter for houses. The value of flats for owner occupation became greater than their value to landlords for renting. In these market conditions, traditional residential investment companies are replaced by an aggressive breed of speculative break up companies who are not "landlords" but asset strippers.[75]

Existing tenants were persuaded to purchase the long leasehold interest and new tenants bought flats on this basis so that the blocks now contained both leaseholders and tenants. Problems and conflicts rapidly emerged with these changed relations between the landlord and tenant which eventually led to the establishment of the Nugee Committee in 1985 (DoE, 1985). The terms of reference of the committee constructed the problem as one of management failure:

"poor maintenance, excessive service charges, lack of consultation over works, not knowing who the landlord was, little contact between

---

[74] Hamnett and Randolph, *op. cit.,* p. 32.
[75] Hamnett and Randolph, *op. cit.,* p. 6.

landlords and tenants, inadequate leases and lack of management expertise."[76]

The 1987 Landlord and Tenant Act reinforces this construction of the problem. The tenant is entitled under Part 2 to apply to the court to appoint a manager when the landlord is in breach of the repairing obligations and has failed to comply with a notice to remedy. In cases of persistent failure to carry out management obligations the tenants are entitled to acquire compulsorily the landlord's interest (Part 3). The tenants collectively are given under Part 1 a right of first refusal on sale by the landlord. Also if the landlord sells without notice, tenants all have a right to purchase the block at market value from the new landlord.

Therefore the tenants' claim to enfranchise is only recognised where the landlord is in serious breach of his/her management obligations. In all other instances the property rights of freeholders are recognised. However, the claims of leaseholders through the construction of their interests as owner-occupiers continued. Their claim is similar to those of house dwellers. The premium paid reflects the owner-occupied value of the dwelling and yet the leasehold system undermines this value—it is a wasting asset which reverts to the freeholder on reversion.

The Leasehold Reform, Housing and Urban Development Act 1993, Part 1 recognises the changed relationships within this sector and the claims of owner-occupying flat dwellers by granting a right to tenants to purchase the freehold of their block collectively or to extend their leases. The Act once again constructs the property relation between the parties. The rights are only available where the block is seen to be owner occupied. Half of the participating tenants need to be resident, two-thirds of tenants must have a long lease at a low rent and two-thirds of these must support enfranchisement.[77]

Despite the recognition of the leaseholders' claim on the basis of owner occupation, their "equitable" claim is not as strong as those purchasing under the original 1967 Act term. The price includes the purchase of the freehold, at least 50 per cent of the marriage value, injurious affection payments and both the landlords' and tenants'

---

[76] Bright, *op. cit.*, p. 212.
[77] Bright, *op. cit.*, p. 218.

costs. The high prices to be paid not only make enfranchisement unlikely for many but also retains recognition of the freeholder's property rights.[78]

Thus we see that there are three constructions of leaseholders under the 1967 and 1993 Acts which reflect the varying property relations between the parties based on differentially recognised claims to property rights. These claims have arisen in the context of marked changes in the broader regulatory framework for owner occupation and private renting. The dominance of the market in owner occupation, encouraged by Government fiscal policy, has led to the new forms of landlordism based more on trading and asset stripping than on residential investment.

## Conclusion

The relations within the private rented sector are underpinned by the common law form of the lease which itself contains conceptual ambiguities; containing both proprietary and contractual perspectives. These tensions are highlighted in the context of this residualised sector where relations are far more easily characterised as contractual rather than proprietary but which have been unable to generate any of the indicies for contractualisation. Consumerism has not developed, although there is evidence of the emergence of such an approach. Instead the sector has been heavily policed through the courts on the assumption that landlords will be aberrant rather than socially responsible. We see the attempt to stimulate a new socially responsible yet profitable landlordism. These developments will highlight the tensions experienced in more acute form in the socially-rented sectors. At present landlords to a large extent externalise the costs of social and economic marginalisation on to courts and the public regulators such as tenancy relations officers and environmental health officers. A repositioned landlordism will become accountable to the tenants and will have to deal with the costs of this. This is at a time when the other sectors are attempting to externalise "antisocial behaviour" and non-housing costs.

---

[78] There are proposals to introduce a new form of tenure, the commonhold, to deal with the difficulties of freehold flats. See Law Commission (1987); Clarke (1995).

In part these landlords are a product of changes within the other sectors which will be discussed in the forthcoming chapters. These include the creation of a social market in renting and the development of more entrepreneurial social landlords involved in large scale voluntary transfers and the impact of compulsory competitive tendering of the council stock.

# Chapter Four

# Local Authority Housing

## Introduction

I intend to use the same relational concepts as in the other chapters. However, there are some significant differences between the local authority and private rented sector. First, in the former the individual property relation of landlord and tenant structured by the lease has never existed outside the framework of state regulation. The landlord is the embodiment of the state, a public body, a creature of statute. Secondly, this housing form is very much a product of the twentieth-century. Although the local authorities' powers to build housing was established in the second-half of the nineteenth-century, the basic framework for the development and management of local authority housing evolved between 1909 and 1935.

The Housing and Town Planning Act 1909 terminated the requirement for authorities to resell within ten years any dwellings constructed in redevelopment areas and enabled authorities to provide, manage and fix reasonable rents for lodging houses for the working classes without the need to adopt specific powers. The Housing and Town Planning etc. Act 1919 (Addison Act) imposed a duty on local authorities to survey the needs of their area and to make and carry out plans for the provision of housing. Subsidies via the rates and the Exchequer were made available for the first time. The subsidy system was extended and refined by the Housing Act 1923 (Chamberlain Act) and the Housing (Financial Provisions) Act 1924 (Wheatley Act). These two Acts reflected different political

119

philosophies. The latter was a product of the minority Labour Government and established the principle that the Exchequer subsidy was conditional on municipal rate subsidy:

"The Wheatley Act subsidy established a pattern which endured for thirty years: the Exchequer contribution was a fixed amount per dwelling for forty years and there was a statutory rate-fund contribution, which could be supplemented by discretionary local subsidy, depending upon local costs and political priorities."[1]

The Housing Act 1930 (Greenwood Act) tackled the issue of slum clearance, requiring local councils to rehouse all those displaced by the schemes. The problem was how to finance the rehousing of the poor tenants who could not afford economic rents. Standards of building were reduced, local authorities were empowered to charge reasonable rents and to develop local rent-rebate schemes while still being obliged to balance their housing accounts. "This encouraged the development of differential rents, with more affluent tenants required to cross-subsidise their poorer neighbours".[2] Five years later the 1935 Housing Act introduced the requirement to maintain a unitary Housing Revenue Account. All rents, subsidies, debt charges and other current expenditure associated with the dwellings built since the Addison Act were pooled into the one account.[3] Local authorities were also given specific duties to provide sufficient accommodation to alleviate overcrowding.

Thus by 1935 the statutory framework for housing development was in place and made feasible by various general and specific subsidies. Allocation and rent fixing arrangements were established. Cole and Furbey (1994) among others point out that it would be inaccurate to depict a unitary, coherent political history to the development of council housing in the first-half of the twentieth-century. The levels of subsidies altered regularly as did the emphasis on housing for general needs or for slum clearance and overcrowding. The contribution required from the rates varied considerably under the various Acts. Local councils' decisions over how to balance

---

[1] Malpass, *Reshaping Housing Policy: Subsidies, Rents and Residualisation* (1990), p. 41.
[2] Cole and Furbey, *The Eclipse of Council Housing* (1994), p. 55.
[3] Merrett, *State Housing in Britain* (1979), p. 58.

their accounts, in particular whether and how to utilise differential rent and means-tested rebate schemes, also differed substantially. Nevertheless the statutory framework consolidated into the 1936 Housing Act endured.

Thus the structures for the provision and management of council housing were in place well before the post-war welfare state settlement. Indeed, council housing was a major form of tenure before 1939. Some commentators argue that the pre-war form was taken and transformed into one which was seen in the same universalistic terms as the new National Health Service and state education system.[4] We argue that while council housing prospered and received bipartisan support along with the other welfare state services, it was never fully incorporated into the settlement. The dominance of the market in the provision of housing was never broken (Stewart and Burridge, 1989).

However, council housing emerged out of this history with a number of characteristics. First, its form undoubtedly incorporated a number of collectivist elements such as rent pooling, subsidy from rates and general taxation, allocation according to notions of need, not ability to pay, and political accountability. These collectivist elements emanating from statute have interacted with the individual property relationships constructed through the lease in significantly different ways to those relations in the other housing sectors. Secondly, because public landlordism is the product of a historical political compromise with collectivism and welfarism, it was more vulnerable to and sharply affected by the breakdown in political consensus on the welfare state than the other services. We have argued elsewhere that the development of a social market in housing in the 1980s was unopposed precisely because of this history (Stewart and Burridge, 1989). Thirdly, the public landlord has been constructed legally throughout this history in a variety of ways not only through the regulatory framework but also through the judges' interpretation of the relationship between the rights of tenants under the lease and the responsibilities of a public landlord. Prior to 1980 the courts constructed the public landlord through recognition of its collectivist elements when challenged by tenants. Post 1980 it can be argued that the courts have contributed to the reconstruction of the public landlord through challenges primarily in the regulatory sphere.

---

[4] Saunders, *A Nation of Home Owners* (1990), p. 27.

I will argue in this chapter that there has been a substantial repositioning of the public landlord within the housing market over the last thirty years. The collectivist elements within the relationships have been undermined. The sector has been residualised and commercialised. These changes are reflected in the shifting relationships between landlord and tenants. The trend can be characterised by the changing construction of tenants from local people entitled or in need of state provision to consumers of a public commodity purchased through a contract with rent as a consideration.

Until the 1970s, legal relationships provided the backdrop to more important relations structured by the bureaucratic methods of local housing officers and, to a lesser extent, by the activities of the local politicians. Discussions relating to new housing provision would generally be dominated by professional and technical concerns and involve little or no consultation with wider constituencies. Allocation decisions and rent levels would reflect the past development activities of the council far more than the present context of need or market rents. This administrative approach also characterised the regulatory sphere, with the parties manoeuvering within an agreed financial framework. The provision of council housing embodied an overall political consensus on the role of local authorities in the welfare system.

This consensus dissolved in the 1980s requiring central government to resort to legislation rather than bureaucratic persuasion to achieve their objectives. As the conflicts developed, local-central relationships generally became more juridified.[5] The main focus for activity by central government has been in the regulatory sphere, on the financial regimes which affect both the capital and revenue budgets of the local authorities. Financial management and accountancy practices drawn from the private sector have become far more significant as the power and influence of the financial regulators have increased. Housing management has been professionalised in an attempt to demonstrate that landlords can be efficient and effective. At the same time, there has been a renewed interest in tenant consultation and participation, with tenants becoming consumers of

---

[5] See Loughlin, *Local Government in the Modern State* (1986) and "Law, Ideologies and the Political—Administrative System", *Journal of Law and Society*, No. 1, pp. 21–41.

housing services as well as residents. Tenants have been granted, centrally, consultation rights in conjunction with a variety of possible routes out of local authority ownership. Locally, the emphasis has been on developing new accountability structures to encourage tenants to stay. Generally, these new forms have been based on market consumerist ideas as a substitute for administrative and political methods.

It is possible to see a variety of mechanisms through which these changes have occurred. The work of Hirschman (1970) on exit and voice provides a useful way of characterising some of these. Although writing in 1970, his ideas on deterioration within firms and organisations has a distinct resonance with the political contexts of the eighties and nineties. He suggests that there are two options available to purchasers of goods and members of organisations when the quality of the product starts to decline. The first is to exit, to buy elsewhere, the second is to give voice, to complain from within. Exit is an economic mechanism, voice, a political one. He looks at the conditions under which each of these options is used and under which a combination of the two can prove useful in an attempt to improve the performance of a firm or organisation. His view is that both mechanisms are important. In some situations, exit is the main dissent mechanism, particularly where there is market competition, in others there is nearly complete reliance on voice, such as in the family. He suggests that in some situations, where there is less reliance on market profits, exit can weaken the voice capacity because the most economically able or flexible leave without the full economic impact of this being felt within the organisation. The voice option, however, is not strong enough to bring about change or can just be ignored. In these situations, a more difficult exit route or rather a greater use of the voice option would be of benefit to the organisation. In other situations, the absence of exit leads to sluggish or autocratic management or rule. The possibility of exit can, however, in certain circumstances, lead to a strengthening of the voice option. If the cost of exiting is high, either socially or economically, then the incentive will be to give voice.

Hirschman also discusses the negative and positive effects of loyalty. Loyalty will lead to the use of voice when exit would seem to be the most economically rational thing to do. If the loyalty is active rather than passive then again the organisation is given the opportunity to recover. Loyalty, however, can be problematic when it becomes absolute because the worse the situation becomes the more fierce the loyalty without necessarily the commensurate change in the organisation.

Basically, Hirschman is providing a form of economic analysis which is relatively agnostic about the benefits of market mechanisms to cure all ills in either the economic or the political sphere. By emphasising the importance of voice in economic contexts as well as political, he is giving credibility to political mechanisms as a way of producing recovery. His analysis of the relationship between exit and voice and the need to find an optimal, if elusive, mix of exit and voice is useful in a political context which suggests that economic instruments are the only effective remedy for public sector ills. This analysis of exit and voice provides a way of seeing the shifting accountability structures within the council-housing sector. It also offers insights into the plethora of measures directed at this sector over the last 15 years by central government.

The changes that have occurred produce a complex story which I propose to tackle as follows. I intend to examine the three interacting spheres of relationships at four moments in time: the mid-1970s, the early 1980s; the late 1980s; and 1992-5. When the story has been told in this way, I consider changes in the spheres of relationships through time rather than across time in order to highlight the impact of the shifting power relations on those elements of council housing which in the mid-1970s formed the collectivist element of council housing. The discussion will therefore concentrate on allocation, rents, security of tenure and management which is broadly defined to include landlord accountability.

In the previous chapters we have started with a discussion of the individual property relations. However, in this chapter the order has been reversed. This reflects the different interactions between the three spheres of relations. The dominance of the landlord as a public authority heavily enmeshed in wider regulatory contexts has had a major impact on the other spheres of relations. This is illustrated by the way in which the courts, early on, constructed the local authority landlord in contrast to the private landlord. The general statutory powers granted to local housing authorities under the Housing Acts set the context through which the courts understood the relations between the local authority as landlord. The individual property relations seem insignificant in the light of the landlord's collectivist publicly-oriented housing powers.

The development of the legal construction of public landlordism is seen in the case law which considers the management powers of local authority landlords. In 1949 the House of Lords considered the question of security of tenure for council tenants in *Shelley v. London County Council* [1949] A.C. 56. In this case the landlords were using the Small Tenements Recovery Act 1838 to obtain possession from the appellant, who had not committed any breach of her tenancy agreement. Her dwelling was within the ambit of the Rent and Mortgage Interest Restrictions Acts 1920 to 1939 unless the nature of the landlord took away that protection. The relevant statutory provision was section 156(1) of the Housing Act 1936:

> "Nothing in the Rent and Mortgage Interest Restrictions Acts, 1920–1933, as amended by any subsequent enactment shall be deemed . . . to prevent possession being obtained (a) of any house possession of which is required for the purpose of enabling a local authority to exercise their powers under any enactment relating to the housing of the working classes . . .".

Section 83(1) of the same Act vested general management, regulation and control of houses in the local authority. For Lord Porter (expressing the opinion of the majority) the proposition was:

> "If . . . the general management, regulation and control of houses includes the right to oust the tenant, the local authority in giving notice to quit were exercising their powers under an enactment relating to the housing of the working classes and the protection afforded to tenants of private owners does not apply." ([1949] A.C. 56 at 65.)

He found that "management" must include a right to terminate the tenancy as far as the general law allows. In the much repeated passage he says:

> "It is to my mind one of the important duties of management that the local authority should be able to pick and choose their tenants at their will. It is true that a private landlord cannot do so, but local authorities who have wider duties laid on them may well be expected to exercise

their powers with discretion and in any case the wording of the Act seems to me to necessitate such a construction." ([1949] A.C. 56 at 66.)

Lord Du Parcq dissenting did not find it necessary to construe the statute in this way.

> "It is, however, I think, no less possible that Parliament may have thought that all tenants, even those who, being members of what is called the 'working class,' are given the privilege of occupying their houses as tenants of a local authority, should have the same security of tenure." ([1949] A.C. 56 at 71.)

He argued:

> "If I am right in my opinion that a landlord exercises the general management, regulation and control of his property although it is subject to the Rent Acts, it seems to me to follow that a local authority cannot be said to require possession of a house for the purpose of enabling it to exercise its powers under the Housing Acts *when it already owns the house and has let it in proper performance of its duty* under those Acts." ([1949] A.C. 56 at 73.) (emphasis added.)

Thus, Lord du Parcq distinguishes between the exercise of the Housing Act powers of the local authority, for instance to undertake slum clearance, which requires authorities to seek possession of privately rented dwellings so acquired, and the duties of the local authority as a landlord of its own dwellings. He seeks to treat public tenants in a manner similar to private tenants who obtain security of tenure under the Rent Acts.

The majority distinguishes the local authority as landlord from the private landlord because of their wider Housing Act powers. The public position of the local authority ensures that it can be trusted to act in a public-spirited and fair way in the general public interest as a landlord. Here the relationship of the local authority tenant is constructed by the collectively organised management arrangements of the landlord not by the individual property relations with the landlord.

The construction of the landlord's collective need to manage as antithetical to the tenants' security was not challenged again in the courts until the late 1970s when, as we shall see shortly, the outcome was very similar. However, statutory intervention through the Housing (Homeless Persons) Act 1977 (now Part 3 of the Housing Act 1985) was by then reinterpreting the respective needs of landlord and tenant. The homeless provisions require the landlord to consider the individual housing need of certain categories of persons who are statutorily defined, not picked or chosen locally.

The dominance of the regulatory context can be seen in the determination of rent in the council sector. Understanding the history of rent fixing in local authorities is not an easy task. It is necessary to grasp a number of elements in the equation. The first point to make is that the consumption aspects of council housing have been socialised, but the production aspects were not.[6]

> "Although tenants on the whole do not pay market rents, the total cost to be borne by rents and subsidies reflects the fact that local authorites have to buy land at market prices, they have to borrow money at market rates of interest, and the great majority of council houses have been built under contract by private builders, whose prices are in turn influenced by the market prices for labour and materials, and by their own need to make a profit."[7]

Secondly, "despite these interactions with the market system council housing in Britain has been, and even now remains, characterised by non-market based approaches to pricing".[8] The starting point for council rents is historic cost pricing *i.e.* rents are related to the original cost of production not what the dwelling is worth on the open market. However:

> "the rents of individual council houses have not been closely related to their own historic costs, but total rental income in each local authority has been related to the aggregate costs of its housing stock."[9]

The 1935 Housing Act provided the legal mechanism for this aggregation to occur by requiring that housing authorities keep Housing Revenue Accounts for their stock as a whole. Not only were rents pooled but also all forms of subsidies, including Exchequer and

---

[6] Malpass, *Reshaping Housing Policy: Subsidies, Rents and Residualisation* (1990), p. 60.
[7] *ibid.* pp. 60–61.
[8] *ibid.* p. 61.
[9] Malpass, *op. cit.*, p. 61.

the contributions from the local rate fund which were required under specific legislation such as the Wheatley Act of 1924 (which remained the operative statute for building until 1933) together with any discretionary sums.

Local authorities had wide discretion over rents within the general statutory requirement to fix them at a "reasonable" level (section 24 of the Housing Act 1985 as amended by the Local Government and Housing Act 1989). As Malpass has pointed out, while central government provided fixed subsidies for every house built by a local authority, rent decisions locally had no impact on Exchequer spending and could therefore be more or less ignored.[10] These fixed subsidies were related to production. When the focus moves to subsidies for consumption after 1972, central government is far more concerned to regulate expenditure.

If authorities wished to use pooling as a generalised device to keep all rents down then they would pool both rents and subsidies comprehensively. If they wished to subsidise poor tenants in a specific welfare way then they could use the subsidies and also rent pooling to finance rent rebate or differential rent schemes.[11] The authority could also add voluntary contributions from the rate fund. These three sources of funds, rents, Exchequer subsidy (eventually in two forms, general bricks and mortar and needs related) and local contributions (both mandatory and discretionary) put into practice through rent pooling and rebate schemes, provide the basis for the administrative process of rent fixing until 1972 and still form key elements in the contemporary equation.[11a] Rent rebates and differential rent schemes were extremely unpopular with tenants and most local authorities refused to introduce them.[11b] Leeds, however, was one of those authorities which attempted to introduce a comprehen-

---

[10] ibid. p. 59.

[11] Merrett, State Housing in Britain (1979), pp. 173–174.

[11a] A further way of tackling the cost of providing for poor tenants is to build poorer quality dwellings and to sort the body of tenants on quality and income grounds. This method was also used and has obvious impact on allocation policies as we shall see later. It also had the effect of avoiding the introduction of rebate schemes.

[11b] In 1939 there were only 80 authorities in England and Wales out of a total of 1,400 operating such schemes and even these were using a tiny proportion of the subsidy pool for these purposes (Malpass, 1990: 45). Most of the schemes were directed at tenants from clearance areas. Only 14 of the schemes were available to all tenants (Parker, 1967: 40).

sive rebate scheme in the early 1930s. It led to bitter opposition from the tenants and the first legal challenge on a local authority's legal capacities in this area.

The tenant defendant in *Leeds Corporation v. Jenkinson* [1935] 1 K.B. 168 refused to pay the additional rent resulting from the scheme and was served with a notice to quit. He appealed arguing that:

> "the notice to quit was not served *in the ordinary course as between landlord and tenant*, that it was served by these particular landlords, who were subject to statutory limitations and statutory duties, for the purpose of carrying out a policy of relief or public assistance by way of rent relief which was alien to the powers and duties possessed by the Corporation." (emphasis added) [1935] 1 K.B. 168 at 171.

and as a result the Corporation's action was *ultra vires*. The tenant's argument was that the landlord in acting as a welfare institution, increasing all rents and aggregating them in order to contribute to a means-tested benefit was *ultra vires*. The authority as landlord should use its rights arising from the tenancy in the same way as a private landlord.

The Court of Appeal rejected the appeal unanimously, distinguishing between the legislation which set out the subsidy regimes and the legislation granting the powers of management to local authorities, including the duties to determine rents. The legislation in relation to subsidy did not set the rents. The Master of the Rolls also held that the local authority had powers to give "reasonable preference to large families" in letting houses and that preference could extend to rent determination.[12] As in *Shelley's* case, but significantly earlier in its history, the court constructed the landlord differently, as a public-welfare body entrusted with very broad and flexible powers to determine rent which changed the property relations between landlord and tenant.

Pre-war schemes were directed at the problem of low and falling tenants' income. In the post-war period, particularly after 1955, rent pooling and rebates became increasingly linked together. Now rent

---

[12] In practice, "5,202 of 5,771 tenants were receiving a full or partial rebate at the end of the first six months of operation; that is 90 per cent of the tenants were judged unable to meet the cost of the 'average economic rent' for the type of house" (Parker, 1967: 41).

pooling enabled local authorities to raise rents on the older houses above historic levels and use the surplus earned to transfer to newly built stock which was becoming far more expensive to build in an era of inflation.[13] The pooling reduced the subsidies needed to bring rents down to levels which tenants could afford. However, by raising rents of the older properties in this way, authorities came under increasing pressure to introduce rebate schemes or to increase their rate-fund contributions.

The tenants in *Belcher v. Reading Corporation* [1950] Ch. 880 once again failed to convince the court that the rebate scheme was *ultra vires*. Romer J. introduced the need to balance the interests of tenants, particularly those of small means, with the interest of ratepayers, the majority of whom were people of comparable means to the tenants. In 1955 the tenants of Cardiff Corporation tried to challenge their differential rent scheme. The scheme under consideration in *Smith v. Cardiff Corporation (No. 2)* [1955] 1 Ch. 159, unlike the previous two cases, involved an increase in rent for tenants within higher income bands. Dankwerts J. held that this method of surcharging the tenants of particular houses according to their means was not *ultra vires* and was within the powers of the Corporation.

The Housing Subsidies Act 1956 significantly altered the financial equation for authorities by withdrawing some Exchequer subsidies and lowering others for new building but, more importantly, removed the necessity for councils to make any rate contribution to their Housing Revenue Account. Not surprisingly, this new context stimulates more legal challenges to individual authority's decisions in the courts.

There are three cases which attempt to tackle aspects of rent pooling and rate contribution. In *Summerfield v. Hampstead B.C.* [1957] 1 All E.R. 221 the tenants challenged the pooling system which cross-subsidised the newer properties but to no avail because there is no duty to fix "economic rents" and because there is "no justification in the Housing Acts" for "the notion that a council house must necessarily be run at a loss" ([1957] 1 All E.R. 221 at 226). The challenge in *Luby v. Newcastle-under-Lyme* [1964] 1 All E.R. 84 came because the authority did not operate either a rebate or a differential-rent scheme. The tenant argued that the authority had

---

[13] Merrett, *op. cit.*, p. 72.

failed in its duty by not considering his personal circumstances before fixing his rent. Lord Justice Diplock in the High Court held that there was no need for the authority to do so. He goes on to introduce another element in the equation:

". . . there is also involved a choice whether the individual impoverished tenant should be assisted at the expense of the general body of ratepayers by a reduction in rent, or at the expense of the general body of taxpayers, by national assistance." [1964] 1 All E.R. 84 at 89.

The appellant in the third case, *Evans v. Collins and Another* [1964] 1 All E.R. 808 was a ratepayer who objected to the accounts on the ground that London County Council rents are unreasonably low contributing to loss on the general rate fund. The LCC at the time was opposed to differential rent schemes and means tests in principle, instead it assessed the level of rents which its tenants could afford to pay as a whole and then balanced this with a contribution from the rates. Its methods were considered to be appropriate by the court. The authority was not required to consider the needs and capacities of individual tenants. The LCC rents had for some time been considerably less than rents in the private sector.[14] The court held there was no requirement to fix "economic" rents as long as it could show that it had considered the various interests of rent and rate payers.[15]

Thus the courts allowed local authorities to set their own political priorities and to translate these into whatever rent scheme suited them in relation to their own stock. The power to set reasonable rents was in effect the power to set any rent which did not transgress the general public law requirement to exercise discretion reasonably. Diplock, L.J. made this clear in *Luby* when referring to section 111 of the Housing Act 1957 (now section 24 of the Housing Act 1985 as amended). "I doubt whether the addition of the adjective 'reasonable' has the effect of narrowing the wide discretion which the local authority would have if that word were not present" ([1964] 1 All E.R. 88).

---

[14] In the pre-war era council rents would generally have been as high or higher than the private sector but this relationship between public and private rent levels had changed significantly after the war, so that rents in the public sector were often well below those in the private sector. This was partly due to the Rent Act 1957 which had introduced phased de-control of rents.

[15] The 1949 Housing Act had removed the requirement to have regard to the rents ordinarily payable by persons of the working classes in the locality.

It is interesting to compare the courts' response to attempts by a local authority to use a rate contribution to subsidise private tenants' rents. In *Taylor v. Munro* [1960] 1 W.L.R. 151 the Labour controlled St Pancras Urban District Council objected to the de-controls introduced by the Rent Act 1957 and to means testing. Tenants of de-requisitioned dwellings were entitled by legislation to continue to pay the rent which they had been charged during the requisitioned period. This had been initially fixed by central government but responsibility had passed to local councils. However, landlords were entitled to the rent payable under the Rent Act 1957. The local authority was required to pay any difference in the two figures. St Pancras U.D.C. refused to consider any increases in the rents of dwellings which they could legitimately charge to these tenants. Opposition councillors, acting in their capacity as ratepayers, complained to the District Auditor that this was an unreasonable use of rate funds. The District Auditor agreed and surcharged the councillors involved who appealed to the court. They were unsuccessful. The court considered that the councillors acted in a political manner and had not exercised their discretion reasonably by refusing to consider an increase in rents. In doing so they had failed to take account of the interests of ratepayers.[16]

The 1972 Housing Finance Act marked the end of the era of local laissez-faire. Like the Housing (Homeless Persons) Act 1977, it heralded the direct legal intervention of central government into local authority discretion, reduced local autonomy and challenged the "welfarist" aspects of council housing. It was very unpopular with both tenants and local authorities.[17] The Act was a highly complex piece of

---

[16] H.W.R. Wade commented in *The Listener* "To raise the general levels of wages, to introduce the principle of equal pay, to give free travel to old people, to subsidise rents abnormally – these are all, in effect, new social services. . . . A borough council must not use the general powers which do belong to it in order to encroach on fields which do not belong to it. To pay for novel social experiments is the privilege of the taxpayer, not of the ratepayer" (1960: 921).

[17] The government anticipated resistance and added default powers to the Act so that councillors could be fined and disqualified from public office for failing to implement the legislation. Councillors could be replaced by a centrally appointed Housing Commissioner. Two authorities, Clay Cross and Bedwas and Machen, were the standard bearers of resistance. A Commissioner was imposed on the latter, while councillors from the former ended up in prison for refusing to pay their fines. For more detailed accounts of reactions to the Housing Finance Act see Skinner and Langdon, 1974; Sklair, 1975; and Beirne, 1977. See also *Asher v. Lacey* [1973] 1 W.L.R. 412 and *Asher v. Secretary of State of the Environment* [1974] 2 W.L.R. 446.

legislation but, in essence, it introduced the fair-rent system which had been operating in the private sector, since the Rent Act 1965, into the public sector. Local authority rent increases would be determined externally and would be obliged to increase to a point where they reflected market rents.

The 1972 Act required local authorities to provide a mandatory rent-rebate scheme which would also be available to council tenants on supplementary benefit. There had been a low level battle between central and local government on which should be responsible for paying the rents of those on state benefits. (In 1967, 21 per cent of council tenant heads of households were in receipt of supplementary benefit.) Until 1972, this was decided by negotiation at district office level but generally fell to the centre. Now local authorities were to receive a specific subsidy to cover a high proportion of the cost of the scheme, although in the longer term the aim was to move to a position where rental income would be sufficient to cover it. In the meantime, the balance was made up from the rates. A new general subsidy system based on deficit financing was also introduced so that subsidy would cease to be payable once rents had risen sufficiently to cover costs. Opposition to this Act produced the only case in which a local authority's powers to fix a reasonable rent was successfully challenged. A rent increase from £7.71 to £18.00 per week for one house (to avoid the provisions of the Act) was thought unreasonable in *Backhouse v. Lambeth B.C., The Times*, October 14, 1972.[18]

To summarise, the local authority landlord and tenant relationship has been imbricated within the public collectivist elements of the provision and management of council housing. The courts have helped to shape the relations between landlord and tenant in such a way as to facilitate the collectivist elements. Claims based on the individual property relations between the parties have been far less powerful.

---

[18] The Greater London Council, under Conservative control, had in the late sixties introduced on their own initiative a scheme very similar to that in the 1972 Act. Rents were raised substantially to move towards the private sector in exchange for which tenants were offered means-tested benefits. There was considerable tenant resistance, particularly in East London, to these increases. Five per cent of the quarter of a million GLC tenants refused to pay the increases. The issue eventually found its way to court but not as a dispute over the reasonableness of the rents. In *Greater London Council v. Connolly* [1970] 2 Q.B. 100 the tenants failed to defend possession proceedings for non-payment of rent on grounds that the rents were not validly increased due to uncertainties in the conditions of the tenant's lease.

# Relationships in the Mid-1970s

## A. REGULATORY SPHERE

By the mid-1970s the developmental aspects of council housing were faltering. The huge urban clearance programmes were winding down while criticism of the results were emerging. The politics of council housing had been through a turbulent period. Rent increases in the 1960s had met with considerable opposition from tenants with a number of high profile rent strikes. Through political ineptness central government had managed to unite tenants and many of their landlords in opposition to the Housing Finance Act. Although the incoming Labour Government repealed the most contentious elements of the 1972 Act, it left the national rebate scheme intact, an indication that the political opposition to means-tested benefits in this sector had died out.

The problems of housing finance had not, however, disappeared. The incoming Labour Government announced a fundamental review of housing finance across the sectors in November 1974. Although the review took two-and-a-half years and generated much very useful material on housing issues, its recommendations (DoE, 1977) were seen as a great disappointment by most housing experts (see Merrett, 1979). It considered in some detail questions of council house management, maintenance and tenant control and argued strongly for greater tenant control over a variety of aspects of council housing. In hindsight, this document reflects the crisis of legitimacy which hit welfare-state provision in the seventies. Its concern with consumption issues, rather than production, mindful of Treasury dictates on economic policy, rather than with setting clear political priorities to tackle the growing difficulties in the sector all point to this.

While this review was proceeding, the Government was introducing the ascendant prescriptions of monetarism by cutting public expenditure on housing very substantially in the midst of a major economic crisis.[19] Nevertheless, by 1979, average net rents were at an historically low level in relation to both costs and wages. One innovatory recommendation which was introduced in the financial

---

[19] Malpass, *Reshaping Housing Policy: Subsidies, Rents and Residualisation,* (1990), p. 130.

year 1977–8 was the housing strategies and investment programmes (HIP) to regulate the capital expenditure activities of local authorities.

"The HIP system allowed central government to set a limit for total local authority housing investment and to distribute that allocation between individual authorities, with the authorities choosing their own mix of spending. . . . When introduced, the new system was said to be in the interests of local discretion as well as giving central control of aggregate spending. In fact, the system has accompanied as almost continuous fall in net public capital spending on housing . . .".[20]

Tenants at this time renewed their attempts to use the courts to regulate a number of management issues. Undoubtedly, this recourse to the law was related to the development of law centres and the growing expertise of housing lawyers who were discovering public law and widening their horizons to challenge public as well as private landlords. Also, as the Public Health Advisory Service commented at the time:

"Perhaps part of the reason for the quickening growth of law centres, housing aid centres, community groups, etc., is a reaction to the changing role of local government from protector and protagonist to opponent and antagonist."[21]

As we have seen, local authorities had been granted broad powers to manage, regulate and control their houses and the courts had decided that the need to exercise these powers collectively was antithetical to individual tenant's occupational rights particularly in relation to security of tenure and rent regulation. In the 1970s almost all the major functions, allocation, occupational security, rent determination and consultation and other forms of accountability were exercised within the general regulatory sphere. (Repairing responsibilities were to some extent an exception, a point to which I will return.)

In selecting tenants, authorities have been required by the various Housing Acts to give reasonable preference to persons occupying insanitary or overcrowded houses, persons having large families, and

---

[20] Hills, *Unravelling Housing Finance: Subsidies, Benefits, and Taxation,* (1991), p. 81.
[21] Public Health Advisory Service, *Interim Report,* (1976), p. 26.

persons living under unsatisfactory housing conditions. Those found to be homeless were added to the list in 1977 (section 113(2) of the Housing Act 1957, subsequently section 22 of the Housing Act 1985). No further procedural requirements were laid down by statute and the courts were reluctant to establish any such requirements. Local authorities also have housing responsibilities in relation to persons displaced by public action under the Land Compensation Act 1973. Under section 39(1) the local authority must secure accommodation in circumstances where suitable alternative residential accommodation on reasonable terms is not available. One of the questions which arose in *R. v. Bristol Corporation, ex p. Hendy* [1974] 1 All E.R. 1047 was the priority to be given to a person housed under these powers in comparison with those housed under the general powers. The court held that there was no priority over those on the general waiting list, thereby refusing to interfere with local discretion.

Tenants also attempted to prevent the process of eviction through public law challenges. There are two types of cases, the first when the local authority is seeking possession because the tenant is in breach of a term of the tenancy usually arrears of rent, the second when there is no such breach.

Local authority landlords had developed practices over the years which involved the use of suspended possession orders in the county court to persuade tenants in arrears to pay off arrears and maintain their existing rents. In *Bristol District Council v. Clark* [1975] 3 All E.R. 976 the tenant fell into arrears and after due warning he was served with a notice to quit. After the notice had expired the tenant paid off the rent arrears. However, he had failed to repay a rent rebate which he had wrongfully obtained. The county court judge had refused to grant the landlords an order for possession on the ground that they had failed to give evidence that they required possession of the house in order to house others in accordance with their powers under section 158 of the Housing Act 1957.[22] The Court of Appeal upheld the appeal holding that a local authority did not have to rely on section 158 but could rely simply on its common law right to obtain possession on the expiry of the notice to quit.

---

[22] Under s.158(2) local authorities could recover possession for the purpose of exercising their powers under any enactment relating to housing.

In *Bristol City Council v. Rawlins* (1977) 34 P. & C.R. 12 at the county court proceedings to obtain an order for possession, the deputy registrar gave possession to the plaintiffs but ordered that the judgment be not enforced without leave of the court because the authority had made an agreement whereby the defendants undertook to pay off the arrears of rent over a 12-month period. The defendants subsequently fell into arrears and the authority sought a warrant for possession. When the matter came before the deputy registrar the defendants had managed to pay off a substantial part of the arrears. He decided not to issue a warrant but to stipulate that the outstanding arrears were to be paid off. He suggested that there would be no further extensions. The question for the Court of Appeal was to determine the extent to which the judge could exercise his discretion in favour of a tenant who is not protected by the Rent Acts and whose tenancy has been properly brought to an end by notice to quit. Geoffrey Lane L.J. held that:

> "Provided that the local authority are acting properly according to their duties . . . and provided that it has been shown . . . that the tenants have failed to observe the terms of the informal arrangement with the local authority, . . . the discretion of the judge or the registrar is very strictly limited indeed. . . . By breaking the terms of the agreement, the tenants cast themselves back . . . on what rights they had at common law. Those rights are very strictly confined." *Bristol City Council v. Rawlins* (1977) 34 P. & C.R. 12 at 20.

The Court of Appeal took a similar view in cases which did not involve rent arrears or other breach of the tenancy terms. In *Cannock Chase District Council v. Kelly* [1978] 1 All E.R. 152 the local authority served the tenant with a notice to quit with no reasons. The judge found Mrs Kelly to be a good tenant but also that it was open to a local authority to evict a good tenant. The tenant appealed, contending that the local authority had abused its powers by taking into account some factor which it ought not to have taken into account or omitting to take into account a factor which it ought to have taken into account. The Court of Appeal dismissed the appeal holding that any allegation of bad faith required dishonesty. It was possible for the tenant to construct a defence of abuse of a local authority's power of management but the burden of proof lay with the tenant. The fact

137

that the tenant was a good tenant and had complied with the terms of the tenancy did not give rise to an inference of abuse of power.

The tenant in *Sevenoaks District Council v. Emmott* (1979) 39 P. & C.R. 404 attempted to raise a defence of abuse of power in possession proceedings. He argued that the plaintiffs relied upon untested complaints by neighbours without informing him and they failed to ensure that he had a fair hearing. He further contended that in arriving at their decision the plaintiffs took into account irrelevant matters such as arrears of rent when there had been none since 1975 and the alleged refusal of the defendant to attend meetings. The Court of Appeal dismissed the appeal. Under its statutory powers of management, the local authority was not required to give reasons for a notice to quit, it had no duty to give the tenant the opportunity to make representations or to conduct a formal inquiry as to the merits of any allegations.

Thus the courts were unable to offer any support to tenants challenging the decision-making processes of their landlords. Their attitude is perhaps best summed up by Lawton L.J. in *Bristol District Council v. Clark*:

> "this court should be most reluctant to interfere with the exercise of Housing Act powers by a local authority. Local authorities have to meet the electors from time to time. The electors are in a far better position than this court could ever be to decide whether the powers have been exercised in a way which meets with general approval." ([1975] 3 All E.R. 976 at 981.)

While the courts seemed to place considerable faith in political accountability, others were questioning it. Tenants' campaigns over rent increases and other housing issues in the late sixties and early seventies had fuelled scepticism over the ability of representative democracy to offer an effective service to tenants.

Local authorities were under no obligation to consult with tenants or encourage them to participate in the decison-making processes. Indeed, a study by Chamberlayne (1978) of the politics of participation in four London boroughs between 1968–1974 found considerable hostility to the concept of participation by local groups. In two of the four boroughs, she found outright hostility, in one, a degree of tolerance and in the fourth, active encouragement. Attitudes to tenants' associations were found to be on the whole patronising and controlling.

While housing practitioners were attempting to use public law to regulate the activities of local authority landlords, academic public lawyers were concentrating on the politico-administrative context for the provision of certain housing services.

A study of council house allocation policies by Lewis and Livock (1979) found the process to be highly discretionary with "slapdash" administrative systems in some authorities, little or no publicity of the rules (where they existed), no public involvement in policy formulation or review (other than that provided by councillors) and few if any procedures for redressing grievances. The authors found in their fieldwork considerable evidence of inappropriate use of discretion by both officers and councillors. It also must be said that they found a number of examples of authorities trying hard to create and operationalise more open and appropriate systems. Their recommendations were for more publicity, more public consultation and involvement in policy review and the provision of suitable grievance redress.

The establishment of the Commission for Local Administration in England under Part 3 of the Local Government Act 1974 had provided an alternative method of challenge for tenants. The ombudsman deals with issues of maladministration, with the way in which decisions are reached rather than the decision itself. A substantial number of complaints from the outset concerned allocation and transfers. Hoath and Jones (1979) studied the ombudsman's investigations on the subject in the first four years, concentrating particularly on the issue of bias. They concluded that bias was likely to creep in where council members were concerned with applications and recommended that councillors should not be involved in the day-to-day process of allocation. They also recommended that there should be more public information available to applicants and that there should be national guidelines on the subject.

Concern over allocations was also being expressed by tenants' organisations and pressure groups, including the growing consumer lobby. (See for instance Welsh Consumer Council (1976)). However, the legislation introduced at this time in the area of allocation was not a result of these activities. The Housing (Homeless Persons) Act

(H(HP) Act) introduced in 1977 represented a distinctly different form of intervention into the relationship between central and local government in the area of housing. It was the product of considerable campaigning which had brought the plight of the homeless to public attention. In particular, it was intended to stop administrative buck-passing between social service and housing departments for responsibility for the homeless. The statute established a number of duties in relation to various categories of homeless persons. Although local authorities retained considerable discretion over the execution of their duties, their actions in this area have been subjected to substantial review by the courts.

The construction of public landlordism during the first half of the century as primarily a politico/administrative arrangement, with little resemblance to a relationship based on the private law lease, was revealed in the 1970s when tenants, motivated in part by changing economic and political priorities, began to challenge their landlords. The court actions exposed the vulnerability of tenants within the other spheres of relations.

B. Individual Statutory Relations

Over the same period, the relations of power contained within the individual property relations in the private sector were modified by a variety of statutory interventions. Security of tenure and rent regulation formed the focus for these measures. However, the increasingly residual nature of the sector prompted further statutory regulation of the individual relations. While directed at the private rented sector, these measures were based on the tenancies and almost by default included public sector tenants.

Council tenants, therefore, have been included in the protection offered by the legislation on unlawful eviction, which was prompted by the activities of private landlords in the era of deregulation between 1957–65. The Protection from Eviction Act 1977 (as amended by the Housing Act 1988 and the Criminal Justice and Public Order Act 1994 imposes procedural requirements on landlords wishing to evict tenants, such as the need to serve a notice to quit in a prescribed manner, and criminalises harassment and unlawful eviction (section 1, PEA 1977 as amended by the Housing Act 1988, section 29).

140

Council tenants have also been included to some extent in the legislation which is aimed generally at providing "a poor man's lease".[23] The Landlord and Tenant Act 1985, section 4, obliges landlords to provide a rent book where the rent is payable weekly unless the rent includes a payment in respect of board which forms a substantial proportion of the whole rent. The rent book must contain the landlord's name and address and a summary of the statutory provisions relating to overcrowding (Housing Act 1985, section 322(1)). Local authority landlords are obliged to provide less information than their private sector counterparts.

Sections 11–16 of the Landlord and Tenant Act 1985 imposes repairing and maintenance covenants on all landlords who lease dwelling-houses for terms of less than seven years (on leases granted on or after October 24, 1961). These oblige the landlord to keep in repair the structure and exterior of the dwelling and to keep in repair and proper working order the installations in the dwelling for the supply of water, gas and electricity, for sanitation and for space heating or water heating. The Defective Premises Act 1972 added a tortious liability in situations where a landlord has an obligation for maintenance or repair.[24]

However, public landlordism had been constructed within the general regulatory sphere to make specific statutory protections unnecessary. Landlords, because of their positioning, were deemed to be more responsible.


C. INDIVIDUAL PROPERTY RELATIONS

Until the 1970s council housing policy was development-oriented. The aim was to overcome housing problems through slum clearance and rehousing in the public sector. This expansion faltered in the early 1970s under changed economic, social and political pressures.

" . . . sharp swings in the economy, steep rent increases and growing dissatisfaction with the treatment they received from both public and

---

[23] Partington and Hill, *Housing Law: Cases, Materials and Commentary*, (1991), p. 94.
[24] For further discussion of repairing covenants see Partington and Hill, 1991: 338–394; Hughes and Lowe, 1995: Chap. 7.

private landlords accentuated two central issues for tenants: housing costs and the quality of housing and related services provided by landlords."[25]

Tenants campaigned strongly against rent increases, using in most instances political rather than legal channels, achieving successes on local rent policies and nationally against the Housing Finance Act. However, reflecting the changing national housing priorities, the organised tenants' movement started to produce charters with an emphasis on rights to security of tenure, to consultation, particularly on rent increases, to decent quality housing and an efficient repair and maintenance service (see for instance the National Tenants' Organisation, 1978).

By the mid-1970s, the idea emerged that tenants' interests could be protected through consumer rights. This approach emphasised the need both for a fair contract between landlord and tenant covering the terms of the relationship and the quality of services received by individual tenants and for systems of redress to be available to individual tenants when things went wrong.[26]

Attention therefore turned to the relationship of an individual tenant with their local authority landlord. Most council tenancies are periodic, being granted on a weekly basis. There are no general legal requirements for short-term tenancies not exceeding three years (section 54(2) of the Law of Property Act 1925). In the 1970s a number of reports revealed local authority practice in relation to tenancy conditions. The first came in a circular to local authorities from Derek Fox, adviser on housing management at the Department of the Environment in which he suggested that authorities were stipulating vast numbers of conditions, "most of which were printed on rent cards in such a way that many tenants will not be able to read them let alone understand – and agree – to them" (Fox, 1973).

The National Consumer Council (1976) (NCC) in its very influential report on tenancy agreements found agreements to be wholly one sided, wrongfully excluding council liability, paternalistic, punitive and incomprehensible. Subsequently, the Housing Services

---

[25] Kay, Legg and Foot, *The 1980 Tenants' Rights in Practice: A Study of the Implementation of the 1980 Housing Act Rights by Local Authorities 1980–1983*, (1986), p. 1.
[26] Kay, Legg and Foot, *op. cit.*, p. 1.

Advisory Group (1977) issued an equally critical report. Both the HSAG and the NCC drafted a model tenancy agreement which set out in some detail the rights and obligations of both parties. The courts had a chance to consider tenancy conditions in *Liverpool City Council v. Irwin* where both the Court of Appeal [1975] 3 W.L.R. 663 and the House of Lords [1976] 2 W.L.R. 562 commented on the tenancy agreement. Lord Wilberforce provides a clear description:

> "As is common with council lettings there is no formal demise, or lease or tenancy agreement. There is a document headed "Liverpool Corporation, Liverpool City Housing Dept" and described as "Conditions of Tenancy". This contains a list of obligations upon the tenant – he shall do this, he shall not do that or he shall not do that without the corporation's consent. There is an amalgam of obligations added to from time to time, no doubt, to meet complaints, emerging situations, or problems as they appear to the council's officers. . . . At the end there is a form for signature by the tenant stating that he accepts the tenancy. On the landlords' side there is nothing, no signature, no demise, no covenant." ([1976] 2 W.L.R. 562 at 566.)

In some ways the nature of these documents was legally irrelevant in relation to tenants' occupational status in the seventies. The landlord, as we have seen, did not have to rely on breach of tenancy condition to evict a tenant. As long as the authority follows the procedural requirements set out in the PEA 1977 and acts in good faith, it could do what it liked with its tenants. What these tenancy conditions reveal is the relationship of power which existed between landlord and tenant.

The history of the local authority as developer had its legacy in the way in which tenants were treated. Little or no concern was focused on the consequences of development, mass landlordism. Tenants entered and were then expected to be silent to adopt Hirschman's terms (1970). They were provided with no legal voice mechanisms, no rights to be consulted or to participate. A very few authorities had developed systems for consultation, often as a result of organised tenant action in the earlier seventies, many others were antipathetic or openly hostile.

The attempts by collective tenant bodies to introduce charters represented a struggle to alter the balance of power, politically. The model tenancy agreements suggested by the consumer lobbies also recognised the power imbalance and sought to redress it through legally constructed contracts.

## Relationships in the 1980s: 1980–88

A. INTRODUCTION

The election of the Conservative Government in 1979 under Margaret Thatcher heralded a new era in the relationships of council housing. The failure of political confidence in the public sector in the seventies, accentuated by serious economic difficulties, presented the opportunity for restructuring the sector. Central government policy was dominated by a desire to curb local authority spending and to facilitate the right to buy. The period under present discussion saw the local authority landlord recast from (faltering) developer to (flawed) manager of a declining stock. The period involved some significant changes in power, through centralisation and juridification of relationships. We see also the development of exit rights for tenants but very muted "voice" mechanisms.

B. REGULATORY SPHERE

Loughlin (1986; 1994) has argued that during this period the relationship between central and local government became increasingly politicised and juridified.

> "Juridification arises from two sources. First in the short-term, it results from the consequent breakdown in traditional administrative practices; the legal relationship, of minor importance traditionally, now defines the limits of central departments and local authorities' ability of independent action. Secondly, in the longer-term, it is a product of the particular form which the Conservative Government's attempted solution has taken."[27]

Over these years there was a plethora of legislation directed at the provision of council housing. The form it took was far more directive

---

[27] Loughlin, *Local Government in the Modern State*, (1986), p. 188.

and interventionist than in the past, attempting either to reduce the wide powers available to local authorities or to replace these with specific duties. The overwhelming objective of the Conservative Government at this time was to control, curb and direct public spending on housing with the aim of reducing the size and influence of this sector. It is also, however, important to remember that many of the housing policies adopted had their origins in the seventies and that many of the mechanisms were adaptations or refinements on existing models. This section will concentrate on the financial issues while in a later section we will return to housing management issues.

The Local Government, Planning and Land Act 1980 formalised the capital spending activities of local government. Local aggregation was permitted and initially considerable flexibility was built into the system. In particular, local authorities were permitted to use a prescribed proportion of their net capital receipts from the sale of assets (initially set at 50 per cent in any one year) to supplement their allocations. This flexibility was gradually eroded over the next few years (to 20 per cent in 1985–86) as the struggle between central government, intent on keeping expenditure down, and certain mainly urban, metropolitan local authorities, determined to maximise their ability to spend, developed. The struggle was conducted in the main through drafting and redrafting regulations and produced a cat and mouse game between central and local government in the latter's attempt to outwit and push to the very limits their legal powers under the legislation. Nonetheless, the system did produce a massive reduction in public spending on housing during the eighties and shifted the balance of activity from new development to maintenance of the existing public stock.[28]

However, the inability of this system to deliver the year to year control over total spending which the Government wanted[29] and the successful evasions by local authorities eventually led to more comprehensive controls in the 1989 Local Government and Housing Act. The system introduced by the 1989 Act tightened the central

---

[28] The real gross public capital spending on local authorities and new towns in £bn at 1988–89 prices in 1976–7 was 5.8 (4.7 on new build, 0.9 on capital repairs) whereas in 1988–9 it was 2.9 (0.7 on new build, 2.3 on capital repairs). Thus expenditure had been halved. (Hills, 1991: 31).

[29] Hill, *Unravelling Housing Finance: Subsidies, Benefits and Taxation*, (1991), p. 82.

controls by setting an annual basic credit approval for each authority. This is the maximum amount that can lawfully be spent through conventional borrowing and credit arrangements. It takes account of capital receipts. Authorities are required to use 75 per cent of their receipts to redeem outstanding debt or to use them for future commitments. The Act also introduces an equal instalments principle for debt repayment which increases the immediate burden on the Housing Revenue Account.[30]

The Housing Act 1980 initially tackled the revenue and subsidy issues. Whereas the earlier subsidy systems had been related first to the unit cost of providing a dwelling and later to a percentage of the debt charges on the loans, the system introduced in the 1980 Act was based, like the Housing Finance Act 1972, on the concept of deficit financing. The subsidy was therefore related to the state of the entire Housing Revenue Account: if there was a deficit, then it was covered by subsidy, but, if income rose faster than expenditure and the deficit disappeared, then no subsidy was paid.[31]

> "The [Act] did no more than set up a formula for the annual calculation of local authority subsidy entitlement – what actually happened to rents and subsidies would depend on the figures fed into the formula each year."[32]

"Subsidy entitlement was therefore based on central government *assumptions* about changes in costs and incomes in each authority".[33] Thus the system gave considerable discretionary power to the Secretary of State which was used to increase actual rents through the use, for subsidy purposes, of assumed rent increases.

Subsidy was very rapidly and massively withdrawn so that soon the majority of authorities were receiving no subsidy at all. The impact

---

[30] See Malpass et al., 1993, for a good explanation of the post-1989 financial regime for council housing.

[31] Briefly, the starting point was the amount of subsidy received by the authority in the previous year to this was added the housing costs differential which was the amount by which each authority's "reckonable" expenditure for the year exceeded the previous year. From the sum of these two would be taken the local contribution differential which was the amount by which "reckonable" income for the year exceeded the authority's reckonable income for the previous year. The figure left represented any subsidy payable centrally.

[32] Malpass, *Reshaping Housing Policy: Subsidies, Rents and Residualisation*, (1990), p. 139.

[33] *ibid.* p. 139.

on rents was substantial; as McCulloch has commented, the rent increases were "considerably larger in real terms over a three year period than those which caused all the uproar under the Housing Finance Act 1972".[34] The impact on new building was equally dramatic. "Under the 1980 Housing Act, for the first time since the First World War, many local authorities arrived at the position that any new building was unsubsidised".[35] The cost of new building therefore acted as a powerful disincentive.

Raising council rents and withdrawing general subsidy necessitated an increased reliance on means-tested benefits, the cost of which rose substantially during the period. After 1982, expenditure on housing benefit was taken out of the national housing budget and relocated within the social security budget. The system for the delivery of means-tested housing benefits was also restructured in Part 2 of the Social Security and Housing Benefits Act 1982 which moved the administration of the system to the local authority.

> ". . . whilst the housing benefit reform was effectively removing the issue of means tested assistance with rent from the area of housing policy altogether, at the same time the administration of housing benefit was being handed over to the housing authorities."[36]

Malpass argues that there is a conceptual distinction between general subsidies and means-tested benefits. The former refers "to some notion about an appropriate price level applicable to all consumers and is part of housing policy, being a means by which the state influences the price of rented housing paid by consumers"; while the latter is "related to the financial circumstances of individual tenants and can be seen as technically a form of income maintenance".[37] It has been argued that this restructuring of the form of subsidy was designed to undermine the collectively based historic cost financing system and to replace it with an individual income-related allowance (Loughlin 1986, Stewart and Burridge, 1989).

Another way in which local authorities were able to subsidise collectively the provision of council housing was by the transfer of

---

[34] McCulloch, "The New Housing Finance System", *Local Government Studies,* (1982), Vol. 8, No. 3, pp. 98–99.
[35] Malpass, *ibid.* p. 144.
[36] Malpass, *op. cit.,* p. 146.
[37] *ibid.* p. 146.

funds from the General Rate Fund into the Housing Revenue Account (HRA). The 1980 legislation preserved the power to undertake this transaction but increasingly penalised authorities financially for so doing. The central assumption was that HRAs would move towards surpluses, and indeed the 1980 Housing Act abolished the requirement that authorities should not budget for such a surplus. In 1982–83, 84 authorities transferred funds from their HRAs to the rates. By 1988–89 the figure had risen to 130. Thus the system allowed the income from higher rents to be converted into a benefit for taxpayers rather than better services for council tenants. As Malpass points out:

> "a system which initially appeared to have major implications for local autonomy was soon characterised by wide variation in local impact and outcomes as councils found ways of exercising discretion in implementation."[38]

Having determined on a method of implementing rent increases by subsidy entitlement, central government lost its leverage over local decisions when authorities moved out of subsidy. The 1990 system introduced under Part 6 of the Local Government and Housing Act 1989 tightened up the existing system by prescribing the credits and debits to the account (section 75 and Schedule 4). Local authorities have a duty to prevent a debit balance on the account (section 76). The first significant change is the ring fencing of the Housing Revenue Account allowing neither payments in nor out to the general account. All Housing Revenue Account income must be spent on housing services. The second is the change in the subsidy regime. The Housing Revenue Subsidy, created by section 79, combines entitlement to general subsidy with that paid to authorities to cover housing benefit. As all authorities receive means-tested subsidies this brings virtually all of them back within central control. The effect of both changes is far greater central control over rent levels. It also facilitates the use of "negative" general subsidy. Thus it is possible to reduce the subsidy notionally payable to cover housing benefit by the assumed surplus on the account generated by rent increases. The Exchequer will now benefit from real or notional surpluses generated through those tenants who pay rents.

---

[38] Malpass, *op. cit.*, p. 149.

Overall, the regulatory relations changed very substantially in this period with much tighter controls on local authority financial decisions in relation to housing. Without any direct intervention on rents, central government raised council rents substantially and altered dramatically the balance of expenditure. Subsidy became individualised rather than collectively provided. Rent payers in many areas were subsidising ratepayers and now taxpayers.

The exercise of discretion by local authorities in relation to housing finance has been substantially curtailed. However, within the authority, housing departments have found that they can rely on the changed legal regime to protect themselves against reductions in corporate spending. Precisely because the housing account is ring fenced it cannot be used to bolster expenditure on other services.

## C. INDIVIDUAL STATUTORY RELATIONS

The Housing Act 1980 introduced financial mechanisms which facilitated a profound change in the relationship between central and local government. However, this aspect of the proposed legislation attracted very little comment or debate during the parliamentary process.[39] The emphasis instead was on the consumptionist aspects of the Bill, known as the tenants' charter, which included the tenant's right to buy.

As we have seen there had been a growing lobby calling for change in the relationship between tenants and local authority landlords. This eventually led to the drafting by the Labour Government of a Housing Bill which included a charter of tenants' rights. These proposals formed the basis for the incoming administration's Housing Bill with some notable amendments. As Kay et al. (1986) point out the charter which was eventually enacted did not necessarily reflect the priorities of the tenants' movement and met with considerable opposition from local authority associations.

The Housing Act 1980 constructed a new status for the majority of council tenants: they were now to be secure. This status brought with it a range of individual rights which were added to over the next six years by legislation. These formal rights were granted to tenants

---

[39] Malpass, *op. cit.*, pp. 137, 138.

while the financial provisions reduced local autonomy and substantially cut back the resources available to landlords. The flagship right was to exit through the secure tenant's right to buy. While Hirschman suggests that the ability to exit can encourage change within an organisation, it often needs to be coupled with "voice" mechanisms. The Housing Act 1980 contained very weak concepts of voice and limited mechanisms to increase collective accountability. These aspects were contained within the general regulatory framework with political, rather than legal, accountability.

In this section I will consider the legal status of secure tenants before moving on in the next section to consider the consequential rights provided to individual secure tenants. The source is the present legal provision, the Housing Act 1985 as amended.

Secure tenants gained security of tenure in 1980. The tenancy cannot be brought to an end by the landlord except by obtaining a court order (Housing Act 1985, section 82). The court shall not make an order for possession except on one or more grounds set out in Schedule 2 (section 84). The grounds for possession set out in the Act are divided into three parts.[39a] Part 1 (grounds 1–8) contains the grounds on which the court may order possession if it considers it reasonable. These are often described as the tenant misconduct grounds. Ground 1 covers rent arrears and breach of tenancy obligation, and ground 2, conduct which is a nuisance or annoyance to neighbours. Part 1 grounds account for the overwhelming majority of actions, rent arrears being the most significant. The court has the discretion to adjourn proceedings, stay, suspend or postpone the order on proceedings in relation to Part 1 and 3 grounds (section 85). A secure tenancy is not generally assignable (section 91). Thus, secure council tenants "have no ordinarily saleable interest" (Ralph Gibson J. in *Wiseman v. Simpson* [1988] 1 W.L.R. 35 at 42.

Obtaining a consistent set of statistics on possession actions in the county courts which would allow comparison before and after the introduction of security of tenure is not easy. However, the number of orders for possession made by the courts in 1978–89 to social

---

[39a] Grounds within Pt. 1 of Sched. 2 require the court to consider reasonableness; those within Pt. 2 require the court to be satisfied that suitable accommodation will otherwise be available; those within Pt. 3 require both reasonableness and suitable accommodation (section 84).

landlords (this would include most housing associations) was 43,010 in England and Wales. In 1982 the figure was 22,399 for possession actions under the Housing Act 1985 (this would also include most housing associations). By 1985 the statistical base had changed but it is reliably estimated by Burrows (1986) that there were over 40,000 orders made to social landlords. Figures provided by the Lord Chancellor's Department show nearly 63,000 orders made in local authority non-mortgage possession proceedings in 1988. (This excludes housing associations.)[39b] By 1992 this figure had risen to 63,412. Given that the council sector has lost about 1.5 million dwellings since 1980, this represents a significant increase in the use of the courts.

The court exercises its power to suspend on what seems to be a consistently high proportion of cases. This varies from year to year but is in the region of 75 per cent of cases. Only a proportion of orders will eventually lead to eviction.[40] There has been much criticism of court procedures and "possession" days in the county court (see Burrows, 1986).

"The low level of attendance by defendants; the almost predictable outcomes; the lack of information on which judgments are based; and the confusion between possession and debt are but a few of the problems."[41]

The overwhelming majority of possession proceedings against tenants are for rent arrears; only 1 to 2 per cent are based on other grounds.

"Of the 16 grounds for possession in the 1985 Act grounds 2–16 are scarcely used at all, as ground 1 (breach of a condition of tenancy) covers both rent arrears cases and the most common non-arrears cases.[42]

---

[39b] Figures provided on request to author November 23, 1993.
[40] Burrows (1986) reliably estimated on Lord Chancellor's Department figures that from the 40,000 orders made in 1985, 22,000 warrants were issued and 9,000 executed. It would, however, be risky to extrapolate a similar percentage for subsequent years. Much would depend on the proportion of suspended orders, local authority policy, any amendments to the social welfare system and the state of the national economy.
[41] Leather and Jeffers, *Taking Tenants to Court,* (1989), p. 18.
[42] *ibid.* p. 13.

Authorities have well-established procedures for rent arrears cases. However, tensions arise when the landlord wishes to uphold social responsibilities through the tenancy terms to curb nuisance, harassment and anti-social behaviour. The court must be persuaded not only that the term of the tenancy has been broken but also that it is reasonable to grant the order (see *Woodspring D.C. v. Taylor* (1982) 4 H.L.R. 95). This latter requirement protects the tenant from the more petty or arbitrary terms. These types of problem and the mechanisms to deal with them have been the subject of considerable recent public debate and now government intervention. We will return to them.

We saw in the discussion of the pre-1980s period that tenancy agreements with their outmoded conditions had little relevance to the legal relationship between the local authority landlord and its tenants. Statutory protection has increased the significance of these contracts, particularly in relation to possession proceedings on the basis of breach of a condition of tenancy.

## D. INDIVIDUAL PROPERTY RELATIONS

While the statutory security provisions have given increased significance to the terms of tenancy agreements, there is no requirement for these agreements to be in writing. There are, however, various information obligations imposed upon landlords which require landlords to provide a statement of the tenancy terms (section 104 of the Housing Act 1985 as amended by section 123 of the Leasehold Reform, Housing and Urban Development Act 1993).

Apart from the basic right to security of tenure, secure tenants have a bundle of rights which are described as a tenants' charter.[43] These rights are implied in secure tenancies. Some re-establish common law rights which have been commonly excluded in tenancy agreements. There is a right to take in lodgers (section 93(1)(a)); a right to sub-let with the consent of the authority (such consent not

---

[43] The rights were originally contained in the Housing Act 1980 but were subsequently added to by the Housing and Building Control Act 1984. Further amendments have been made by the Housing and Planning Act 1986 the Local Government and Housing Act 1989 and the Leasehold Reform, Housing and Urban Development Act 1993.

to be unreasonably withheld) (sections 93(1)(b), 94); and the right to exchange the tenancy with any other secure tenant or certain assured tenants with the consent of the landlord (such consent not to be unreasonably withheld) (sections 91 and 92 as amended by the Local Government and Housing Act 1989, Schedule 3).[44] The Housing Act 1985 provides succession rights to spouses or other members of the family (sections 87–90).[45] There is a right to make improvements with the consent of the authority (such consent not to be unreasonably withheld) and to receive compensation on termination (sections 97–101 as amended by the 1993 Act). A right to carry out certain repairs and recover certain sums from the landlord was introduced in the Housing and Building Control Act 1984. The original unsuccessful scheme has been replaced by another under the Leasehold Reform, Housing and Urban Development Act 1993 (section 96 of the Housing Act 1985 substituted by section 121 of the 1993 Act) (see Hughes and Lowe, 1995 for detailed discussion of these rights).

These rights in practice offer little to tenants. The economic disadvantage of most tenants limits their right to undertake improvements. The landlord's own improvement programmes have been severely affected by cuts in capital spending although more resources have been directed towards day-to-day maintenance and repairs over the 1980s.[46] Tenants have found it exceptionally difficult to use the existing statutory provisions under section 11 of the Landlord and Tenant Act 1985 (whereby the landlord is responsible for the repair of the structure and exterior of the dwelling) to counter underfunded or inadequate council repairs programmes. The right to repair proved a non-starter and has had to be redrafted. The right to succeed in most authorities formalises existing practice but is still welcomed as are schemes to increase mobility.

Kay et al. (1986) found in their study of the implementation of the Housing Act 1980 that many tenants were unaware of the charter rights (Chapter 8). Enforcement of these individual rights lies

---

[44] Section 91 prohibits disposition of the whole tenancy with three exceptions: assignment by way of exchange; in pursuance of an order made under the Matrimonial Causes Act 1973; and assignment to a family member eligible for statutory succession.
[45] The right is limited to one succession, less generous than the right in the Rent Act 1977 (two successions) and more generous than the right in the Housing Act 1988 (one succession limited to spouses).
[46] Hills, *Unravelling Housing Finance: Subsidies, Benefits, and Taxation*, (1991), pp. 29, 30.

through the county court but there is very little evidence to suggest that tenants pursue them but perhaps they are, as Kay et al. suggest, more symbolic.

"The main reason why tenants wanted legal rights was that they felt that only the power of the law and the independent mediation of the Courts would ensure that local authorities would meet their obligations. . . . Many also hoped that the existence of legal rights would improve the public status of council tenants and lead to changes in attitudes and treatment of tenants by local authorities."[47]

The hoped for improvement in the status of the sector has not materialised, indeed the very reverse has happened in the past 15 years. Council housing has been "residualised" increasingly housing those unable to go elsewhere and on the whole economically and socially vulnerable. Security of tenure is important in these circumstances, although there is growing evidence to suggest that tenants on some estates are very anxious indeed about wider security issues such as fear of attacks and harassment generated by this residualisation process.

The most valuable and legally powerful of the rights granted to tenants was the right to buy, the right to exit, to be a secure tenant solely for the purpose of ceasing to be one. Local authorities had the power to sell prior to the 1980 Housing Act but the new Act compelled sales on terms very favourable to tenants at a time when the ability to replace dwellings was being curtailed. The legislation anticipated landlord opposition and was drafted in ways to encourage sales and to prevent obstruction. Secure tenants of two years standing are eligible to acquire the freehold of their house or a long lease of their flat. The purchase price is based on market value, with the right of referral to the District Auditor for final determination (section 128) but the tenant is entitled to a discount (section 129). The discount for a house is 32 per cent which rises by one per cent for each year of previous occupation up to a maximum of 60 per cent. The discount for a flat is 44 per cent plus two per cent for each previous year up to a maximum of 70 per cent. The minister has

---

[47] Kay, Legg and Foot, *The 1980 Tenants' Rights in Practice: A Study of the Implementation of the 1980 Housing Act Rights by Local Authorities 1980–1983*, (1986), p. 219.

power to fix higher discount percentages. The procedure for purchase is tightly drawn with time-limits on key stages (sections 122–
125, 138).

There are a number of enforcement mechanisms.[48] First, the
tenant can pursue the matter in the county court; the duty to
complete the transaction is enforceable by injunction (sections 138(3)
and 150(3)). The tenant should also be able to enforce the rights by
way of a tortious action for breach of statutory duty and obtain
damages. Secondly, the tenant is provided with a self-help remedy
introduced by the Housing Act 1988 (sections 153(a), 153(b)). The
tenant can initiate a notice of delay procedure, after which rent
payments can be deducted from the purchase price. Thirdly, the
minister has been granted very wide powers of intervention where it
appears to him that tenants have or may have difficulty in exercising
effectively and expeditiously the right to buy (section 164). The
Secretary of State has powers directly to vest the freehold or long
leasehold interest, to recover the costs with interest from the local
authority (sections 165–166) and to provide assistance to the tenant
including legal assistance and arranging legal representation (section
170).

The decision to intervene under the Secretary of State's default
powers can only be challenged on judicial review. The Court of
Appeal in *Norwich City Council v. Secretary of State for the Environment*
[1982] 1 All E.R. 737 described them as coercive and draconian and
deliberately framed by Parliament to maximise the minister's power
and to minimise any power of review by the court.

> "Having given tenants rights in law by Parliament it was felt tenants
> should be placed in a position to exercise them without the necessity to
> go to court: 'it cannot be right that tenants should have to embark on
> complex and expensive legal proceedings simply to exercise their
> statutory rights' (Parliamentary Debates (H.C.) 1983, Standing Com-
> mittee B, col, 338)."[49]

The fourth way in which the tenant can seek assistance is through
the audit process. The tenant in his capacity as local government

---

[48] Hoath, *Public Housing Law*, (1989), pp. 355–359.
[49] Cooper and Qureshi, *"Through Patterns Not Our Own: A Study of the Regulation of
Violence on the Council Estates of East London"* (1993).

elector can make an objection to the auditor.[50] Finally obstruction by the council can be deemed to be maladministration as a result of a tenant's complaint to the local ombudsman. (The last two mechanisms are not restricted to the right to buy.)

Not surprisingly there is a body of case law on the right to buy. The key question centres on when the right to buy has been established and may be exercised in a context where the landlord issues possession proceedings during the procedure. The courts consider the rights of the tenant very carefully finding analogies with private property concepts such as options to purchase and are wary of the council's actions in pursuing the possession proceedings.[51]

We have seen the way in which some elements of the relationship between the tenant and the landlord were transferred to the sphere of individual property relations by granting tenants the status of secure tenant. We now turn to those collective elements, not included in this transfer to individual property rights, which remained with modification in the regulatory sphere.

## E. REGULATORY SPHERE REVISITED

The Housing Act 1985 does not interfere with the landlord's powers of allocation. (We have seen earlier the impact of the Housing (Homeless Persons) Act.) It does, however, require the authority to maintain a set of rules in relation to the procedure for allocation and exchange. A summary of these rules must be published and made freely available to members of the public (section 106). Thus the authority must have some rules: those operating merit schemes cannot comply with this duty.

---

[50] Where councillors or officers have deliberately obstructed the right to buy, then in respect of any loss or deficiency suffered by the authority due to their wilful misconduct the auditor may recover the amount of that loss or deficiency from them: Local Government Finance Act 1982, s.20 (Hoath, 1989: 359).

[51] See *Enfield London B.C. v. McKeon* [1986] 2 All E.R. 730, *Dance v. Welwyn Hatfield D.C.* [1990] 3 All E.R. 572 and *Taylor v. Newham L.B.C.* [1993] 2 All E.R. 649, where the court has considered whether the claim for possession can annul the exercise of the right to buy. The secure tenancy must subsist throughout the time of the negotiations up to the moment of completion and grant. See *London Borough of Sutton v. Swann* (1985) 18 H.L.R. 140 and *Jennings and Jennings v. Epping Forest District Council* (1992) 25 H.L.R. 241.

The tenants' charter does not require a written tenancy agreement. Local authorities still determine the detailed terms of tenancy under the exercise of their general management powers (section 21) and the courts have no general discretion to interfere with oppressive tenancy conditions.[52] However, the legislation imposes a duty to provide secure tenants with a written statement of the terms of the tenancy if they are not already contained in a written tenancy agreement (section 104). The authority must also publish information concerning the terms on which secure tenancies are held and make this available to every secure tenant (section 104(1)).[53]

The legislation provides tenants with a form of accountability over management. Every authority is required by section 105 to make and maintain such arrangements as it considers appropriate to enable those of its tenants, who are likely to be substantially affected by a matter of housing management, to be informed of any proposals and to make their views known to the authority. Consideration of rent is excluded. The authority must also publish its arrangements. The section provides very little further procedural support for collective consultation and participation by tenants. The method is left to the discretion of the landlord. However, we shall see in subsequent sections that tenant consultation to facilitate processes of exiting has been the subject of considerable legislative intervention.

The "rights" are less strictly drafted retaining very substantial discretion for the authorities. Any enforcement is still via judicial review. There are no specific remedies or powers of enforcement: no default powers held by the Secretary of State, no self-help remedy.

An illustration of the changing relationships generated by the legislation can be seen in *Palmer v. Sandwell D.C.* (1988) 20 H.L.R. 74. We have seen that local authority landlords are not obliged to provide written tenancy agreements, but they are required to provide tenants with information on the terms of the tenancy. The authority must consult with secure tenants who are substantially affected by proposals relating to a matter of housing management (excluding

---

[52] Initially the obligation was to provide this from time to time. The Leasehold Reform, Housing and Urban Development Act 1993 requires information in relation to the right to buy and to the statutory landlord repairing obligations to be provided annually, but not information in relation to the terms of the tenancy.

[53] Hoath, *Public Housing Law*, (1989), p. 177.

157

issues of rents and charges). They are not obliged to consult with tenants on the provision of information. If the authority wishes to bring about a change in the terms of the tenancy agreement then the duty to consult will probably arise. Under the common law the obligations agreed by two parties can only be altered by the mutual consent of the parties or under the terms of the tenancy. Prior to 1980, local authorities would insert a unilateral variation clause into their agreements to avoid the need to terminate the tenancy and enter into the new tenancy which incorporated the changes.[54]

The Housing Act 1980 altered these rules in relation to secure tenants. Section 102 provides that the terms of a secure tenancy can only be varied by one of three methods set out in the section. These are: by ad hoc agreement; by the authority or the tenant alone for a term relating to rent, council tax or services (i.e. providing statutory force for a unilateral variation clause); and by the authority alone by notice of variation, the procedure for which is set out in section 103.

Sandwell entered into a widespread consultation process with the tenants' organisations over the implementation of the tenants' charter. However, it seems that no final agreement as to the form of a new tenancy agreement was ever reached between the Charter Campaign and the council. The council subsequently produced a "tenant's handbook and charter" which included among its many sections a draft tenancy agreement. The handbook was described in court as a "ragbag" containing over 25 pages, most of which were closely printed. This handbook was distributed to all tenants without a covering letter but with an introduction by the chairman of the housing committee. Included in this document was a clause in the section entitled "tenants' charter" headed "repair of design or material defects" which significantly increased the landlord's liability for the consequences of design faults, in the present case, chronic condensation. Ms Palmer sought to rely on the clause in her action against the council for damages and specific performance. She succeeded at first instance. The council appealed contending that

---

[54] See *Greater London Council v. Connolly* [1970] 2 Q.B. 100 for discussion of such a unilateral variation clause which in that case related to the rent increases. The question before the court was whether the particular clause in the agreement was uncertain. The Court of Appeal found that it was certain enough.

there had been no variation in accordance with section 102 and therefore the clause was not valid.

The debate in the Court of Appeal centred on the two methods set out in section 102. Ms Palmer contended that the terms of the tenancy were unilaterally varied by the council by a notice of variation (*i.e.* the booklet) and that, in so far as the procedural requirements were not complied with by the council, the plaintiff was entitled to waive such requirements as being for her benefit. The Court would not accept such a complete waiver of the procedural requirements. The second contention on behalf of the plaintiff was that there was an agreement between the parties. The Court was willing to consider the delivery of the booklet as an offer, but could not find sufficient evidence of acceptance from Ms Palmer. Her continued payment of rent was equally consistent with non-acceptance as acceptance. While the Court was very scathing of the behaviour of the council in putting out such a document, it was unable to find evidence of variation. The court felt obliged to rely on individual contractual concepts in this collective context. The lack of a clear procedure for collective consultation and implementation of the new terms caused confusion. The council's muddled attempt to disseminate led to increased expectations but no legal liability. The question to ask is what should Ms Palmer have done? Written a letter to the council accepting the terms? Would that have been enough? In that case would she have had a unique tenancy agreement? The case has echoes of the cases discussed earlier in this chapter in which the courts distinguished between the local authority *qua* landlord and as a public body. The consequences for the tenant of the dominance of the regulatory context in relations with the landlord are highlighted here.

The interaction between the two spheres of relationships can also be seen in a series of cases which challenge various aspects of the rent-determination process. The Housing Act 1980 did not alter the statutory context for rent determination: a local housing authority may make such reasonable charges as it may determine for the tenancy or occupation of its dwellings (Housing Act 1985, section 24). These changes will be reviewed from time to time. The Local Government and Housing Act 1989 added a convoluted subsection (3) to section 24 which attempts to introduce some market-based concepts into the process:

"a local housing authority shall have regard in particular to the principle that the rents of houses of any class or description should bear broadly the same proportion to private sector rents as the rents of houses of any other class or description."

The first case relates to the epic legal battle between Mr Winder and Wandsworth L.B.C.[55] Wandsworth has been a flagship authority for Conservative policies during the eighties. The authority increased its rents very substantially from the outset of the legislation. Mr Winder's rent rose from £12.06 to £16.56 in April 1981 to £18.53 in April 1982. He refused to pay the increase. Eventually, Wandsworth brought an action in the county court for possession for arrears of rent. Mr Winder entered a defence that Wandsworth's notice of increases were *ultra vires*, perverse and unreasonable. This defence raised the question of whether it was possible to use a public law defence in a private law action. After *O'Reilly v. Mackman* [1983] 2 A.C. 237 and *Cocks v. Thanet District Council* [1983] 2 A.C. 286 it was thought that the only way to challenge the conduct of a public authority was by an application for judicial review under R.S.C. Order 53. The House of Lords eventually distinguished their previous two cases and held that the defendant in the present case was defending existing private law rights under his contract of tenancy. The court preferred in this context to preserve the rights of private citizens to defend themselves rather than protect the public authorities against unmeritorious or dilatory challenges.

The case was then referred to the High Court for discussion of the substantive issue. Mr Winder lost and appealed. In the Court of Appeal the defence questioned in a number of ways the decision of the council to alter the relative contribution of ratepayers and tenants to the cost of providing council housing. Mr Winder contended that the council failed to take sufficient account of the relative means of council tenants as a group and of council ratepayers as a group because it did not undertake precise statistically-based calculations to establish this; that the council had relied only on the rise in real incomes of council tenants over ten years and not ratepayers as a

---

[55] *Wandsworth London Borough Council v. Winder* [1985] 1 A.C. 461 (C.A.), 493 (H.L.(E)); *Wandsworth London Borough Council v. Winder* (No. 2) (1988) 20 H.L.R. 400, C.A.

whole; and that raising rents by 37 per cent when inflation was only 10.5 per cent while reducing the rate contribution simultaneously was unreasonable. The Court disagreed holding that:

> "this was no doubt a political decision, in one sense, about the manner in which the finances of the Council should be borne by council tenants on the one hand and ratepayers on the other. It was no doubt a decision which was controversial. But, . . . to say that it was unreasonable in the context of all the evidence given is . . . well nigh unarguable." (May L.J.: 409).

Lord Justice May also pointed to the availability of means-tested benefits to cushion the substantial increases.

The applicant in *Hemsted v. Lees and Norwich City Council* (1985) 18 H.L.R. 424 was also concerned with the relative contributions of ratepayers and tenants. In Norwich the council increased the rate fund contribution to compensate for loss of general subsidy. Using the powers granted to ratepayers to query and object to an item of expenditure under section 159 of the Local Government Act 1972, the applicant contended that it was unreasonable for the council to make a contribution from the general fund to the Housing Revenue Account for social expenditure and that the council should fix its rents prior to making a contribution from the rate fund. McCowan J. dismissed the application, holding that there was nothing in the material put before the court to indicate that the authority was not holding the scales fairly between the two branches of the community to which they owe a duty.

These two cases concern challenges by individuals, albeit representing wider constituencies, over the rent policies of authorities which are the political consequences of the changes in the regulatory sphere. Despite the changed relationship between central and local government, the courts adopted the same stance in relation to "reasonable" rents: that the landlord has very wide discretion, adding to the attempts to challenge rent levels which (with one exception) have failed. We next see the cases which result directly from the changed regulatory relations, which not only reflect the juridification of these relationships but also the cat and mouse game played in the context of changing power relations. They result from the attempts of local government to use the subsidy systems to support their policies. The concept of rent is once again debated but within the regulatory sphere.

*R v. Secretary of State for Health and Social Security, ex p. City of Sheffield* (1985) 18 H.L.R. 6 concerned the interaction between rent-rebate subsidy and reasonable rent. The Secretary of State is empowered by section 28 of the Social Security and Housing Benefits Act 1982 to draw up statutory schemes for housing benefit. The statutory scheme was contained in the Housing Benefit Regulations 1982. Under section 38 of the 1982 Act the Secretary of State is required to pay subsidies to the local authorities who administer the schemes. The procedures for payment were set out in the Housing Benefits (Subsidies) Order 1984, S.I. 1984 No. 110.

Sheffield Council developed a scheme whereby tenants could opt for one of two levels of repairs service. Under the full service the council took responsibility for a number of minor repairs in exchange for a higher rent. Central government saw this as a way of increasing rents and therefore housing-benefit subsidy. It changed the definition of rent with the regulations for the purposes of subsidy to foil the scheme. Sheffield amended its scheme so that tenants in receipt of housing benefit were excluded from the limited repairs scheme. Those not in receipt of benefit who opted for the full service were entitled to a repairs grant. The Secretary of State changed the rules again to refine further the definition of rent in the regulations. Amounts attributable to any services, facilities or rights with which a tenant could choose not to be provided were excluded from the definition of rent for the purposes of subsidy. In the action Sheffield sought a declaration that the Secretary of State was under a duty to provide subsidy for the scheme.

The court was reluctant to interfere in the field of policy and held that it was appropriate for a council to take account of the impact of subsidies, although it would be an improper exercise of discretion to consider solely the increase in subsidy. The court found that Sheffield had exercised its discretion in an appropriate manner bearing in mind legitimate housing management matters. However, the court went on to find that the Sheffield scheme fell within the amendment and was therefore excluded from subsidy. Thus Sheffield was able to introduce a differential rent scheme under its powers to set "reasonable rents" but unable to claim subsidy for the differential rents under the different definition of rents for the purposes of subsidy. The regulations, while written generally, were altered successively to catch these two schemes.

Prior to making such regulations the Secretary of State is required to consult with local authority representative bodies. The requirement is waived if the matter is urgent (Social Security Administration Act 1992, section 176(1),(2)). This use of central powers to create regulations rapidly and for specific purposes has been challenged in subsequent cases for lack of consultation.

In *R v. Secretary of State for Social Security, ex p. AMA* (1986) 17 H.L.R. 487, Webster J. held that consultation involved a genuine invitation to give and then consider it. This in turn required sufficient information to be provided. However, the Secretary of State will determine the timetable for consultation, according to the political urgency. Webster J. held in the specific case that there had been inadequate consultation on proposed changes to the regulations, but refused to exercise his discretion to quash them because they were already in force and being administered by local authorities. In the subsequent case of *R v. Secretary of State for Social Security, ex p. AMA* (1992) 25 H.L.R. 131, Tucker J. came to the same conclusion. This case concerned a scheme developed by Hackney L.B.C. to tackle their rent arrears problem. After the 1989 Local Government and Housing Act ring-fencing provisions the authority was unable to make a general fund contribution to assist with this debt. The only method of dealing with the bad debt was to increase rents. Generally, this is achieved through an across-the-board increase thereby penalising all tenants. Hackney's scheme involved specific increases in rent for tenants in arrears which reduced the overall increase necessary. The scheme was entitled to a Rent Arrears Supplement (RAS). The Secretary of State notified the authority (and others) in February 1992 that he intended to alter the regulations so that payment of RAS by tenants was not eligible for housing benefit. The amendment came into effect in April 1992 without any consultation because the minister had considered it to be a matter of urgency. Tucker J. found that the minister was within his powers to make such amendments to the subsidy arrangements, although he considered the scheme to be a very sensible, fair and practical approach to a difficult and sensitive problem. The minister had been aware of the Hackney scheme for some time so the matter could not be treated as urgent. However, he found that no useful purpose would be served by quashing them for lack of consultation.

We saw earlier in this section that there were two significant changes to the regulation of the revenue accounts of local authorities introduced by the Local Government and Housing Act 1989, the ring fencing of the Housing Revenue Account and the new form of subsidy, the Housing Revenue Account Subsidy. The effect of the changes was to give central government far greater control over the housing budgets of local authorities and greater leverage on rent increases.

Both ring fencing and subsidy calculation have been the subject of litigation. In *R v. Secretary of State for the Environment, ex p. London Borough of Greenwich* (1990) 22 H.L.R. 543, Greenwich Council challenged the basis on which the minister calculated housing revenue account subsidy under section 80(1) on the ground that the minister's discretion was fettered by a predetermined sum made available nationally for this subsidy, whereas section 76 required that any shortfall in the housing revenue account had to be met by subsidy. Secondly, that in calculating the subsidy entitlement, the minister had determined that sums spent by local authorities on repairs financed from capital should be ignored (a practice which although legal was used as a way of avoiding expenditure controls under the previous legislation). This inevitably meant that those authorities which had capitalised their repairs were penalised under the new subsidy regime. Both contentions were dismissed. The court stressed the wide discretion available to the minister under the legislation which entitled him to include or exclude any item of expenditure for subsidy purposes. Also it did not fetter his discretion to have regard to the general limits of the national budget.

While the legislation gives a very wide discretion to the minister, it has tightened up very considerably on the form of the housing revenue account. In *R v. Ealing L.B.C., ex p. Jennifer Lewis* (1992) 24 H.L.R. 484, Ealing, under Conservative control, determined to raise rents by over 100 per cent, amounting to an average increase of £28.48 per week. Ms Lewis did not challenge the reasonableness of this increase, rather she challenged the construction of the newly ring-fenced housing revenue account under sections 74 to 78 of the Local Government Housing Act

1989. Schedule 4, Part 1, lists the items which must be carried to the credit of the housing revenue account, Part 2 lists the debit items. The Secretary of State is given considerable (on some items unlimited) discretion to make directions on these items. The present case related to item 1 in Part 2, the expenditure of the authority in respect of the repair, maintenance, supervision and management of houses and other property. Here the Secretary of State is given discretion to direct which items shall or shall not be included under the general heading of repairs, maintenance and management. The applicant challenged some of the expenditure on the homeless persons' unit, the housing advisory service and the wardens of the sheltered accommodation. The Court of Appeal, while expressing a wariness about the use of judicial review in this highly policy-oriented area, held that some elements of the warden and homeless services did not fall within item 1. It found that where items of expenditure could be described as borderline, the authority retained a discretion, subject to ministerial direction, to include or exclude them.

However, it is the case that local authorities now have much less freedom to organise their accounts and will be subject to legal challenge on specific items of expenditure. The 1935 legislation which established housing revenue accounts and facilitated the development of collectivism within council housing has been severely eroded by the 1989 legislation. The flexibility over their budgets which local authorities used to reflect their political priorities has been curtailed. The ability of tenants to challenge rent decisions at an individual level has been unaffected by the changes at the regulatory level, although there are now a variety of constructions of "rent": reasonable for tenants, appropriate rents for the purposes of central subsidy and rental income for the purposes of the housing revenue account.

## Relationships in the Late 1980s

The financial regimes of the eighties had transformed the local authority housing function. Local authorities were no longer developers but landlords managing a shrinking stock in the developing social rented market encouraged by the Housing Act 1988. The

165

aim of the Act was to reposition relationships within the rented housing market generally by redefining the security available to private tenants and tenants of housing associations and by introducing market-related rents.

As far as the council sector is concerned, the focus moves from the individual tenant's right to buy to the collective transfer of council stock to alternative landlords.[56] The longer term implication for local authority owned housing is clear from the 1989 amendment to section 9 of the Housing Act 1985, entitled the provision of housing accommodation:

> "that nothing in the Housing Act shall be taken to require (or to have at any time required) a local authority itself to acquire or hold any houses or other land for [this] purpose" (Local Government and Housing Act 1989, section 161).

However, the measures to strengthen social market forms within the rented sector can be seen both as an attempt to reduce the size of the council sector through transfer of stock and also as an attempt to increase tenants' power by providing the choice of exiting. In this section I will discuss both the mechanisms for collective tenant involvement and the extent to which tenants are involved in the processes of collective exiting.

Tenants need information to be involved. We have seen that tenants are entitled to receive some information from their landlords under the Housing Act 1985 tenant's charter provisions (sections 104–106). The 1989 Local Government and Housing Act (section 167) requires that tenants receive an annual report which must give details of the landlord's housing management performance (including certain performance indicators prescribed by the Secretary of State to whom a copy must also be sent). The analogy is with a company report to shareholders and represents a continuing shift in accountability mechanisms from political to economic.[57]

---

[56] The Government was still exploring ways of extending individual routes to ownership: the Housing Act 1988, s.129 authorises local authorities to give grants to assist tenants wishing to buy a dwelling in the private sector (or to extend their existing property) DoE, *Cash Incentives for Local Authority Tenants*, Housing Research Summary, No. 36 (1994).

[57] For an evaluation of the measures, see Marsh et al., 1992.

We have seen that section 105 of the Housing Act 1985, as amended, obliges local authority landlords to consult with tenants over matters of housing management. Until recently, few local authority landlords have enthusiastically implemented these measures (see Birchall, 1992). The early difficulties facing tenants in using this provision to exercise effective voice rights in the context of privatisation plans can be seen in *Short v. London Borough of Tower Hamlets* (1985) 18 H.L.R. 171 and *R. v. Hammersmith and Fulham London Borough Council, ex p. Beddowes* [1987] 1 All E.R. 369. In the former case an agreement in principle by the council to embark on an exploratory marketing exercise with a view to privatisation of a council estate was held not to require consultation. In the latter case, the council wished to sell an estate consisting of a number of tower blocks to a developer to renovate and then sell the majority of the flats to individual buyers. As the scheme was to be phased, the council sought to impose restrictive covenants in the transfer documents for the first block to prevent the occupation in the other blocks of anyone other than a long leaseholder, *i.e.* owner-occupiers. The decision to include these covenants had been bitterly opposed by the opposition party and tenants. The applicant sought judicial review of two aspects of the process; first, that the council had not carried out its responsibilities to consult. Tenants had been consulted at an earlier stage when the potential purchaser was anticipated to be a housing association landlord and before the idea of the covenants had developed. In fact the developers were a profit-making builder/developer and the covenants guaranteed a change of tenure. However, the Court of Appeal held that the consultation duty had been fulfilled. Secondly, had the council fettered its discretion in adopting these covenants? A majority of the Court of Appeal thought not. The purposes of the Housing Act 1985 could be met by the provision of owner-occupied dwellings and as such the covenants were in furtherance of that statutory duty and no fetter. Kerr L.J. in dissent considered that the decision was so influenced by irrelevant political considerations that it fettered the council's future policy.

The general duty to consult under section 105 now excludes a range of situations relating to the privatisation of council housing which have their own statutorily prescribed consultation schemes.[58]

---

[58] See Hoath, 1989: 310–312 and Hughes and Lowe, 1995: Chap. 2.

Many local authorities during the 1980s gradually came to realise the importance of tenant consultation and participation and some developed management initiatives which were based on a desire to provide a more responsive service and greater accountability. The most popular mechanism has been decentralisation of services to neighbourhood or area bases.[59] Often these initiatives are coupled with formal involvement of tenants representatives on area committees. Some authorities granted tenants formal representational rights on the housing committee. However, these political voice rights have been curtailed by the Local Government and Housing Act 1989, section 13, which removes tenants' voting rights.

A number of initiatives have also been developed in the late 1980s whereby tenants become more directly involved in the management of their dwellings. These include joint management through Estate Management Boards and self-management through Tenant Management Co-operatives. Section 27 of the 1985 Housing Act, as amended, allows authorities to transfer specified management functions to "another person" subject to ministerial consent. Another person can mean the tenants or, since the advent of compulsory competitive tendering of housing management, alternative professional managers.[60] The transfer is by way of management agreement. Until 1993 tenants could not force their landlords to enter into such an agreement, but under the Leasehold Reform, Housing and Urban Development Act 1993, section 132, tenant management organisations are given a right to manage. There are a number of relatively daunting procedural stages for any tenants' organisation wishing to exercise this right (see Envis, 1994) which have limited the overall success of this scheme.[61] In a small number of instances tenants have established an ownership co-operative to which the dwellings have been transferred.[62]

We now turn to a discussion of the measures aimed at the privatisation of housing. The most successful exit power by far has been the individual right to buy. The Housing Act 1980 not only granted this right to tenants but also provided financial incentives in

---

[59] Cole and Furbey, *The Eclipse of Council Housing*, (1994), pp. 217–223.

[60] See Hughes and Lowe, *Social Housing Law and Policy*, (1995), pp. 132–135.

[61] Crossley, "Time to give tenants a hearing", *Roof*, May/June 1995, p. 13.

[62] Birchall, 1992, provides a very good discussion of tenants' rights, particularly this area of consultation and accountability.

the form of discounts. Undoubtedly, this right was very valuable to tenants and has a major impact on landlords, not only because of the loss of stock (over 1.25 million dwellings have been sold) but also because of the threat that potential sales posed for overall housing management.

Subsequent measures to reduce the public stock have been directed at changing the landlord, not tenure. There are three ways in which this potential for exit can take place: Housing Action Trusts; Tenants' Choice; and Voluntary Transfer. The statutory rights of tenants are affected by these measures. As Birchall points out:

> "With hindsight, the Conservative government might well regret the granting of even such a basic right as security of tenure. During the second half of the decade, ministers set out to break up council monopolies, and security of tenure got in the way."[63]

However, tenants do generally retain the right to buy which is transferred with them, although not available to tenancies entered into after the transfer (sections 171A to 171H (as amended) of the Housing Act 1985). Also tenants can use their potential to exit, particularly their rights to be consulted and balloted on potential transfers, as a bargaining tool.

Housing Action Trusts (HAT) involve a form of compulsory purchase in reverse. The Secretary of State designates "an area of land where in his opinion it is expedient that a corporation should be established" (section 60 of the Housing Act 1988). A transfer of the land is then made from the local authority to the HAT. The Housing Act 1988 granted tenants the right to be balloted before any transfer takes place. The Secretary of State can proceed unless in his opinion "a majority of the tenants, who, on that ballot or poll, express an opinion about the proposal . . . are opposed to it" (section 61). This right shifts the balance of power in the relationships in very unexpected ways. In a number of the originally proposed HATs, tenants negotiated very favourable terms for themselves, which their existing landlord could not hope to match, as a condition of their yes vote in a ballot (Gregory and Hainsworth, 1993). Thus transfer

---

[63] Birchall, "Council tenants: Sovereign Consumers or Pawns in the Game" in Birchall (ed.) *Housing Policy in the 1990s*, (1992).

seemed to offer very substantial advantages to tenants by way of physical and environmental improvements. Yet none went ahead.

This stems in part from the difficulties for tenants in each of the spheres of relations discussed earlier. Ultimately, there was no way that tenants could enforce the bargains they had so vigorously negotiated by incorporating them into their tenancy agreements because they were not parties to the contract between the landlord and the HAT. They had to trust the parties concerned to stick to their promises on future repair and rent levels. The uncertainty of the conditions for sale might have been the reasons why tenants gave up the immediate advantages of transfer. In addition, tenants were aware that they were changing not only their individual tenancy terms but also the form of account-ability with their landlords. Once the transfer had taken place their relationship with the new landlord would depend on the terms of their tenancies, the statutory framework provided to secure tenants for the duration of the HAT and any additional representation that they as a group had negotiated but probably could not formally enforce. Sceptical as tenants are of political accountability and secure status, these still seemed to be important.

Recently, there has been a revival of interest in the idea of HATs. This time, the initiative has come from the landlord which sees the transfer as a way of obtaining some investment into an area, even if it is at the expense of its ownership. The funding available to these initiatives has been generous. In this situation, the HAT is not being imposed on the landlord or, in theory, on the tenants and as such has lost much of its original threat for the landlords. The support of the landlord, which seems to be crucial to the success of the ballots, is now forthcoming.

In addition, the rules relating to HATs have been altered to allow the local authority to repurchase the stock on the dissolution of the HAT. The Leasehold Reform, Housing and Urban Development Act 1993 amends the Housing Act 1985, section 84, to require the HAT to notify local authorities within its area that it wishes to dispose. The local authority can then serve a notice on the tenants informing them of the consequences of returning to local authority ownership and notifying them of their right to make representations to the Secretary of State that they would like to take up that option. If a majority of tenants wish to return then the Secretary of State shall provide for their transfer. The transfer price is left to the discretion of the Secretary of State. Six HATs had been established by October 1995, and it is unlikely that there will be many more.

Tenants affected by a possible HAT have somewhat fleeting voice powers, valuable at the time of negotiation but limited in extent. Tenants' choice under Part 4 of the Housing Act 1988, whereby tenants can choose a new landlord, offers slightly more opportunity to entrench negotiated terms but reduces statutory rights. Although structured as a tenant initiative, the focus of attention has been on the potential new landlords who must be approved by the Housing Corporation. The legislation sets out very detailed procedural requirements for the transaction although the policing body, unlike right to buy, is the Housing Corporation, not the Department of the Environment. Tenants must be balloted on their wishes (section 102). The transfer cannot proceed unless 50 per cent of tenants in the area respond or if over 50 per cent of those balloted wish to continue with the existing landlord (section 103). In this case, efforts have been made to strengthen the tenants' ability to enforce the bargains which they have negotiated. This involves a tortuous legal process whereby the Housing Corporation tries to ensure that the purchasing landlord sticks to the agreement as a condition of its approval to the take over process.[64] Tenants' choice has also had negligible impact.

Quite unexpectedly, the largest number of transfers have taken place using powers granted to local authorities to carry out voluntary sales prior to the Housing Act 1980. This power is now contained within sections 32–25 of the Housing Act 1985, as amended by the Housing Act 1988. A number of individual estates and, increasingly, the whole stock of an authority, have been sold under these powers (Kleinman, 1993). The procedural requirements for such sales, known as large-scale voluntary transfers (LSVT), are less extensive than in the first two methods, although they still involve the consent of the Secretary of State (sections 32 and 34 of the Housing Act 1985, as amended) and a majority of affected tenants. (The balloting method is not specified although the majority use a straight majority voting system.[64a] Once again the consultation gives tenants a degree of power to negotiate

---

[64] Alder and Handy, *Housing Association Law* (2nd ed., 1991), pp. 256–266.
[64a] DoE, The Council Tenant's Charter, (1992).

advantageous terms. Legally, their position is very similar to that discussed in relation to the HAT, although their legal status after transfer is different. Unlike tenants' choice, all the stock involved is transferred not just the dwellings of those who voted in favour of the transfer. Because the conveyance takes place between the existing and new landlords, the tenants' wishes are not legally binding unless they have persuaded their existing landlord to change the terms of their tenancy prior to the transfer.[65] In addition, if the tenant is transferring to a housing association, the statutory context is changed. The tenant becomes an assured tenant with none of the public sector charter rights referred to in the earlier section (except the retained right to buy). Tenants must rely on the Housing Corporation to enforce a tenants' guarantee (for details see Chapter 5).

The reasons for the popularity of this type of transfer relate first to the financial regimes of local authorities. The authority obtains a substantial capital receipt if the properties are not in too bad condition on transfer. The 1988 Act, however, gives the Secretary of State power to direct how the receipts should be used (section 34 (4B)). The new owners have access to the financial markets using the asset base of the stock, a process which is denied to local authorities. LSVTs have, therefore, been criticised as merely a form of refinancing. "John Perry, policy director at the Institute of Housing, estimates that less than 15 per cent of the money raised through transfers has been invested in development."[66] Secondly, the overwhelming majority of transfers have involved a single new housing association set up by the local authority and registered with the Housing Corporation and have included strong tenants' representation. Amendments in the Housing Act 1988 now allow the Secretary of State to consider the extent to which the purchaser is controlled or influenced by members or officers of the authority (section 34 (4A)).

The success of the schemes also highlight the tension which we have seen between social welfare support, in the form of housing benefit, and housing subsidy. Under the 1989 financial regime, some authorities now obtain negative housing subsidy because the housing

---

[65] It is possible to entrench the negotiated terms but it is not simple legally and will require the help of experts in this area. Even if tenants realise the need, the cost of this will be prohibitive in most cases unless the landlord pays.

[66] Grant. "Voluntary Transfer", *Housing Report, The Observer*, July 5, 1992, p. 5.

revenue account subsidy does not fully compensate for housing benefit payments. Thus council tenants' rents are subsidising means-tested benefits by almost £8 per week.[67] Once the stock moves out of local authority ownership, and out of Department of the Environment control, the cost of the housing benefit must be borne by the Department of Social Security, thereby increasing substantially the burden on the Exchequer. Two departments and policies collide.

Thus we see, in the Leasehold Reform, Housing and Urban Development Act 1993, restrictions on the ability of local authorities to privatise their stock. The Secretary of State is now empowered to draw up a disposals programme which is limited by Treasury cost estimations, including the increase in housing benefit costs (section 135). It also imposes a levy on the disposal, in favour of the Secretary of State, so that central government receives a proportion of the receipts from the sale of local authority assets (section 136). These restrictions have at least temporarily reduced the number of such transfers.[68]

To summarise, local-authority tenants have been granted legal powers in the context of a changed set of relationships within the regulatory framework. They are potentially in a far stronger position than before. This strength lies in their ability to purchase their property and to negotiate in the shadow of the ballot in the collective transfer situations. For those transferring to new landlords, their individual contract rights become far more significant as their rights which result from statute are eroded. They lose the accountability structures of the local authority and enter the uncertain regulatory framework of the social market.

## Relationships in the 1990s

A. INTRODUCTION

We have charted the reconstruction of the occupants of council dwellings from tenants in need of decent housing, through tenants

---

[67] Roof. "Who's paying the rent now?" Fast Facts, *Roof*, September/October 1994.

[68] The 1995 Housing White Paper and the accompanying consultation paper on the development of the social rented sector (DoE, *The Legislative Framework for Private Renting*, (1995) places heavy emphasis on the use of LSVT to increase choice within the social rented sector while recognising the financial difficulties associated with these types of transfer.

with rights, to tenants with choices in a social market. The nineties can be characterised as the era of public citizenship: we now see the transformation of tenants into consumers of public commodities. However, there are major difficulties in this construction which result from the impact of the policies pursued in the eighties. The council sector has been "residualised" and impoverished, socially and economically. Yet there is an attempt to entrench market approaches to the landlord and tenant relationship with tenants who have less and less relationship with the market system and who rely very heavily on state benefits to pay for the "commodity". The aim of transforming tenants into individual consumers sits uneasily with the expectation that the local authority as landlord will intervene in the social manifestations of residualisation, such as racial harassment, crime on estates and the disintegration of families.

B. INDIVIDUAL PROPERTY RELATIONS

Tenants gained few additional individual rights over the 1980s. This trend has continued into the nineties. The most recent legislation, the Leasehold Reform, Housing and Urban Development Act 1993, substitutes a new right to repair for the wholly unworkable earlier scheme, a right to be compensated for agreed improvements on the termination of the tenancy and a right to receive annual information. The other new measure is the "rent to mortgage" right which allows certain tenants to transform rent into mortgage payments (section 143 of the Housing Act 1985, amended by sections 108–120 of the 1993 Act). Many commentators have been sceptical about the scope of this right: few tenants would seem to qualify. It is not available to tenants in receipt of housing benefit nor with the means to purchase under the right to buy provisions. The response to the pilot scheme in Milton Keynes and Basildon was low: between March and October 1991, 67 in Milton Keynes and 39 in Basildon (DoE, 1994). It could be said that this is another relatively elaborate scheme (like the right to shared ownership, to repair and to manage) which has extremely limited impact but a large amount of bureaucracy.

The attempt, however, has been to reconstruct the tenant as a consuming citizen. The council tenant's charter was one of the first to be produced under the tenant's charter initiative introduced by the Local Government Act 1992. It offers the tenant nothing new, only a way of seeing the relationship between themselves and the landlord. The emphasis is on the individual contractual "rights" of tenants although much of the material included in the charter is aspirational: "the services the council should provide, and how it should provide them".[69]

## C. REGULATORY RELATIONS

We see the increasing pressure on the housing finance system, the key element of which is the growth in the cost of housing benefit in the wake of the creation of the social market. It is now far cheaper for the Treasury if tenants remain in the public sector because of the restructuring of the subsidy systems. Consequently we have seen the restrictions on the voluntary transfer arrangements introduced in the 1993 Act. It is still seen as an important part of central housing policy when "there will be benefits for the tenants from more investment at the same time as reductions in the burden on taxpayers".

The most recent white paper on housing recognises that:

> "providing a subsidy to a local authority or housing association to enable them to charge a below market rent can be cheaper over time than paying housing benefit on a market rent for several decades."[70]

It also suggests that "we are now approaching the limits of what can be achieved through higher rents" when two-thirds of social sector tenants [local authority and housing association] receive help with their rents through housing benefit (DoE, 1995b). The proposals on rents are, therefore, restricted to encouragement to set rents which reflect market criteria, such as location, rather than social need.

However, privatisation initiatives persist. These are now focusing on ways in which the asset base of local authority stock could be used

---

[69] DoE, *The Council Tenant's Charter* p. 6. The 1995 version of the tenants' charter distinguishes more clearly between existing rights and good practice (DoE, *The Legislative Framework for Private Renting Consultation Document*, (1995).

[70] DoE, *Our Future Homes. Opportunity, Choice, Responsibility: The Government's Housing Policies for England and Wales*, (1995) Cmnd. 2901, p. 4.

as collateral for private finance while allowing local authorities to retain more influence than is presently possible under Large Scale Voluntary Transfer (representation must not exceed 20 per cent). The latest idea which has met with considerable political consensus is the idea of housing companies (DoE, 1995b; DoE, 1995c; Wilcox et al., 1993; CIOH, 1995). As long as council representation on the board remains in a minority, this will not affect their status as private corporations nor require their borrowing to be classified as local authority capital spending (and therefore public expenditure). Other "stakeholders" such as tenants can also be represented.

The major change presently underway at the regulatory level is not at the level of changes in the ownership structure but with the separation of ownership and management functions through the compulsory competitive tendering (CCT) for housing management services (Local Government Act 1988 and the Leasehold Reform, Housing and Urban Development Act 1993). Certain prescribed tasks must be specified and put out to tender, potentially transforming the relationship between the tenant and landlord. This requires the local authority landlord to specify and cost the services involved. The incentive for consultation with tenants has finally been provided for some authorities. In anticipation of the tendering process, local authorities are attempting in some instances to draw up "agreements" with estates on the nature and level of service which tenants would like to receive. This involves an attempt to "contractualise" the relations between landlord and tenants on a collective basis. We return to this idea in the subsequent chapter.

The introduction of CCT affects the existing accountability structure of consultation on housing management and exposes another tension in government policy. What if consultation with tenants reveals a strong desire not to put the management out to tender? Is it the tenants' right to be managed by their existing managers? It seems not. The consultation process for the introduction of CCT is exempted from section 106 of the Housing Act 1985 and, the duty to consult on matters of housing management, replaced with a specific arrangement by the 1993 Act. This involves a tenant's right to be informed of the terms of the agreement and a right to inform the authority of his/her views at the outset and throughout the duration of the contract (sections 27A and 27AA of the Housing Act 1985 introduced by section 130(1) of the 1993 Leasehold Reform, Housing and Urban Development Act). It does not entitle tenants to take part in the contract specification process.

There is increasing contractualisation of the relations of local government, particularly in the area of housing, with the tenant being recast as the self-activating responsible consumer. CCT is based on the assumption that it is appropriate or possible to manage public sector stock on a commercial basis. It marginalises the social collective elements of public housing. There are, however, considerable difficulties with this view of the relationships within the sector. I intend to develop this point by looking at the last of the collective elements of council housing yet to be covered in this chapter: allocation policies.

We have seen that local authorities were granted very wide powers to manage their stock under section 21 of the Housing Act 1985, and that the courts have been reluctant to interfere with the exercise of these powers. Some of these powers have been limited by legislation in the eighties, although the collective process of allocating council housing has been subject to very little statutory intervention other than the need to publish the rules by which such allocation is undertaken. Yet running alongside these administrative systems has been the very substantially litigated area of the individual duties to the homeless.

The collective system for allocation stems from section 22 of the Housing Act 1985, which requires the local housing authority to give reasonable preference to persons: living in bad conditions or overcrowded houses; having large families, and towards whom the authority owes a duty under the homeless provisions. The section has stimulated very little challenge in the courts. In *R. v. Canterbury City Council, ex p. Gillespie* (1986) 19 H.L.R. 7 it was held that an authority may not operate such a rigid policy as to fetter its discretion in consideration of its application to individual circumstances. Thus blanket exclusions from waiting lists are inappropriate if there is no retained discretion. (See *R. v. Forest Heath District Council, ex p. West and Lucas* (1991) 24 H.L.R. 85 in which the Court of Appeal granted leave where the local authority had denied housing to a couple alleged to be in arrears with their community charge.) However, pursuing this approach has its limitations as shown by *R. v. Bristol*

*City Council, ex p. Johns* (1992) 25 H.L.R. 249. The applicant and her husband were denied housing despite the fact that both of them suffered from severe health problems. The council had an allocation policy which did not consider owner-occupiers for rehousing unless they were in severe difficulties or fell within the homelessness provisions. The Johns, who were owner-occupiers, argued that the authority had fettered its discretion by having this blanket policy. The court dismissed the application because the authority retained some discretion despite the exclusion from the points system for those in severe difficulties. On the facts, one is left wondering what a severe difficulty would look like.

The lawfulness of a heavily pressed London borough's system for allocation came under scutiny in *R. v. London Borough of Newham, ex p. Watkins* (1993) 26 H.L.R. 434, when the applicant sought judicial review of the points system for failure to furnish a reasonable preference to categories of applicants cited in section 22 of the 1985 Act. (Mr Watkins had a large family living in a small house. He had considerable medical problems and one child had a medical condition). Blom Cooper J. thoroughly reviewed the socio-legal issues involved. While finding that the system did not give preferential treatment to some of the categories mentioned in section 22 of the Housing Act 1985, he also held that a local authority, in applying these provisions is bound to perform its duties within the context of its overall public law duties and not only those that are directed exclusively to its duties under the housing legislation. In these circumstances he declined to find the lettings policy unlawful. Once again the passing of the regulatory sphere in the landlord and tenant relation is demonstrated.

Numerous reports over the years have argued that it is inappropriate for councillors to take part in the detailed administration of the allocation system.[71] However, in some parts of the country, they are still involved.

> "In six out of 37 Welsh local authorities local councillors are directly involved in decisions about the allocation of properties. In a further seven, . . . published allocation policies state that local councillors are

---

[71] CHAC, 1969, HSAG, 1978, see more generally Cole and Furbey, *The Eclipse of Council Housing*, 1994, pp. 120–128.

involved in approving or selecting applicants for priority, while in six, allocations are made by officers in consultation with local councillors."[72]

The allocation policies of a number of these authorities have been criticised in Ombudsman reports recently.[73] The issue has also surfaced in the courts in *R. v. Port Talbot Borough Council, ex p. Jones* (1987) 20 H.L.R. 265. A member of the council was allocated a council dwelling for which she was not entitled under the published allocation rules. The normal procedure was bypassed and the effective decision was taken by the Chair and Vice-Chair of the Housing Tenancy Committee. The leader of the council challenged the decision. The court allowed the application because of the inappropriate delegation and the irrelevant considerations used to come to the decision (that she would be better able to fight an election from that property).

However, these few cases pale into insignificance when compared against the volume of case law on the homeless duties. It is the most litigated area of housing law despite the absence of an appeal structure. Every aspect has been subject to extensive judicial scrutiny. I do not intend to discuss this wealth of case law here but discussion can be found in Arden et al., 1994; Hughes and Lowe, 1995; Partington and Hill, 1991.

One of the key reasons behind the original 1977 Housing (Homeless Persons) Act was to stop the shuffling of families back and forth between different departments or authorities. Yet it has emerged again. Under the Children Act 1989, Part 3 the social services authority has a duty to safeguard the welfare of, and provide accommodation for, children in need within its area. Do social service authorities have to secure accommodation for children with their families in situations where the family has been deemed intentionally homeless and, therefore, owed limited duties by the housing authority? In *R. v. Northavon District Council, ex p. Smith* [1994] 3 All E.R. 313 the House of Lords had to decide whether the 1989 Children Act amended the 1985 Housing Act to enable a social service authority to require a housing authority to exercise its powers to provide accommodation for "intentionally" homeless applicants

---

[72] Stirling, "Blast from the past", *Roof*, September/October 1994, p. 12.
[73] *ibid.* p. 12.

with children. The court held that the 1989 Act imposed a duty of co-operation between the authorities both of which had to do the best they could in carrying out their respective responsibilities for children and housing. It further held that judicial review was not the appropriate means of obtaining co-operation.

The impact of the homeless provisions has come under considerable scrutiny recently. Lord Brightman in the House of Lords in *Puhlhofer v. Hillingdon L.B.C.* [1986] 1 All E.R. 467 caused alarm to housing law practitioners when he stated that leave to apply for judicial review should no longer be granted for challenging decisions under Part 3 "save in the exceptional case". There is evidence to suggest that leave for applications have since become more difficult to obtain.[74] Partington and Hill argue that:

> "there are large question-marks surrounding the effectiveness of the legislation in securing accommodation for the homeless. It has been argued that the combined effect of judicial decisions and local authority practice has been largely to reduce the extent of the duties as intended by those who proposed the legislation (P. Burkinshaw, Homelessness and the Law: the effect and response to legislation (1982) 5 U.L.P. 255). This is perhaps particularly the case in the context of relationship breakdown and domestic violence."[75]

It is clear, however, that this route into council housing has restructured the allocation processes of local authorities, particularly in the context of reduced supply and increasing need. Research carried out on behalf of the DoE reviewed local authority waiting lists in 1986 and 1991 (DoE, 1994b). The key findings were first that there was a marked reduction in the age profile from an average age of 49 to 34 in 1991, secondly that there was an increase in the proportion of people waiting with children, from 19 per cent to 30 per cent, and thirdly, that only 46 per cent of households have either the applicant or partner in work – three-quarters of applicants have total joint incomes below £200 per week.

The research also found that twice as many applicants in London considered their need for housing as urgent than either metropolitan

---

[74] Sunkin, "What is happening to applications for judicial review?" *Modern Law Review,* (1987), Vol. 50, p. 432.

[75] Partington and Hill, *Housing Law: Cases, Materials and Commentary,* (1991), p. 600.

or non-metropolitan local authorities (51 per cent compared to 24 per cent and 25 per cent respectively). Of those housed:

> "there has been a considerable increase in the number of households containing children under 16 – from 38 per cent in 1986 to 50 per cent in 1991. The fastest rising group amongst these households is lone parents who represented 19 per cent of new tenants in 1986 and 28 per cent in 1991, although the proportion of couples with children has also increased over the same period from 19 per cent to 22 per cent."[76]

Two thirds of new tenants are jobless; average incomes are lower than those for applicants – with nearly half (47 per cent) having an income of £75 per week or less.

The same research suggests that around half of new tenancies go to general waiting-list cases, with 29 per cent going to homeless allocations. However, this average masks the regional differences. In London 43 per cent go to homeless allocations, compared to 20 per cent in the North, 34 per cent in the Midlands and 40 per cent in the South. "Just under half (43 per cent) of those offered a tenancy as a homeless acceptance are lone parents and 31 per cent are couples with children".[77]

These statistics have been interpreted by the Government to suggest that the homeless legislation is not fulfilling its original function as a safety net. The consultation document issued by the DoE on proposals for amending the legislation states:

> "By giving the local authority a greater responsibility towards those who can demonstrate 'homelessness' than towards anyone else in housing need, the current legislation creates a perverse incentive for people to have themselves accepted by a local authority as homeless."[78]

The proposals redefine homelessness and downgrade the duty owed so that in future there will be a responsibility to assist persons in priority need who, through no fault of their own, are without

---

[76] DoE, *Routes into Local Authority Housing.* Housing Research Summary No. 16, (1994), p. 4.

[77] DoE (1994), *op. cit.,* p. 4.

[78] DoE, *Access to Local Authority and Housing Association Tenancies: A Consultation Paper,* (1994), p. 4.

accommodation of any sort in an emergency. The duty will be to provide accommodation for a limited period. All permanent allocations will be from persons whose names appear on the waiting list.

These proposals have met with hostility from almost every quarter including the local authority associations (Shelter, 1994). They offer a simple answer to a complex issue while increasing the discretion of local authorities at the expense of individual applicants. However, the Housing Bill 1996 replaces the existing homelessness provisions and introduces reduced duties towards a number of categories of homeless.[79]

The 1996 Bill establishes a new framework for the general allocation of "social tenancies". Local authorities will be required to establish a register of those who seek local authority or, through nominations, other types of social tenancies. Allocations must in future come from the register. Further, the government intends to prescribe the key principles on which allocation schemes should be based, "keeping regulation to the minimum compatible with ensuring fairness". This marks the first central intervention in local authority allocation systems since their outset. As Cole and Furbey point out allocation in a context of scarcity requires discrimination.

> "Equality demand that public housing is administered according to distinctive 'social' criteria. But steps towards this goal can make public housing less attractive to more affluent white households, so confirming its status as a residual tenure for the poor and stigmatised".[80]

The dissatisfaction with the allocation systems of local authorities is a sympton of much wider issues, one of which is the impact of racism. There has been considerable body of research documenting racism

---

[79] There is a strong argument to suggest that the recent House of Lords decision in *R. v. London Borough of Brent ex p. Awsa* (1995) *The Times*, July 7, has more than achieved judicially the objectives of the proposed legislation. The decision has been summarised as follows by a leading practitioner;

"a person may be housed in something less than settled accommodation, may not be homeless in something less than settled accommodation, and may be intentionally homeless from something less than settled accommodation" (Arden, 1995: 22).

The court suggested that an offer of accommodation for only 28 days would be sufficient to satisfy the housing duty.

[80] Cole and Furbey, *The Eclipse of Council Housing*, (1994), p. 144.

within local authority allocation schemes.[81] Much of the research reveals the tensions caused by competing policy priorities between, for instance, government imposed performance indicators on void levels and a multiple-offer policy. An example of these tensions can be seen in *R. v. London Borough of Tower Hamlets, ex p. Mohib Ali et al.* [1993] 25 H.L.R. 218. Until 1986 the authority used a standard lettings criteria (SLC) for rehousing all applicants including the homeless. Thereafter it adopted an amended letting criteria (ALC) for homeless families which was much less generous. The change had been provoked by the amount of time homeless families were spending in temporary accommodation (2–4 years). The Commission for Racial Equality expressed its concern about these changes and the authority introduced a number of safeguards into the system. These were subsequently abandoned. In 1991 the authority radically decentralised its housing functions to seven autonomous neighbourhood offices. These offices had discretion on whether to use SLC or ALC. Some did and some did not.

The evidence showed that a significantly higher proportion of homeless Asian families were allocated under ALC than homeless white families. To some extent this was due to the larger families of Bangladeshis but the majority of Bangladeshi families were not homeless. The applicant was offered a three bedroomed maisonette on the fourth and fifth floor of a tower block for his wife and himself and their six children aged between one and 18 under ALC. He refused the offer because of the size and appealed to the authority. The appeal was turned down. He sought judicial review. The court held that the ALC policy was not unlawful and found no evidence of direct or indirect discrimination under the Race Relations Act. However, the court allowed the appeal because the removal of the safeguards to those housed under ALC coupled with the arbitrary and random way in which the ALC operated in the neighbourhoods demonstrated unfairness and irrationality.

Some authorities have made considerable efforts to tackle the issue of racism with attention being focused on racial harassment on council estates. (See Commission for Racial Equality, 1987; Mac-

---

[81] See Handy, *Discrimination in Housing*, (1993) for a comprehensive discussion of this issue.

Ewen, 1989; Legal Action Group, 1990.) Concern about the rise in the incidence of harassment has led to some authorities adopting extensive procedures to try to counter the violence and terror. These procedures usually add a non-harassment condition to tenancies to increase the ability of the landlord to evict a perpetrator. Despite these efforts, the results have not been very encouraging. First, it has proven very difficult for a variety of reasons to achieve evictions. These include reluctance of witnesses to come forward and difficulty in persuading the court that eviction of the tenant is the appropriate action. Secondly, research conducted in Newham LBC, a borough noted for its very committed approach to tackling the problem, revealed very considerable dissatisfaction from victims with the processes. The authors argue that:

"The primary function . . . of a housing department . . . is to manage the property and to collect the rents. . . . it is unrealistic to expect the same personnel . . . to exercise the quasi-judicial, quasi-policing, quasi-mediating function of a caseworker . . . in circumstances of racial harassment. Housing officers cannot command the unconditional trust of the tenant by virtue of their landlord function."[82]

Concern over racial harassment is one manifestation of a wider anxiety about social conflict on council estates. There are increasing reports of the fear with which tenants live and housing staff work (Birch, 1995b; Kelly, 1995). Local authorities are finding that tenants are less interested in repairing policy and more concerned about the antisocial behaviour of neighbours. One response is to evict the perpetrator but this has proven slow and ineffectual. Some authorities have turned to the use of civil injunctions (under section 222 of the 1972 Local Government Act) to deal with the problems.

"Since the late 1980s, housing officers and courts have together revolutionised the use of injunctions. Since *Sutton Housing Trust v. Lawrence* in 1987, injunctions have been available, almost as of right where tenants breach 'negative covenants' in their tenancy agreements. Injunctions are similarly available to restrain acts of nuisance and trespass."[83]

---

[82] Cooper and Qureshi, *Through Patterns Not Our Own: A Study of the Regulation of Violence on the Council Estates of East London,* (1993), p. 63.
[83] Campbell, "Putting security on protection", *Roof,* May/June 1995, p. 19.

Despite these developments, some authorities have sought amendments to the security of tenure provisions to make eviction easier. The 1996 Housing Bill clauses 91 and 92 introduce probationary tenancies whereby council tenants will not become secure tenants until the end of the first year of their tenancy. If they misbehave in the meantime the authority will be able to recover possession with ease. The tenant's position will be as vulnerable during this period as it was prior to 1980 which causes anxiety to some (Campbell, 1995).

The public landlord is required to manage the consequences of economic and social residualisation of the council sector in a context where the emphasis is on the local authority as housing facilitator and purchaser of housing services. What is the meaning of public landlordism in this context? Is it as Cooper and Qureshi (1993) suggest no different to that of the private landlord? If so, why are landlords responsible for racial violence and general antisocial behaviour? Can the costs of an anti-harassment policy be attributable to the ring-fenced Housing Revenue Account? If they are not, the cost of residualisation will have to be externalised. If the public landlord is simply another landlord, collective social policies should have no place in the council tenancy. Arguably their presence represents a new and confused power relationship between landlord and tenant.

## Conclusions

The period since the mid-seventies has been one of enormous change in the provision of council housing which reflect those occuring within the welfare state. However, the market has always been a major provider of housing and much involved in the production, but not consumption, of council housing. State housing has therefore always functioned in the midst of a market.

There are two strands to changes in the relations of council housing. The local authority has been transformed from a developer to first and foremost a landlord. The stock is reducing because it is being sold off and is not being replaced. In the eighties privatisation was achieved by providing tenants an individual right to buy. However, the focus in the nineties, now that the backlog of potential purchasers has been reduced, is on wholesale transfer of the stock to private constituted bodies. The other strand has involved the change of relations within the sector so that the local authority landlord resembles other landlords more closely. This has involved the creation of free-standing accounts and pressure to treat rents in a more market-oriented way, no longer based on historic cost within the regulatory sphere. Council tenants in the 1980s were given statutory rights which strengthened to some extent the individual property relations between landlord and tenant. The greatest recognition of the tenant's property claim in the lease was granted in the individual right to buy for those with sufficient economic resources. Security of tenure and consultation rights has proven valuable to tenants in the context of the moves to collective transfer.

Tenants in the nineties are considered to be consuming citizens, provided with choice in the social market of housing. This choice is, however, a chimera given the lack of choice available to the majority of tenants. For many "choice" is limited to whether they are eligible for the duties under the homeless provisions or not. The introduction of compulsory competitive tendering, which involves the contractualisation of relations between purchasers of housing management services and their providers, is producing a similar way of relating to tenants. The form of the relationship between landlord and tenant has changed substantially from one based on public administration to one encapsulated in a contract. The tenants' charter provides the framework for the individual relationship but increasingly the contract is providing the basis for collective relationships. Whether the change in the form of these relationships will translate into increased accountability to tenants is an open question.

# Chapter Five

# The World of Housing Associations

## Introduction

Housing Associations are the product of their long and diverse history. In order to understand the issues which confront the contemporary housing association movement, it is necessary to provide a brief history of their development. One key feature is that they are all non-profit making organisations although they have a variety of constitutional formats, structures and aims (Cope, 1990). Another is that they are voluntary organisations. "Housing association provision is not undertaken through statutory duty but is the result of the energy and commitment of lay volunteers who combine to form an association to meet perceived housing needs".[1] The Housing Associations Act 1985, section 1, describes them as a:

> "society, body of trustees, or company (a) which is established for the purpose of, or amongst whose objects or powers are included those of providing, constructing, improving or managing, or facilitating or encouraging the construction or improvement of, housing accommodation, and, (b) which does not trade for profit or whose constitution or rules prohibit the issue of capital with interest or dividend exceeding such rates as may be determined by the Treasury, whether with or without distinction between share and loan capital."

Some "facts and figures" show their diversity. There are about 4,000 associations in the United Kingdom, meeting a variety of housing

---

[1] Cope, *Housing Associations—Policy and Practice* (1990), p. 1.

needs. Some of these specialise in particular needs: for the elderly, ex-offenders, single homeless, mentally or physically disabled; others offer general housing. Thus, some complement and others overlap the activities of local authorities. Between them, these associations own nearly a million homes, compared to over 4 million in local authority ownership. Almost half of the associations own between one and 50 dwellings and less that six per cent own 1,000 or more.[2] In 1994, 2,276 of these were registered with the Housing Corporation in order to be eligible for public funds. However, only about 500 associations have received significant public funding. Of these about 100 have been responsible for the majority of new developments since the mid-1970s. The sums involved, however, are significant: between 1988 and 1994 associations have invested over £8 billion of public funds and £2.6 billion of private money to produce 200,000 homes.[3]

Some organisations can trace their origins back to the almshouses of the middle ages:

"These were founded by individual benefactors, or guilds concerned with the charitable provision of accommodation as part of their Christian duty, . . . [they] also provided health care and other supportive services."[4]

Almshouses still provide over 26,000 homes. They are now legally and administratively distinct from housing associations.

Significant development of the voluntary housing movement occurred in the mid-nineteenth century at a time when almost all housing provision was privately rented and housing conditions in the cities were abominable. At this time there was little support for direct state intervention in market processes,[5] instead there was the formation of charitable housing trusts by philanthropic capitalists in "an attempt to demonstrate that private provision for the working class

---

[2] Alder and Handy, *Housing Association Law* (2nd ed., 1991), p. 4.
[3] NFHA, National Voluntary Committee Members' Forum paper on Issues and Options for the NFHA Inquiry into Housing Association Governance. Internal document (1994), p. 3.
[4] Cope, *Housing Associations—Policy and Practice* (1990), p. 8.
[5] Steadman Jones, *Outcast London: A Study in the Relationship Between Classes in Victorian Society* (1976), Part II.

could be of a higher standard than that provided by speculative house builders".[6] The twin objective of assisting the labouring classes whilst attracting private investment by providing a limited return on capital came to be known as five per cent philanthropy.[7] The attempt eventually failed (Stedman Jones, 1976; Merrett, 1979) leading to the development of direct state provision and the eclipse of the housing trusts. However, as we saw in the previous chapter, state housing did not become fully established until 1919 by which time a number of the trusts, still in existence, such as the Bournville, Rowntree, Peabody, Guinness and Sutton Trusts had been founded. The 1919 Housing and Town Planning Act permitted local authorities to pass subsidies on to specified housing trusts.

The inter-war years were a period of quiesence in the development of housing associations, although legally they were defined for the first time in the Housing Act of 1935. This definition forms the basis for the present 1985 Act, section 1 quoted above.

Although they are independent organisations, the associations have been the subject of a variety of government initiatives since the 1960s. The next major development within the movement came in 1961 with the encouragement by the Conservative Government of cost-rent housing associations and co-ownership schemes. Both schemes offered attractions to property "professionals" at the time. Cost-rent associations were intended to provide unsubsidised accommodation at economic rents, thereby providing a model for the private sector and encouraging the regeneration of private renting. Co-ownership schemes were a new idea: they were designed for the "indigent middle class"[7a] for whom this type of scheme offered a share in the increase in the value of their home on leaving. Legally, co-ownership organisations are mutual housing associations: the governing rules of the association must ensure that all members are tenants or prospective tenants of the association and that tenancies cannot be granted or assigned to persons other than members. They

---

[6] Back and Hamnett, "State Housing Policy Formation and the Changing Role of Housing Associations in Britain", *Policy and Politics* (1985), Vol. 13, No. 4, pp. 393–394.

[7] *ibid.* p. 394.

[7a] This phrase was coined by the then Housing Corporation Chairman, Lord Goodman, quoted in Alder, 1983: 30.

must also be incorporated by registration under the Industrial and Provident Societies Act 1965.[8]

The Housing Corporation, an unelected body, was established in 1964 to promote and assist the development of housing societies (now section 1 of the Housing Associations Act 1985) with powers to provide loans to housing societies for these schemes. The Corporation "represented a body independent of local authorities receiving central government assistance to promote a form of quasi-private renting in the case of cost renting, and a form of owner occupation in the case of co-ownership housing societies".[9]

These initiatives represented a very different function for associations, part of the creation of a new private-rented sector rather than a response to its inadequacies. They did not prosper with the changed economic circumstances of the seventies and with regulation of fee earning.

The sixties had also seen the formation of local, community based associations which acquired and rehabilitated homes in inner-city areas that were threatened with demolition through slum clearance programmes. Many were set up with the help of Shelter, the campaign for the homeless, which was established in 1966.[10] Some are mutual co-operatives, sharing the same basic legal requirements as co-ownership societies described above but attracting different statutory protections. Others would fall into the non-mutual category whereby not all members are tenants although all tenants are members.

The 1974 Housing Act marked the full scale move away from slum clearance policies to those of rehabilitation. While in opposition, the Labour Party had not supported the cost-rent and co-ownership initiatives. However, they did see a different role for housing associations, undertaking the rehabilitation of the private-rented stock in inner-city areas. This process, which replaced private landlords with housing associations, offered an alternative to municipalisation. Back and Hamnett argue that the Labour approach to housing associations was to see them as quasi-public bodies.[11] We shall see

---

[8] Alder, "Housing Associations—The Third World of Housing Policy", *Journal of Social Welfare Law* (1983), June, pp. 22–37 at 25.

[9] Back and Hamnett, *op. cit.*, p. 400.

[10] Cope, *Housing Associations—Policy and Practice* (1990), p. 11.

[11] Back and Hamnett, *op. cit.* (1985), p. 404.

that the ambiguous nature of association activity and shifting government policy has continued to construct them at various times as alternatives to both the private and public sectors. Some in their purpose and legal form seem more private than public, others the reverse. Many seem to be both private and public bodies. As Alder and Handy point out:

> "because there is no distinctive form of housing association tenure the law is very complex. Housing association tenancies must draw upon the many different legal regimes applicable to residential tenancies in general. Any features peculiar to the needs of housing associations must therefore be sculpted out of particular tenancy agreeements within a legal context designed mainly for the private sector."[12]

The way in which these constructions have occurred and the consequences for tenants of housing associations will be discussed in the subsequent sections where I adopt the tripartite classification of general regulatory, individual statutory and individual property relations. In a similar manner to the chapter on local authority housing, I intend to divide the discussion into eras in order to illustrate the changing relationships and constructions over time. I will consider the period 1974 to 1980, then 1980 to 1988 and finally 1988 onwards. I also intend to concentrate on certain aspects of the landlord-tenant relationship. These will be allocation, security and succession, rents and certain management issues, in particular consultation and participation, mirroring those in the local authority chapter. I am once again interested in highlighting changes in accountability structures.

Although there are major differences in the legal regimes relating to mutual and non-mutual housing associations, my primary concern will be with the latter because they are the form of association which is responsible for most of the new developments since the seventies. My discussion will also be limited to the position in England. Since 1989, Wales has had its own body, Housing for Wales, to fund and oversee the activities of housing associations.

I intend, generally, to limit my discussion to those occupying as tenants. Some housing associations provide accommodation for those with special needs and may use licences either because the residents

---

[12] Alder and Handy, *Housing Association Law* (2nd ed., 1991), p. 81.

are sharing or because special caring facilities are required.[13] Licences grant occupiers personal permission to occupy premises rather than a property interest as in the case of tenancy.[14] Licensees are more vulnerable than tenants under common-law principles and statutory protection has been significantly reduced for new licensees after the commencement of the Housing Act 1988.[15]

In Chapter 4, we saw that the individual property relations in local authority housing have never existed outside of the regulatory sphere because the landlord is the state, and that individual statutory protection came late to the relationship. This position can be contrasted with housing associations. Although the individual property relationship of landlord and tenant reflects the independent, voluntary origins of the housing associations, these organisations have been moulded as landlords by the various regulatory relations. Regulation has taken a variety of forms over time and has contributed to whether the housing association is seen as a public or a private entity. Some associations existed before the Housing Corporation, others are very much a product of its existence. While the landlord has been moulded by the regulatory context, the tenant's relationship with the landlord has been constructed in the main by the individual statutory relations which have shifted the tenants conceptually from the private sphere to the public and back again. The combination of these two spheres of relationships, the regulatory and the individual statutory regimes, has had a major impact on the individual property relations. We now see a complicated and convoluted set of arrangements designed to place associations within the private market sphere yet accommodate the need for associations to remain in the realm of social responsibility.

I will, therefore, commence my discussion with the construction of the landlords through the various regulatory frameworks, move on to consider the various individual statutory regimes and finally reflect on the interactions of these spheres with individual property relations.

---

[13] Alder and Handy, *op. cit.*, p. 87.
[14] See Partington and Hill, *Housing Law: Cases, Materials and Commentary* (1991), pp. 28–84.
[15] For a detailed discussion of special needs housing, see Alder and Handy (1991), *ibid.*, Chapter 10; Cope, *Housing Associations—Policy and Practice* (1990), Chapter 7.

# Relationships Between 1974 and 1980

## A. GENERAL REGULATORY FRAMEWORK

The legislative and financial framework established in the 1974 Housing Act provided the basis for the development of the housing association movement until 1988. These provisions led to the proliferation of the non-mutual form of the housing association which provide rented accommodation. In these associations there is no necessary nexus between members and tenants.[16] About 90 per cent of all housing-association stock is owned by non-mutual associations. In 1991, there were 1,956 non-mutual associations registered with the Housing Corporation.

The Housing Act 1974 transformed the role and significance of the Housing Corporation. Its first ten years were spent pump priming new private-sector initiatives which were ultimately unsuccessful. The incoming Labour Government stimulated the most intensive period of expansion and development of housing associations as a quasi-public rented bodies. The powers of the Housing Corporation were extended, making it responsible for sponsoring, promoting, funding and supervising the work of the associations.[17] All housing associations wishing to obtain public funds via the newly introduced Housing Association Grant and the other subsidies were required to register with it.

The legal definition of a housing association set out in section 1(1) of the Housing Associations Act 1985 does not require any particular constitutional form.[18] Some, such as housing trusts operate completely privately. Associations can be unincorporated, but most are incorporated. They can be companies registered either by guarantee

---

[16] Alder, "Housing Associations—The Third World of Housing Policy", *Journal of Social Welfare Law* (1993), June pp. 22–37 at 32.

[17] Cope, *Housing Associations—Policy and Practice* (1990), p. 12.

[18] Some associations, known as secondary housing associations, do not provide homes but limit their activity to giving advice or assisting other providers and facilitating and encouraging the construction or improvement of housing accommodation. The representative bodies of the housing association world, the National Federation of Housing Associations, the National Federation of Housing Co-ops, the Housing Association Charitable Trust and the National Association of Almshouses are all secondary housing associations.

or shares under the Companies Act 1985. However, unless a company association is also a registered charity it cannot be registered with the Housing Corporation. A housing association can also be a trust, although it must also be a charitable trust. Whatever the form, it must not trade for profit. This does not prevent the association from making a surplus which is then reinvested for housing purposes.

Housing associations are not obliged to register with anyone, although about 75 per cent of associations are registered as industrial and provident societies under the Industrial and Provident Societies Act 1965. This gives the society a separate identity, with limited liability, able to carry out activities authorised by its rules. Once an association has satisfied the statutory conditions for registration, the Registrar of Friendly Societies has a duty to register it. There is no discretion, in contrast to the Housing Corporation. There is a right of appeal to the High Court against the decision of the Registrar to refuse, cancel or suspend registration (Industrial and Provident Societies Act 1965, section 18).

The statutory conditions include the requirement that the society has at least seven members; that its rules cover such matters as objects of the society, qualifications for membership, appointment of a management committee and voting and that the society is either a bona fide co-operative society, or that the business of the society is conducted for the benefit of the community, and there are special reasons why the society should be registered under the 1965 Act rather than as a company. As registration as an industrial and provident society is usually a prerequisite for registration with the Housing Corporation, access to public funds is probably a sufficiently special reason.

The Registrar is not concerned with the housing activities of an association but rather with its financial procedures and whether the society operates within its stated rules.[18a] Some associations are registered with the Charity Commission.[19] Some are registered as industrial and provident societies and as charities.

---

[18a] Alder and Handy, *Housing Association Law* (2nd ed., 1991), pp. 240–242.
[19] For a discussion of charitable housing associations, see Alder and Handy, 1991: 64–76.

Alder and Handy (to whom I am indebted for much of the information in this section) describe a hierachy of privilege.[20] At the top are bodies registered with the Housing Corporation. This provides access to public funding and legal privileges. Such societies must also be registered either as an industrial and provident society or as a charity. In the middle are "specific kinds of housing association which have special privileges other than access to public funds". These include charitable bodies, co-operative housing associations and "certain associations which have entered into agreements approved by the Secretary of State with local authorities to take on some or all of the local authorities' housing duties". At the bottom are unregistered housing associations, often incorporated as companies. In 1995, of the 2,276 housing associations registered with the Housing Corporation, 1,337 are industrial and provident societies, 675 are charitable trusts and 264 are charitable companies limited by guarantee (NFHA, 1995).

The National Federation of Housing Associations (1995) has concluded that although a single corporate status for associations would resolve this multiple regulation, it would require primary legislation of great complexity and that the difficulties of trying to achieve it would far outweigh the likely benefits. Instead it recommends that as regulation by the Registry of Friendly Societies, Companies House and the Charity Commission adds little to the much more rigorous regulation of the Housing Corporation, housing associations should be exempt from the routine regulation of whichever body currently oversees their status.

Generally speaking those at the top of the ladder are constructed as "public" bodies receiving public funds and consequentially the most regulated, while those at the bottom operate as private landlords with few specific privileges. Thus the introduction of large scale public subsidy in 1974, with the concomitant supervision by the Corporation, repositioned the associations within the rented sector, reconstructing them as quasi-public bodies for financial and supervisory purposes.

The primary task of the Housing Corporation at this time was to register some 3,000 housing associations. The registration require-

[20] *ibid.* p. 28.

ments are now contained in sections 3 to 7 of the Housing Associations Act 1985 (as amended by the Housing Act 1988). Section 4 prescribes eligibility for registration: the association must be either a registered charity or a registered industrial and provident society; it must not trade for profit; its purposes must include the provision, construction, improvement or management of houses available for letting or it must be a mutual society. Associations are permitted additional purposes or objects which have been extended by the Housing Act 1988. The Corporation's decision on whether these conditions have been satisfied cannot be challenged in the courts and if an association appears on the register it is conclusively presumed to be eligible (section 5) (see *Goodman v. Dolphin Square Housing Trust* (1979), below). However, if an association does not fulfil the statutory conditions it is possible to apply for mandamus to compel the Corporation to remove it from the register (section 6(2)).

Unlike the Registrar of Friendly Societies, even if the association fulfills the statutory conditions, the Corporation has a discretion whether or not to register it. The exercise of this discretion is subject to review in the courts. While there is no right of appeal on the merits against a refusal to register and reasons do not have to be given, there is a right of appeal to the High Court against a decision by the Corporation to remove an association from the register (sections 6(1) and 7(1) of the Housing Associations Act 1985). The power of removal is very limited (section 6(2)–(4)) (see also *Goodman v. Dolphin Square Housing Trust* (1979) 39 P. & C.R. 257 esp. pp. 261–2). Section 5(1) requires the housing corporation to establish criteria for the exercise of its discretion which are varied from time to time (section 5(2)). We will discuss the implications of the present criteria in a later section.

Despite registering over 2,600 associations within three years, the Corporation gained an uneviable reputation "for remoteness, incoherence, bureaucratic muddle, error and cumbersome procedures".[21] It was also criticised for its rudimentary financial monitoring which contributed to its failure to prevent some dubious practices within housing associations during the seventies, par-

---

[21] Alder, "Housing Associations—The Third World of Housing Policy", *Journal of Social Welfare Law* (1983), June, pp. 23–37 at 27.

ticularly in relation to financial gain by those involved with associations.[22]

The Corporation's other major task was to administer the grants and subsidies available to housing associations. The system for funding housing association development introduced in 1974 was based on different principles to those operating in the local authority sector. Housing associations obtained a capital grant, the Housing Association Grant (HAG) (Housing Associations Act 1985: sections 41 to 52) from the Department of the Environment via the Housing Corporation to fund development in contrast to the local authorities which merely obtained consent to borrow on the money markets.

The Housing Association Grant was:

> "equal to the sum required by an association to reduce its loan repayments in the first year after completing a development scheme to the amount equal to its income from the fair rents set by the rent officer service (net of defined allowances for management and maintenance costs)."[23]

This covered on average 85 per cent of the costs of most schemes, 100 per cent for many special needs schemes.

Associations were also eligible for discretionary subsidies to cover revenue deficits (Housing Associations Act 1985, sections 54 to 57) "covering annual deficits which arose because of stock development under pre-1974 regimes, the effect of rent restrictions after the calculation of HAG . . .".[24] This system placed the risk of development within the public expenditure system rather than with the individual housing association and was primarily responsible for

---

[22] The main concern was over duality of interest of staff and committee members, particularly in relation to possible material or financial gain. The position was formalised by the Housing Act 1980 (re-enacted in ss.13 and 15 of the Housing Associations Act 1985). Associations cannot make gifts or payments to members or families of members. They cannot pay or grant a benefit including a tenancy to current members, officers or employees or those who have held these positions within the last 12 months (Cope, 1990: 49–50). The National Federation of Housing Associations considers the provisions in relation to gain are too restrictive and recommends that the Housing Corporation be given a new statutory power to issue guidance concerning the treatment of conflicts and dualities (NFHA, 1995).

[23] Langstaff, "Housing Associations: A Move to Centre Stage", in Birchall (ed.), *Housing Policy in the 1990s* (1992), p. 31.

[24] Langstaff, *op. cit.*, p. 31.

development of the housing association stock which had trebled in size by 1989 to nearly 600,000.

A considerable amount of housing association activity in this period was directed at rehabilitation of private rented housing in inner-city areas. Many Labour controlled local authorities did not share the national government's enthusiasm for this alternative rented sector. The government preferred housing association owner-ship of rehabilitated stock to that of the local authorities and provided more generous subsidies to associations than to authorities. In addition, since 1964, an increasingly large share of state support of housing associations has been channelled through the Housing Corporation rather than through the local authorities, despite the powers available to authorities to promote and assist housing associa-tions (now Housing Associations Act 1985, sections 58 to 61). This trend has continued so that now in 1995–96 the Housing Corpora-tion's Approved Development Programme of £1.2 billion was only slightly smaller than the capital spending allocation for the local authorities of £1.27 billion.

The seeds of social market landlordism were sown at this time and can be seen as another aspect of the failure of the Labour Govern-ment to set a confident agenda for public sector housing (see Stewart and Burridge, 1989). We will return to the relationship between local authorities and housing associations later.

## B. Individual Statutory Relations

Despite this incorporation into the realm of public regulation, the positioning of housing associations by government as private landlords continued. We have seen in Chapter 4 that the controver-sial Housing Finance Act 1972 extended external rent regulation to the local authority sector. It also extended rent regulation in the form of fair rents to tenants of traditional housing associations. Tenants also became eligible for means-tested rent allowances. Thus, housing association tenants were provided with a similar rent regulation regime to that of private tenants. When the public sector rent regulation scheme was repealed in 1975, housing association tenants covered by the fair rent provision retained their entitlement.[25] In 1977 they were included in the Rent Act provisions on fair rent (see Rent Act 1977, Part 6).

However, most tenants of housing associations were excluded from the security of tenure provisions available to private sector tenants by sections 15 and 16 of the Rent Act 1977 as amended.[26] Thus tenants were deemed in need of rent regulation by an independent body but not in need of the security of tenure provisions available to tenants of private landlords, presumably because their landlords were non-profit making bodies and considered to be socially responsible.

## C. INDIVIDUAL PROPERTY RELATIONS

Housing association tenancies did not give rise in the seventies to the type of scrutiny and criticism levelled at the local authority sector. The disparate nature of the sector and very small size would partly account for this. The main housing association tenancy is periodic and short term. These tenancies are not required by property law to be in writing, although the tenancies would be covered by the same basic statutory provisions as other tenants in relation to the provision of rent books, protection from eviction and repairing obligations (see Chapter 3). Thus, the security of the tenant depended on the terms of the agreement between the landlord and themselves subject to the notice to quit requirements of the Protection from Eviction Act 1977.

Two cases illustrate the insecurity of tenants under this regime but also the positioning of housing associations in law which arise from the interactions of these spheres of relationships. In *Peabody Housing Association Ltd v. Green* (1978) 38 P. & C.R. 644 the housing association was registered both under the Industrial and Provident

---

[25] A special housing association fair rent regime applies to all tenancies, other than co-ownership tenancies, that are outside full Rent Act protection solely because of exclusions contained in ss.15 and 16 of the Rent Act 1977 as amended see next footnote

[26] It is difficult of make generalisations about housing associations: non-mutual unregistered associations, which do not qualify as charitable housing trusts, and full-mutual associations constituted under the Companies Act were covered as long as there was no other reason for their exclusion such as the occupier holding the status of licensee rather than tenant.

Societies Act 1965 and with the Housing Corporation. It had taken an assignment of the remaining years of a long lease of the building in which the defendant resided. The assignment was taken from the Peabody Donation Fund, a housing trust. The terms of the tenancy agreement entered into in 1975 for the defendant's flat stated that the occupation was temporary because the freeholder intended in the future to demolish the building and redevelop the area. The plaintiffs served a notice to quit in July 1978.

The tenancy was not protected by the Rent Act 1977 and as such the tenants had no defence against the notice to quit. Instead they argued in the Court of Appeal that because the association was registered with the Housing Corporation and, therefore, its activities and objectives were strictly delineated by statute, it had a statutory duty to provide housing. When it exercised its power to give notice to quit it was exercising a statutory power. Therefore the courts were entitled to review that exercise of power in order to decide whether or not there had been an abuse of power by the association. The Court of Appeal rejected this argument. The association, in issuing a notice to quit, was empowered by its own rules, one of which stated that the association shall have the power to do all things necessary or expedient for the fulfilment of its objects. Thus judicial review is not available to tenants in these circumstances: they must rely on the terms of their private tenancy agreement. The housing association in its relationship to its tenants is a private body despite its public regulation and funding. We shall see that this approach to the position of housing associations in law is coming under increased pressure in the light of subsequent developments in the regulatory framework but still seems to reflect the present legal position.

The second contemporaneous case involves another attempt to defend a notice to quit by reference to the status of the landlord in relation to its regulators. In *Goodman v. Dolphin Square Trust* (1979) 39 P. & C.R. 257 the tenant argued that the association was not entitled to be registered with the Housing Corporation, because the association was profit making. If the association was not registered with the Housing Corporation her tenancy would be protected by the Rent Act. The Court of Appeal was unwilling to consider the substance of her claim. As we have seen the relevant statutory provision (now section 5(4) of the Housing Associations Act 1985) states that for all purposes a body shall be conclusively presumed to be, or to have been, a housing association eligible for registration at any time when it is, or was, on the register. The Court held that the association must be presumed to comply with the requirements. The Court considered the powers to remove housing associations from the register and held that these were the exclusive responsibility of the Corporation. Thus the tenant of an association cannot directly challenge the landlord's relationship with the Housing Corporation.

The housing association tenant's legal position was defined by the terms of the tenancy which reflected the private landlord and tenant relationship. The landlord was obliged to meet the requirements of its regulators and elements of this relationship can be challenged in the courts via judicial review. Thus the landlord was in effect a private landlord in relation to its tenants but a public landlord in relations to its regulators. Tenants were unable to make use of the regulatory system in their relationship with their landlord.

## Relationships Between 1980 and 1988

A. GENERAL REGULATORY RELATIONS

Housing associations did not experience fundamental reform under the Conservative Government until late in the decade and were in policy terms largely ignored (Langstaff, 1992). They did experience a cutback on their funding as part of the general attempts to reduce public expenditure on housing. In the late seventies the development programme had involved about 50,000 approvals a year. After an initial moratorium on new schemes in 1980–81 which reduced new approvals to 11,000, thereafter housing associations managed 15–20,000 new approvals per year until 1988.

However, Back and Hamnett[27] argue that the Labour Government's positioning of housing associations in the quasi-public area did have an impact. This can be explained by activities within the different spheres of relationships. At a general regulatory level,

---

[27] Back and Hamnett, "State Housing Policy Formation and the Changing Role of Housing Associations", *Policy and Politics* (1985), Vol. 13, p. 405 at p. 411.

significant changes did not occur until after 1988. Both the regulatory and funding systems remained broadly the same. However, within the individual statutory sphere there was considerable change.

It is appropriate here to consider in a little more detail the relationship between the Department of the Environment and the Housing Corporation and the powers of the Corporation. I will be concentrating on the constitutional position of the Corporation which has not been affected by the changes introduced by the 1988 Housing Act. The Corporation's changing responsibilities in relation to supervision and funding of the broader social housing sector will be considered in the later section.

Alder and Handy argue that the capacity of government to influence housing association policy is virtually unlimited.[28] This influence operates through the Secretary of State for the Environment, the Registry of Friendly Societies and the Charity Commissioners and the Housing Corporation. The Secretary of State has no direct legal relationship with individual housing associations but has a battery of statutory powers in relation to the Housing Corporation. Much of the central control is gained through patronage and informal influence. The Housing Corporation's finance is almost exclusively derived from central government. The Department of the Environment negotiates the size of the Corporation's Approved Development Programme with the Treasury. Prior to the 1988 Act Housing Association Grants were the direct responsibility of the Secretary of State, although this responsibility was delegated to the Corporation. Now both Housing Association Grant and Revenue Deficit Grant are the responsibility of the Corporation, although the principles to be applied are approved by the Secretary of State.

The Housing Corporation is a statutory agency, a non-departmental public body. It is not formally part of the Crown. Ministers are not therefore directly responsible for its activities. Parliamentary control is limited to the laying before it of an annual report and accounts. The latter activity is subject to monitoring through the Public Accounts Committee. The Corporation has no elected element: the board of up to 15 members is appointed by the Secretary of State who also appoints the Chair and Deputy Chair. It

---

[28] Alder and Handy, *Housing Association Law* (2nd ed., 1991), p. 211.

is subject to the jurisdiction of the Parliamentary Commissioner (Ombudsman).

The wide-ranging functions of the Corporation offend the principles of the separation of powers. It is promoter, banker, policeman, judge and executioner to housing associations. It exercises wide discretionary powers derived from the Housing Associations Act 1985 (Part 3) and the Housing Act 1988 (Part 2), yet few of its decisions are subject to any right of appeal. It has no general statutory duty to publicise its policies, nor to consult with interested parties nor to give reasons for its decisions. It manages by circular. Although judicial review is available, these characteristics reduce the effectiveness of any court action.

The Housing Corporation has been administratively and politically reviewed a number of times in its recent history. In 1980 it was reviewed along with other non-departmental public bodies by Sir Leo Pliatsky as part of the Conservative Government's stated desire to reduce the number of quangos. His report supported its continued existence because of its dual functions of channelling finance and also promoting registered housing associations. He considered it better suited than either central or local government to mobilise voluntary effort and personal initiative (House of Commons 1992–93, memorandum submitted by the DoE and Housing Corporation, page 3). However, changes were made in its structures to tighten up its performance and its staffing level was reduced by a fifth. A further government review in 1985–86 of financial management and policy implementation concluded that the Corporation had effective systems of financial management and was capable of greater delegation of responsibility from the DoE. This vote of confidence is reflected in the new powers contained in the Housing Act 1988. In 1992–93 the House of Commons Select Committee on the Environment conducted an inquiry into the Corporation in which it considered its relationship with the DoE.

Alder and Handy argue that "the policies and their method of implementation emanate directly for the Department of the Environment. The Housing Corporation merely cloaks in legal form the wishes of its political masters".[29] This perception was shared by a

---

[29] Alder and Handy, *Housing Association Law* (2nd ed., 1991), p. 212.

number of witnesses to the Select Committee including the former Chief Executive (House of Commons 1992–93 report: xvi). The Select Committee discovered that the relationship had been clarified by a Ministerial Statement issued by the Secretary of State in December 1991 to the Housing Corporation. It considered that the Corporation was not a mere tool of the government and "those who portray the Corporation as the Department's poodle have fundamentally misjudged the present relationship" (xvii). The Committee nonetheless recommended that the Department should only over-rule well formulated recommendations from the Corporation in the most exceptional circumstances. The Government's response was to suggest it would listen but would not change its approach.[30]

The Secretary of State has few formal powers over the Corporation's registration function and its supervisory activities and none in relation to its disciplinary sanctions. We have already discussed the registration powers and now turn to the other powers granted to the Corporation. First, the Corporation has a duty to promote the interests of the voluntary housing movement. This is not a representative function (which is carried out by the National Federation of Housing Associations) rather one of "smoothing the way" for their activities. Secondly, the Corporation provides loans and channels grants to housing associations. This involves both the "traditional" system of grant explained above and the "mixed funding" system introduced by the 1988 Housing Act and explained below. Thirdly, the corporation can provide housing directly although it has not done so. Fourthly, it supervises and disciplines registered housing associations. There are two areas of supervision, the first involves the oversight of development programmes, the second of general management. Traditionally the latter has had two objectives: determining whether the committee of management is in control of the association and determining whether the activities of the association are consistent with the objects of a non-profit making housing body in receipt of public funds (Housing Corporation Circular 19/85). More recently there has been greater emphasis laid upon performance monitoring. Lastly, it supervises the tenant's choice machinery (see

---

[30] DoE, The Government's Response to the Second Report From the House of Commons Select Committee on the Environment Session 1992/3: The Housing Corporation (1993), Cmnd. 2363, p. 2.

Chapter 4). I intend to consider the general supervison of management including the implications of the transfer of local authority stock in more depth in a later section.

The powers available to the Corporation to carry out these activities include the regular examination of accounts, monitoring visits, carrying out inquiries under section 28 of the Housing Associations Act and audit under section 29, making determinations (section 50(2) of the Housing Act 1988) and issuing guidance (section 49 of the Housing Act 1988), imposing sanctions such as removal or suspension of members or officers or transfering property from the association and imposing management schemes.[31]

To summarise, housing associations are enmeshed in complex regulatory relations which construct them as public bodies accountable to their regulators. The regulators wield very considerable power over all aspects of their activities but have little accountability themselves. However, associations are private law bodies constitutionally, so their relationships with tenants are firmly rooted within the individual property relation.

## B. Individual Statutory Relations

The position of housing association tenants altered significantly in 1980 with the passing of the Housing Act. Tenants were now defined as secure tenants for most purposes and as such were granted the same status as council tenants. Further evidence of the positioning of housing associations as public bodies comes from the inclusion of measures in the Act to "privatise" them.[32] The first of such was the extension of the right to buy for tenants of non-charitable housing associations which led to the sale of 19,000 homes by 1989. Attempts to extend the right to tenants of charitable housing associations proved very controversial and led to a Government defeat in the House of Lords. The Government was obliged to introduce a scheme whereby such housing associations acquired a dwelling on the market

---

[31] For further details see Alder and Handy, *op. cit.*, pp. 214–240.
[32] Back and Hamnett, "State Housing Policy Formation and the Changing Role of Housing Associations in Britain", *Policy and Politics* (1985), Vol. 13, p. 405.

which they then resold at a discount to tenants.[33] The second was an attempt to encourage a change of focus in their provision through the development of low-cost home ownership initiatives. Housing associations were given additional powers to carry out such schemes and finance was set aside by the Housing Corporation for them. By 1989, 36,000 homes had been provided under these arrangements (see Chapter 2 above, and Booth and Crook, 1986).

Tenants who entered into their tenancies prior to January 15, 1989 obtain the statutory security of tenure of the public sector and the rent regulation of the private. We have seen that the fair rent system was extended to housing associations by the Housing Finance Act 1972. The provisions were consolidated into the Rent Act 1977 and amended by the Housing Act 1980. This Act was consolidated in 1985 and amended by the Housing Act 1988. Housing associations are obliged by the grant requirements to maximise their rental income by charging the rent registered with the rent officer. The registered rent was reviewed every two years and until 1989 any increase was phased over the two years. However, since 1989 the tenant must pay the full increase at once.

The fair rent provisions are contained in Part 6 of the Rent Act 1977. The rent officer must disregard certain factors, most notably, the personal circumstances of the parties and any scarcity value due to the supply and demand factors in the locality (section 70). The rent officer is not required to follow any particular method in calculating a fair rent but in practice usually uses a system of comparables. There is little relevant case law which relates specifically to housing associations in this area. In *Palmer v. Peabody Trust* [1975] Q.B. 604, the Divisional Court held that the rent officer was entitled to place little weight on the fact that some housing association tenants had no security of tenure. This factor would be of more significance in the private rented sector but the judge considered that housing trusts were fair and respectable landlords not requiring the same supervision as private landlords.

---

[33] This discretionary scheme known as HOTCHA was created by the Housing and Building Control Act 1984, now Housing Act 1988, s.58. The scheme is no longer being implemented (Alder and Handy, 1991: 86). It has been replaced by the Tenants Incentive Scheme which offers cash incentives to tenants to help them purchase dwellings in the owner-occupied sector. Three thousand tenants took up the offer in 1991–92.

An interesting question was raised in *Royal British Legion H.A. Ltd v. East Midlands Rent Assessment Panel* (1989) 21 H.L.R. 42, as to whether the availability of grant assistance was a personal circumstance to be disregarded. In this case the landlord appealed to the rent assessment committee that the rent determined by the rent officer was too high. The rent included sums to cover depreciation in capital equipment which the landlord was able to recover through the housing association grant. In these circumstances, the landlord did not wish to pass on to the tenants any part of the burden of paying for such depreciation. The court agreed with the decision of the rent officer and the rent assessment committee that the nature of the landlord, whether it is a charity or in receipt of government grant, was a personal circumstance which had to be ignored.

This somewhat bizarre case highlights the contrast between this world and the controversy over local authority rents at the time. We have seen that the changes in local authority finances had led to considerable challenge over the determination of rents and the role of tax and rate subsidy in the rent equation. The relationship of subsidies to collective rents was highly controversial whereas here subsidy is clearly separated out of the individual rent assessment. Controversy over definitions and levels of rent only became an issue for housing associations' tenants who entered the sector after 1988.

Housing association tenants were granted the same charter rights as council tenants under the Housing Act 1980 (now the Housing Act 1985). These provide security of tenure: landlords require a court order to evict tenants which will only be granted if the court is satisfied that a statutorily defined ground for possession exists. There is a right of succession. Tenants have miscellaneous rights such as to take a lodger, to sub-let, to exchange, to undertake improvements, to obtain repairs, to be consulted and to obtain information. Most of these rights are limited in one way or another (see Chapter 4, above, and Partington and Hill, 1991).

The regulatory context and accountability structures in which these rights operate differ significantly between the two sectors. Government policy since 1980 has been to reduce the size and influence of the local authority sector in the ways described in Chapter 4, above, while it has supported the development of the housing association sector. Nevertheless a local authority housing

207

department generally manages substantially more stock than any one housing association. Local authority secure tenants can make use of public law actions to challenge their landlords statutory responsibilities, housing association secure tenants cannot. Local authority accountability has been administrative, within a permissive statutory framework, and based on political responsibilities to an electorate, housing association accountability is based on constitutionally defined purposes coupled with responsibilities to their regulators. The individual landlord/tenant relationship is weakly defined in the local authority sector while clearly based on private landlord and tenant law in the housing association sector.

## C. INDIVIDUAL PROPERTY RELATIONS

Secure housing association tenants have obtained a legal status with additional rights, some of which are incorporated into their tenancy agreements. They also obtained the "collective" rights available under the Housing Act 1985 to information and to consultation. Housing associations must make available their allocation rules, although many associations do not seem to allocate according to rules, preferring to rely on a consideration of individual merits, which will be related to the objects of the particular society.

The study by Glasgow University in 1989 found that only 26 per cent of associations used a points scheme in comparison with 65 per cent of local authorities. Twenty-two per cent used a date order system exclusively, compared with only eight per cent of local authorities. Both schemes based purely on merits and waiting time have been heavily criticised in relation to local authority allocation. While housing associations are under no statutory obligations in relation to allocation, they must not discriminate on grounds of sex or race in their procedures (Race Relations Act 1976 and Sex Discrimination Act 1975). Niner and Karn (1985) found evidence of racial and social bias in their study of housing associations in Birmingham. The Commission for Racial Equality has also conducted formal investigations into racism in housing associations (1983, 1992, 1993). The last of these considered the policies and practices of a number of associations in the light of the new duty imposed on associations by section 56 of the Housing Act 1988 to promote equality of opportunity and good race relations and found that, particularly in England, that they had made more progress than local authority housing departments.

Tenants must be provided with a written statement of the terms of the secure tenancy (Housing Act 1985, section 104). Landlords have a duty to publish information about its secure tenancies and the methods to be adopted for consultation on matters of housing management (Housing Act 1985, section 105 (5)). Landlords are obliged to consult with their tenants on some matters of housing management (section 105) although we have seen that this is not an absolute right to consultation and the method is left to the discretion of the landlord.[33a]

There has not been a tradition of tenant organisation within the housing association sector. This is partly because of the specialist nature of the associations and their size which has made individual contact easier, but there is also a strong history of philanthropic paternalism which fits uneasily with support for tenant involvement. We will return to the issue of participation and accountability in the next section.

The impact of these statutory rights seems to have been minimal within the housing association sector, reinforcing the point that the formal legal rights operate within a particular social, economic and political context. In the eight years in which all tenants who were eligible enjoyed secure status, the Government's main concern was to redefine local authority relationships and to increase owner-occupation. Crudely, the rights of housing association tenants were not of concern because the Government was not attempting to use them to change the power relationships within this sector. The Government's interest in housing associations as prime players in a social rented market and, therefore, in the position of housing association tenants did not move centre stage until the late eighties.

---

[33a] It is unlikely that the failure to comply with the consultation arrangements could be subject to enforcement for breach of statutory duty because of the width of the statutory discretion which suggest that it was not intended to create private rights (Alder and Handy, 1991: 348).

# Relationships from 1988 onwards

## A. GENERAL REGULATORY RELATIONS

This period of "benign neglect"[34] came to an end with the passing of the Housing Act 1988 when the policy spotlight was turned on the housing association sector. This neglect has not prevented an increasing proportion of public expenditure for housing development being directed towards housing associations in the 1980s, allowing the sector to continue to develop. This was in sharp contrast to the local authority sector whose development role was dramatically curtailed. The 1987 White Paper on Housing made it clear that housing associations were the vehicle chosen for the future development of the rented sector, in the absence of a suitably developed private sector. "The Government believes that housing associations have a vitally important part to play in the revival of the independent rented sector".[35]

Under the 1988 Housing Act housing associations became responsible not only for the development of new "social" rented dwellings but also the second stage of the privatisation of council housing. This involved the transfer of tenanted stock under the tenants' choice provisions. Housing associations were seen as the only viable recipient landlords for the majority of these transfers. An alternative privatisation method was also emerging, now classified as large scale voluntary transfers, which involved the establishment of new housing associations to whom the entire (or the majority) of a local authorities' housing stock would be transferred. (See Chapter 4, above for more discussion of these processes.)

This emphasis on the development of a social market in rented accommodation necessitated considerable changes in the relationships within the housing association sector, the main requirement being to transform a diverse and often specialist set of housing providers into mainstream social but privately oriented landlords. The process has created considerable tensions.

---

[34] Langstaff, "Housing Associations: A Move to Centre Stage", in Birchall (ed.), *Housing Policy in the 1990s* (1992), p. 32.

[35] DoE, Housing: The Government's Proposals (1981), Cmnd. 214, p. 12.

The Housing Corporation has a key role to play in this repositioning of the housing association sector. We will consider three aspects of its activities: support for the mixed funding regime; the monitoring role in relation to housing associations; and its role in relation to the development of a broader social market in housing, in particular in relation to tenants' choice and large scale voluntary transfers.

The existing generous central government funding for housing associations was not considered appropriate for the future development of housing associations. The new system introduced formally in 1988 involved mixed public and private development funding. Public grants are now used to lever private loan finance with only the grant element contributing to public expenditure under the Treasury's spending conventions.[36] This change had two aims: first, to increase the volume of rented housing that associations could produce for any given level of public expenditure, and secondly "to create incentives to associations to deliver services in the most cost effective manner, bringing to bear the disciplines of the private sector and strengthening the machinery of public support" (DoE, 1987b). Grants toward future major repairs and revenue deficits were also withdrawn. Consequently the right to a fair rent under the Rent Act 1977 is not available to tenants housed by associations after the commencement of the Act.

The rate of the grant is of crucial importance to an association's ability to undertake development. This is fixed by the minister and is based implicitly on some assumptions about rent levels in relation to tenants' average incomes. The minister set an average of 75 per cent of development costs in 1991–92, 72 per cent in 1992–93, 67 per cent in 1993–94 and 62 per cent in 1994–95. It is 58 per cent for the 1995–96 development programme. These changes in the development process have led to considerable debate over "affordable" rents. To quote the House of Commons Select Committee on the Environment:

> "A rent ceases to be affordable when it reaches a level which is so high as to leave the tenant with a residual income from which he or she is unable to provide for other basic needs. . . . The National Federation's

---

[36] Langstaff, "Housing Associations: A Move to Centre Stage", in Birchall (ed.), *Housing Policy in the 1990s* (1992), p. 34.

22 per cent affordability ratio is determined using gross rent and average income, including housing benefit. Calculated on the basis of net rents and income, the Corporation's 'benchmark' figure is 25 per cent. The Institute of Housing suggested that in practice, many tenants cannot afford rents even of less than ten per cent of average income. We also note that by definition, any tenant in receipt of housing benefit must face a rent which, before benefit, is unaffordable."[37]

The Committee also discovered that the Government's "implied affordability level" was 35 per cent net of housing benefit. However, there has been no explicit Government view on what constitutes affordability which reflects the changed climate in which the associations operate by placing the responsibility for rent fixing on the landlord (Kearns, 1992).

There have been two consequences of this change in financial regime. The first is the construction of 60,000 more dwellings than would otherwise have been the case (Housing Corporation, 1995) and a substantial increase in rents. In 1994 rents averaged £38 a week but for new properties the average rent was around £54 per week (DoE, 1995). The number of tenants in receipt of housing benefit has increased from 56 per cent in 1990–91 to 68 per cent in 1994–95. However, there is a significant difference between those living in pre- and post-1988 dwellings: the level is 60 per cent for the former and 83 per cent for the latter.

This change in financial regime shifts the subsidy system from a one-off capital sum payable through the DoE and the Housing Corporation to a long-term revenue subsidy in the form of housing benefit from the DSS. It has not resulted in a reduction in public expenditure but has contributed to a poverty trap whereby tenants cannot afford to obtain paid employment which would result in a sharp loss of housing benefit through the tapering mechanism. The cost of the increased rents to the welfare budget has now been recognised and has heralded a shift in emphasis in Government policy.

> "We need to strike the right balance between getting more homes by keeping grant down and the risks of benefit dependency and the benefit

---

[37] House of Commons, The Environment Committee Session 1992/3, second report on the Housing Corporation, 1993–93, xxviii.

costs of higher rent levels. We recognise there are limits to the reductions in grant which can be achieved. If grant is too low and rents rise too far, this can increase public expenditure in the long term."[38]

From 1995 onwards the Housing Corporation will be required to take account of rent levels when deciding which schemes to support. The Government hopes that this will ensure that funding goes to schemes which offer the best overall value to tenants and taxpayers.[39] Thus, although the responsibility for determining rents stays with housing associations, they will be working with a revised set of regulatory assumptions.

In order to implement the new policy, housing associations have raised nearly £3 billion of private finance since 1988, a substantial proportion of which has been provided by two banks and three building societies. Housing association development programmes and their costs are now dependent on the priorities of the private financiers. In Chapter 1, above, we saw that the building societies are under substantial market pressure from competitors and are seeking to diversify their activities. There are other contenders for any available money. The Government is encouraging the private investment in Housing Investment Trusts to regenerate the private-rented sector (see Chapter 3, above) and in the associations or companies undertaking large scale voluntary transfers of former local authority stock (see Chapter 4, above). It is not clear that they will seek to invest in housing association development or that there are sufficient resources available to meet all these demands (Smallwood, 1992). Investors take a keen interest in Government policy on housing benefit. So any reduction in support for rents makes the position of the associations more vulnerable.

The Housing Corporation has been responsible for overseeing these developments and for channelling the funds through to housing associations. (The Corporation's borrowing powers of up to £3,000 million by order are contained in the House Purchase Assistance and Housing Corporation Guarantee Act 1978, section 5). The 1991 ministerial statement to the Corporation spells out the

---

[38] DoE, *Our Future Homes. Opportunity, Choice, Responsibility: The Government's Housing Policies for England and Wales* (1995), Cmnd. 2901, p. 27.
[39] *ibid.* p. 31.

consequences of the transfer of risk to the private sector. The Corporation is expected to ensure that:

> "registered housing associations are soundly managed, in terms both of good business practice and of the service to tenants [and that] associations manage their housing stock so as to obtain the best value for the public investment made in it."[40]

Thus the Corporation's other main role had been to develop the monitoring systems which are necessary not only to protect public money but also to provide confidence to private lenders.

The powers to undertake this monitoring are contained primarily within the Housing Associations Act 1985. In order to be registered with the Corporation, an association must comply with its registration criteria. These require associations to have effective and experienced internal controls, a sound financial basis and proper accounting mechanisms (the last of these are subject to statutory requirements). The Corporation also considers the social role of the association looking for evidence of specific unmet housing need. Associations must have an equal opportunities policy. They must give the Corporation access to information and provide the Corporation with accounts. Finally, registered associations are required to undertake to comply with the Corporation's requirements in relation to management, maintenance and the treatment of tenants. The Corporation sets out these requirements in guidance or circulars. These powers have been extended by the Housing Act 1988 (now section 36A of the Housing Associations Act 1985):

> "(1) the Corporation may issue guidance with respect to the management of housing accommodaton by registered housing associations and, in considering under the preceding provisions of this Part whether action needs to be taken to secure the proper management of an association's affairs, [legal proceedings with respect to any property belonging to the association] or whether there has been mismanagement, the Corporation may have regard (among other matters) to the extent to which any such guidance is being or has been followed."

---

[40] Para. 8 of the management statement issued to the Housing Corporation by the Secretary of State for the Environment quoted in House of Commons, The Environment Committee Session 1992–93: xxxiv.

Subsection (3) sets out the matters which may be contained within such guidance. The Corporation is required to consult with representative bodies and the Secretary of State before issuing or revising any guidance (subsection (4)). The latter must also approve.

There is now much greater scrutiny of associations applying for registration. The number applying have increased. The number registered low, 33 in 1992–93, 27 in 1993–94 (including seven Large Scale Voluntary Transfers) and 32 in 1994–95 (including eleven Large Scale Voluntary Transfers) (Housing Corporation, 1995a). The Corporation exercises considerable power over associations at this stage. For instance, in the Yorkshire and Humberside region it has decided that it will only register one black association per city. Thus the three black associations in Sheffield, one interested in the Afro-Caribbean community, one specialising in the concerns of Somilian refugees and the third with the Pakistani community, have been unable to obtain registration and are obliged to operate under the auspices of other registered societies. The use of umbrella associations is a policy favoured by the Corporation to assist new associations to establish themselves without too much risk.

Once registered the Corporation traditionallly limited its supervisory activities to meeting two main objectives determining whether: (a) the committee of management is in control of the association, and (b) the activities are consistent with the objects of a non-profit making housing body in receipt of public funds. The way this monitoring activity is achieved has been the subject of considerable criticism for taking an overly bureaucratic interest in the detailed affairs of individual housing associations. It has involved teams of officials scrutinising every aspect of activity and producing a comprehensive report on performance.

However, the Corporation's regulatory machinery has undergone significant changes since the introduction of the Housing Act 1988 regime. Some of these resulted from two reports commissioned by the Department of the Environment. The first reviewed monitoring procedures and argued that inspections should be more selective and targeted on those associations where there was some evidence of their being "at risk".[41] The second review covered the Corporation's

---

[41] DoE, "Review of the Monitoring Procedures of the Housing Corporation" (1988) in Day et al., *Home Rules: Regulation and Accountability in Social Housing* (1993), p. 9.

managerial policies and structures.[42] The proposal which has been adopted brings together the various supervisory functions, registration, monitoring and finance, into a single performance audit division at regional level.[43]

The Corporation has now introduced a performance review system which broadens the Corporation's supervision to cover not only management control and financial discipline but also tenancy matters and the social role of housing association activity (Housing Corporation Circulars, 13/94 and 14/94). Section 24 of the Housing Associations Act 1985 requires associations to prepare accounts in a manner prescribed by the Secretary of State. The Corporation has moved to quarterly accounts (for the 600 or so associations mostly involved in development activity) and a system of accounting similar to that required by the Companies Act to satisfy private investors. The Corporation's powers to police these requirements have been extended by the Local Government and Housing Act 1989 (now section 27A of the Housing Associations Act 1985) and includes prosecuting associations for late submissions, of which there were seven in 1993–94 and three in 1994–95.

The second regulatory method involving monitoring housing association performance. There has been a shift away from pre-arranged, wide ranging inspectorial visits to one based on a desktop review of performance measured against a range of indicators. The information for review is taken from the performance standards returns which associations are required to complete. This system enables the Corporation to undertake a wide review of associations which is then followed up by performance audit visits to associations to validate information and also by targeted investigatory visits to those associations where areas of concern had been uncovered by the review process (Housing Corporation, 1994). The performance standards cover control of the association's activities, conduct of their activities, particularly equal opportunities and accountability to tenants, the association as landlord, and the association as developer.

The Corporation has also produced a set of performance indicators. These, which include ethnic mix of tenants, access to housing,

---

[42] DoE, "Report on the Separation of Strategic Functions" (1990) in Day et al., ibid.
[43] Day et al., *ibid.*, p. 9.

arrears and voids, repair and maintenance responses and an indication of the financial standing of the association, are intended to provide benchmarks against which to rate and rank performance.[44] These indicators are very similar to those used by the DoE to measure local authority housing performance. Performance measured against the indicators are published by the Corporation in a similar way to that undertaken by the Audit Commission for local authorities.

If the Corporation considers that there is serious mismanagement it has a range of powers under the Housing Associations Act 1985 to intervene in the affairs of the association. The appraisal of the performance of associations is also used to decide which associations should receive capital funding.

What is the outcome of this extensive monitoring regime? The research of Day et al. on the implementation of the evolving monitoring process in 1993 found that generally performance improved with size.[45] They also found that most associations welcomed the changing regulatory regime because it assisted them in improving their own performance monitoring and moved them into the modern world. A significant minority found the process of regulation a threat to their organisation: they did not want inspectors telling them how to do things.

In terms of the policies imposed by regulation, twelve out of the 21 associations interviewed had problems with the regulator's policy on tenant participation and 14 were concerned about the future affordability of their housing and the rent policies being imposed.[46] The associations supported the idea of tenants having a good housing deal and being able to complain:

"But they all argued that the blanket notion of participation is ill-thought through and ends up, therefore, in tokenism. . . . many associations will agree to the policy on paper but implement it only symbolically. The associations suggested also that the regulators might eventually find it convenient not to pursue this policy, if it became apparent that it was a regulatory farce. The aspects of the policy that associations found most unacceptable were: the placing of tenants on

---

[44] Day et al., *op. cit.*, p. 12.
[45] *ibid.* p. 14.
[46] *ibid.* p. 23.

the committee, the involvement of tenants in the running of the organisation and forcing tenants to form associations where they plainly did not want to."[47]

On affordability, almost all the associations were worried about future rent levels. The associations felt that the regulators were not providing a clear lead. Nine associations had problems with the allocations policy which expects them to maintain open access:

"The allocation problems of associations varied, with some objecting to 'foreigners' from outside their community and others complaining that they could not find any disadvantaged groups to put in their housing."[48]

Nine associations were critical of policies on equal opportunities:

"To summarise, they saw nothing wrong with the principle but did not like the way the regulators expected them to strive for compliance even where it was to the detriment of the association".[49]

Eight of the 21 associations complained that some of the regulatory demands threatened both their prospects of development and their traditional mission:

"Not only did they risk not getting development funds if they failed to fit with national policy goals, but even some non-developing associations reported that they were under pressure from the regulators to change their client groups to suit national housing needs policies".[50]

These findings highlight a number of issues which will be discussed in more detail later. However, since December 1994 the Corporation has strengthened its regulation of housing management practice by including compliance with the "tenants guarantee" in its performance review process (Housing Corporation Circular 36/94). Thus the terms of the guarantee are defined as performance standards which are subject to the corporation's audit.

However, it is clear that the monitoring process is focused on and receives most support from associations for the public accountability

---

[47] Day et al., *op. cit.*, pp. 23–24.
[48] *ibid.* p. 25.
[49] *ibid.* p. 25.
[50] *ibid.* p. 26.

function: ensuring that the resources invested in housing associations are used economically, efficiently and effectively.[51] This is reinforced by the need to provide assurance to potential private lenders. The Environment Select Committee confirmed that private lenders found the monitoring process reassuring, providing them with further security for their loans. However, the effect on the "good steward-ship" function is leading to considerable strains in some associations. The increasing imposition of general social policy goals generated by their new position as key players in the field of social landlordism is also creating tensions between the form of management and the role of some associations. This issue has been addressed by the National Federation of Housing Associations in its report on the governance of associations (1995) to which we return later.

The Housing Corporation has also been given responsibility under the Housing Act 1988 to oversee the development of a wider independent landlord sector through the transfer of publicly owned stock, the main recipients of which were expected to be housing associations. Indeed, they had already been involved in taking over the ownership of public housing from the new towns under the Housing and Planning Act 1986. The Corporation, however, was given a key role as the supervisor of the transfer of stock under the tenant's choice provisions. The Act creates a complex regime through which this process must be undertaken.

As it has not proven popular, we will simply outline the role of the Corporation.[52] The first requirement is to establish the criteria to be satisfied by persons wishing to become landlords under the scheme, the second is to approve applicants. The Corporation is also obliged to keep a register of approved landlords. The Corporation requires an approved landlord to adopt a code of tenant's rights which is very similar to the tenant's guarantee required of registered housing associations. One significant difference is that tenants retain the right to buy under the tenant's choice regime.

The Corporation has at present no specific responsibilities in relation to the voluntary transfer of local authority stock under section 32 of the Housing Act 1985 (see Housing Corporation

---

[51] Day et al., *op. cit.*, p. 35.
[52] For further details, see Alder and Handy, *Housing Association Law* (2nd ed., 1991), pp. 259–266.

Circular 25/88). As we saw in Chapter 4, above, this has proven the most popular method of transfer and usually involves the establishment of a new housing association to take on the stock. These associations are subsumed within the standard approach to registration: they must be registered either as a charity or an industrial and provident society and with the corporation if they wish to obtain public funds (seven were registered in 1993–94, eleven in 1994–95). They do, however, represent a new subgroup within the housing association traditions. They are mainly staffed by former local authority personnel and come with the traditions of the public sector, including the potentially more collective approach of both staff and tenants to housing issues. However, there have been suggestions that they will quickly transform themselves into bodies which are more akin to private landlords. It will be interesting to see the impact that such associations have on housing association representative bodies and policy in the future.

The 1996 Housing Bill ensures that the Corporation will in the future be responsible for the supervision of the entire range of "social landlords" including those private landlords who will be eligible for public funds, landlords receiving transferred local authority stock and local housing companies.[53] The Government proposes: to end the prerequisite of registration as an Industrial and Provident Society or as a charity for registration with the Housing Corporation to enable Companies Act companies that do not trade to become registered social landlords; to introduce a corporation licensing system for landlords that are financially accountable to parent companies or to shareholders for profits.[54]

Some have argued that these changes within financial and general regulatory spheres are turning housing associations into hired agents of central government operating as branch offices of the Corporation,[55] others that the regulation amounts "to a complete surrender of the association's independence from the state".[56] Day et al. argue that

---

[53] DoE, *Our Future Homes. Opportunity, Choice, Responsibility: The Government's Housing Policies for England and Wales* (1995), Cmnd. 2901.

[54] DoE, More Choice in the Social Rented Sector. Consultation paper linked to the Housing White Paper *"Our Future Homes"* (1995).

[55] Langstaff, "Housing Associations: A Move to Centre Stage", in Birchall (ed.), *Housing Policy in the 1990s* (1992).

[56] Alder and Handy, *op. cit.*, p. 43.

"whereas in the past the regulatory system was itself shaped by its constituency, it is now increasingly shaping the housing association movement".[57]

## B. INDIVIDUAL STATUTORY RELATIONS

The new positioning of housing associations as independent landlords and the changes in the financial regime have had this impact on the statutory relations. Between 1980 and 1988 tenants of housing associations obtained the public sector legal status as secure tenants with the additional statutory protection of rent regulation under the Rent Act 1977 (where the tenant is eligible for such protection). Thus they were constructed as hybrids, partly public, partly private.

The Housing Act 1988 repositioned them within the private sector. All new tenancies entered into after January 15, 1989 are assured tenancies. Thus registered and unregistered housing associations are now treated alike. Assured tenants obtain security of tenure (section 5 of the Housing Act 1988). The landlord must follow the possession procedures specified in section 8 of the Act and must satisfy the grounds for possession set out in section 7 and Schedule 2. These grounds offer somewhat wider scope to the landlord to obtain possession against an assured housing association tenant compared to a secure tenant. There are also reduced rights to succeed to an assured tenancy.

The tenant does not obtain any tenant's charter rights. Thus the rights to assign, sub-let, improve, repair and so on do not apply. The collective rights to be informed and to be consulted are also lost. The right to a fair rent has been withdrawn. Assured tenants have very limited access to rent regulation as we have seen in Chapter 3. The tenant does not have a right to buy, the most economically valuable right. The withdrawal of this right could be seen as a desire to locate associations within the private rented sphere. Nonetheless the Government is proposing, in the 1996 Housing Bill, to offer tenants the opportunity to buy[58] in line with its overall policy to increase home

---

[57] Day et al., *op. cit.*, p. 38.
[58] DoE, *Our Future Homes. Opportunity, Choice, Responsibility: The Government's Housing Policies for England and Wales* (1995), Cmnd. 2901.

ownership, but perhaps also reflecting the suspicion that Housing Association landlords are still quasi-public in nature.

Thus, housing association tenants joining the sector after 1989 have fewer statutory rights and higher rents than those tenants already residing in the sector. However, there has been an attempt to counter this withdrawal of statutory rights by replacing them with contractual rights, regulatory codes and discretionary schemes. Thus we see the emergence of a new relationship between the regulatory and individual property spheres.

## C. INDIVIDUAL PROPERTY RELATIONS

Under the new regime tenants are pushed back on to their contractual rights in line with the repositioning of their landlords as private for the purposes of regulating relationships with their tenants. The tenancy agreement takes on a far more central role in the relationship. Instead of statutory protection and the rights associated with secure status, the tenant is offered a combination of contractual rights and non-enforceable but persuasive indirect rights which have been generated by the regulators. We have seen that the Housing Corporation requires registered housing associations to follow their guidance and circulars and that section 36A of the Housing Associations Act 1985 (amended by the Housing Act 1988, section 49) gives the Housing Corporation greater powers to generate these guidances and specifies the type of matter that may be included.

The Housing Corporation has issued the Tenants' Guarantee (most recent revision December 1994, Housing Corporation Circular 36/94) to replace the rights lost under the secure tenants' charter. The Tenants' Guarantee requires housing associations to incorporate its requirements into their housing management policies and practices. It covers security of tenure, rent levels, assignment and subletting, repairs and improvements, information, consultation, equal opportunities and discrimination. It also makes provision for internal complaints mechanisms and encourages arbitration.

The National Federation of Housing Associations has devised, and the Housing Corporation indorsed, a model tenancy agreement which incorporates some of the elements contained in the guidance. The reduced security resulting from the new grounds for possession (in particular ground 9, availability of suitable alternative accommodation, and 11, persistent delay in payment of rent), are offset by the exclusion of ground 11 in Schedule 2 of the Housing Act 1988.[59] Those parts of the guidance which have been included in tenancy agreements can be enforced by tenants directly.

Enforcement of the provisions not incorporated into the tenancy agreement is more difficult given that the Tenants' Guarantee does not create statutory rights. Alder and Handy (1991) argue that the issuing of the Tenants' Guarantee as guidance gives rise to a "legitimate expectation" in law that it will be followed unless the association can positively justify not doing so. This doctrine is usually associated with public law enforcement, but Alder and Handy argue that it is applicable to private bodies such as housing associations. These questions raise wider questions on the distinctions between public and private law in the changing constitutional and administrative relations of the state. We will return to a more general discussion of accountability including access to the courts in the next chapter.

Thus the elements of the guidance not included in tenancy agreements relies on the compliance of the housing association landlord with the Housing Corporation guidance. We have seen that compliance forms part of the monitoring exercise and that the Corporation has sanctions for those who do not comply with its requirements. We have, however, seen the tensions created within certain sections of the housing association world by the imposition of these regulatory requirements.

Housing association tenants have no statutory right of access to the Housing Corporation. However, the guidance undertakes that the Corporation will investigate complaints when the tenant has exhausted the landlord's own complaints procedure. The Corporation has set up procedures at both national and local levels to deal with tenant's complaints about their landlords. The number of complaints has doubled between 1990 and 1993 and is now running at an annual rate of about 1,000.[60]

The Corporation also introduced in 1994 a tenants' ombudsman scheme. There was considerable discussion within the housing

---

[59] Cope, *Housing Associations—Policy and Practice* (1990), p. 201.
[60] Day et al. *Home Rules: Regulation and Accountability in Social Housing* (1993), p. 37.

association movement about the appropriate location of this service. The argument put strongly by most was that it should be independent of the Corporation. This view was indorsed by the Select Committee on the Environment, although it noted the jurisdictional problems of independent location. If the service is located within the Corporation, it can make use of the Corporation's supervisory and monitoring powers in relation to housing associations to gain access to housing associations. An independent jurisdiction would have required primary legislation. The Select Committee argued for a private member's bill in the absence of any likelihood that the Government would find parliamentary time for it. This was not forthcoming.

The newly established ombudsman forms part of the Corporation. It is autonomous but nonetheless not independent of the Corporation. The service has not been in existence long enough for substantial assessment but the view to date is that its standard of performance is very high (see Chapter 6, below for further discussion). The Housing Bill 1996 provides a statutory footing for the ombudsman, independent of the Corporation. All other types of social landlords will be included in its jurisdiction.[61]

The legal right not replaced either directly through contract terms or indirectly through the enforcement of a code of guidance, is the right to buy. This has been replaced by a discretionary scheme operated by the Housing Corporation which has its origins in the local authority sector. Local authorities paid cash sums to tenants with higher incomes to help them buy homes, thereby freeing up a public tenancy for a homeless person. (This activity became eligible for public subsidy under section 27 of the Housing Act 1988). The housing association scheme offers cash incentives to tenants to assist in the purchase of property. Associations can bid to the Corporation for housing association grant to support the scheme. All dwellings which are vacated under the scheme must be used to rehouse the homeless. All tenants and properties are eligible, including those belonging to charitable housing associations, although tenants have to

---

[61] DoE, *Our Future Homes. Opportunity, Choice, Responsibility: The Government's Housing Policies for England and Wales* (1995), Cmnd. 2901.

rely on their landlord's willingness to operate the scheme. They have no right to apply directly (unlike secure tenants of charitable housing associations under the HOTCHA scheme) or to exercise a statutory right. The scheme is cash limited by the Housing Corporation but it has set aside considerable sums to cover the scheme (£76 million in 1993–94).

The Housing Bill 1996 introduces a voluntary purchase grant scheme to enable tenants of associations to buy their own homes at market value. However, tenants will be eligible for a grant (probably between £8,000 and £16,000) to assist them. The landlord will keep all the sale money and will not be obliged to repay any grant received for the provision of the dwelling. However, the purchase price will be used for the provision of new dwellings. The landlord's participation is voluntary, although the Government intends to make it a condition of future housing association grant that associations participate.[62] This arrangement avoids the difficulty of mandating sales of privately owned dwellings partly funded by private funds at a discount.

I have outlined above the general changes within the different spheres of relationships and pointed to some of their consequences. However, I would like now to look in a little more detail at four areas of housing activity to provide some illustrations of the way in which these changes affect tenants: these are access and allocation, rent determination and its consequences, participation and more generally accountability.

In the private model of landlordism, the landlord's policy in relation to access and allocation of stock is of no concern of his/her other tenants. If the tenant in question dislikes the consequences then in general the remedy is to exit. In certain circumstances the tenant can also resort to voice mechanisms through use of the law, such as if the neighbour is causing a nuisance or interfering with quiet enjoyment. However, generally, it is the responsibility of the aggrieved tenant to take action not the landlord. The public sector model of landlordism has been different. It includes social responsibilities for the collective welfare of tenants on estates. So, for example, we have seen the development of racial harassment procedures by local authority landlords in response to racism on estates.

---

[62] DoE (1995), *op. cit.*

Recent legislation has encouraged tenants to become involved with the landlord's management practices (Leasehold Reform, Housing and Urban Development Act 1993, section 132, adding sections 27A and 27B to the Housing Act 1985, grants a tenant's right to manage.) Where are housing associations positioned in relation to these two models?

Associations are under less statutory responsibilities than local authorities in relation to access and allocation. Nonetheless, housing associations are required by section 72 of the Housing Act 1985 to assist local authorities in their obligations to the homeless. This obligation is usually met through nomination agreements. Subsidised housing associations are currently expected to offer nominations to local authorities on at least 50 per cent of lettings. Their performance in meeting these responsibilities have been criticised by a number of bodies.[63]

However, there are further pressures on housing associations. The first results from the new funding regimes in both the local authority and housing association sectors. Increasingly the two bodies are entering into partnerships to assist each other in their respective activities. In some cases housing associations obtain development land for a nominal figure in exchange for 100 per cent nomination rights. Secondly, there is the prospect of further changes in statutory responsibilities as a result of the Government review of homelessness. One suggestion is the holding of joint waiting lists by housing associations and local authorities. The pressure on housing associations to meet obligations to the homeless will increase in line with the decline of the local authorities' abilities to provide directly for them. The most recent Government proposal is to encourage joint registers but not to require these through statute.[64]

Housing associations begin to face the same tensions as local authorities in relation to allocation policies, which in the past have created concentrations of socially and economically vulnerable households on estates. There is evidence to suggest that such estates are developing within the housing association sector. This is also in part

---

[63] See Bramley, *Meeting Housing Needs*. Association of District Councils (1989); Audit Commission, *Housing the Homeless: the Local Authority Role* (1989).

[64] DoE, *Our Future Homes. Opportunity, Choice, Responsibility: The Government's Housing Policies for England and Wales* (1995), Cmnd. 2901.

a product of the new funding regime which has led to considerable increases in rent and the commensurate increase in the number of tenants on housing benefit being housed by associations. The recent report by Page (1993) on new housing association estates shows the outcome of the pressures to meet general housing need and to meet financial targets on rents: high density estates housing socially and economically vulnerable households.

Housing association allocation schemes are therefore increasingly under pressure to meet social welfare needs. However, we have seen that housing association landlords tend to adopt more discretionary methods of allocation. Research by the Commission for Racial Equality (1983; 1993) has revealed evidence of discrimination in association allocation policies while the research by Day et al. (1993) suggested that some associations were resistant to what they saw as interference by regulators in this sphere of their activities.

What is the position of applications? Housing associations are not open to challenge under the homeless provisions in Pt. 3 of the Housing Act 1985. They are equally not open to legal challenge generally on their allocations policies unless they can be shown to discriminate against the applicant on grounds of race or sex. The position of existing tenants will depend on whether they are secure or assured tenants. Secure tenants have rights to exchange under the Housing Act 1985, assured tenants do not under the Housing Act 1988.

The same set of issues arise in relation to rent determination. The financial context of housing associations has changed substantially since 1988. The mixed funding regime has led to sharp increases in rents, despite attempts by housing associations to cross subsidise from their old regime stock. Rent levels now depend to a large extent on the Housing Corporation and, therefore, the Government's implicit assumptions concerning appropriate rent levels. There has been little that the associations could do to resist rent increases. The most obvious method is to reduce building costs which leads to poorer quality dwellings and higher densities which in turn leads to other problems.[65]

---

[65] Recognising the problems of managing difficult and socially disruptive tenants, the Housing Bill 1996 widens the scope of the nuisance grounds for possession.

Rents are increasingly being met by housing benefit. This has implications for the associations and tenants, both of whom are vulnerable to changes in housing benefit policy. Tenants become locked into a poverty trap. The survey by Glasgow University in 1989 found that rent arrears were higher in housing associations than local authorities (3.5 per cent of gross rent debt compared with 2.1 per cent for local authorities). The average outstanding debt was also higher (9.3 per cent owed more that £100 in comparison with 6.8 per cent in the local authority sector). Eviction rate was also higher (1.5 per thousand dwellings compared with 0.8 per thousand in the local authority).

The Tenants' Guarantee states that associations are expected to set and maintain their rents at levels which are within the reach of those in low paid employment. This will usually entail setting rents below market level. These provisions have no direct enforceability in tenancy agreements. They leave tenants with their theoretical ability to negotiate the rent term within the tenancy at a time when the landlord's source of funding is becoming more expensive and open to the vagaries of the market. The tenant is legally obliged to rely on the assumption of freedom of contract contained in the property relationship between landlord and tenant because their landlords are being transformed into market bodies by their paymasters.

The 1985 Housing Act introduces some measures to facilitate the involvement of secure tenants with certain collective housing management issues, including publication of allocation policies and consultation on housing management matters (sections 105 and 106). The enforceability of these rights is open to question given that the landlord is not a public body. The Tenants' Guarantee sets out the practice the landlord should follow, including publication of the policy which should be open, fair and meet housing need. The policy should provide for equal opportunities. The problem once again is enforceability. These matters are not easily translated into individual tenancy terms. So the tenant will have to rely on the activities of the regulators.

We have already seen that tenant participation is a confused and contested area of housing association activity. The Select Committee on the Environment heard evidence from the Tenants Participation Advisory Service that housing associations were "non starters" on participation and involvement and judged that the Housing Corporations tenant participation strategy issued in July 1992 was poor and undeveloped. Day et al. (1993) confirm this view with their research finding that housing associations thought the policy a farce.

In this context the assured tenant might have terms included within the tenancy agreement outlining consultation and participation rights, but unless the landlord is enthusiastic about such an approach, these will be unenforceable. However, it is important to recognise that lack of participation mechanisms does not necessarily equate to lack of satisfaction. The Glasgow Study (1989) found that there was a high degree of tenant satisfaction with the performance of housing associations both absolutely and in comparison with local authorities. Seventy-six per cent compared to 58 per cent of local authority tenants thought their landlord efficient and 80 per cent compared with 67 per cent were satisfied with their housing management services.

This brings me to the final issue which is presently causing considerable debate within the housing association movement: the governance and accountability of housing associations. These independent housing association landlords are required to carry out increasingly complex social responsibilities in relation to housing. To whom is the association accountable? Answering this question raises a wide range of issues. The first is the conflict between the objective of efficient business management within cost restraints imposed by the financial regime and the fulfilment of social welfare housing management which is costly. The Glasgow research (1989) comparing the management of housing associations and local authorities found that on the whole housing associations were effective but expensive (30 per cent more costly per dwelling than local authorities). It seemed that to increase tenant satisfaction by 10 per cent required the landlord to spend 50 per cent more on management. There is therefore a growing tension between low rent policies and intensive management services. The second concerns the management committees of the housing associations. These voluntary bodies are the core accountability structure: committee members are accountable to their shareholder members. Yet Cope argues that the particular electoral regulations of industrial and provident societies lead to the same members being elected year after year, particularly if the association has few members. They become self-perpetuating oligarchies.[66]

Public accountability to the taxpayer is provided by the monitoring of the Housing Corporation. In recent years the Corporation has broadened its approach to accountability. The Government and, therefore, the Corporation is laying increasing stress on account-ability to tenants at the same time as transforming the monitoring process to take account of the needs of private investors and to protect the public purse in a more risk-prone context. Thus the regulator is obliging landlords to be more accountable to their tenants as part of the regulators objectives. The form of the accountability seems to be market oriented, accountability to individual consumers, although the Government also seems interested in tenant control and collective management. The National Federation of Housing Asso-ciations has described these alternative approaches as Marks and Spencers and the Co-op models.[67]

An alternative way of seeing the position of tenants is to classify them as stakeholders in the enterprise along with other interested parties, such as the local authorities and the local communities in which housing associations operate. This approach recognises the changing relationships within the social rented sector. Local author-ities are now required to be facilitators not providers, to provide the strategic overview, to marshall resources and agencies within the locality. Coupled with their continuing legal responsibilities in relation to housing need, local authorities have arguably a strong stake in the management of housing associations.

The National Federation of Housing Associations has recently put forward proposals which address some of these weaknesses in housing association governance in an era of broader responsibilities (NFHA, 1995). The inquiry team develop a code of governance for associations which concentrates on the constitutional and manage-ment roles of the association, in particular on the operation of the board of the association (see Chapter 6, below, for further discussion of some of these points).

---

[66] Cope, *Housing Associations—Policy and Practice* (1990), p. 43.
[67] Langstaff, "Housing Associations: A Move to Centre Stage", in Birchall (ed.), *Housing Policy in the 1990s* (1992), p. 43.

The final question to consider is the classification of housing associations. Despite the changing positioning of associations within the independent sector, they could be seen as very like local authorities but without democratic accountability. To others they look suspiciously like the local authorities they are supposed to replace and not enough like the private sector they are supposed to emulate. They are open to the complaint that they are public bodies which are impossible to privatise. Coleman argues that:

> "the government is entrusting housing policy to agencies, many of which rather like being within or on the edge of the public sector, which object to profits in housing and which have been protected by the taxpayer from the worry of raising private finance and by the rent officer from the trouble of setting their own rents."[68]

He goes on to suggest that there "may be a case for permitting associations which wish to diversify to privatise themselves: attract shareholder capital, make profits and issue dividends, attract corporate talent to run them by paying their boards"[69] and that the building societies offer a good example. Others are trying to avoid the consequences of a dichotomy between public and private by further repositioning of the two landlord bodies. Thus there are proposals put forward by the Institute of Housing for a national standards agency which would take over the monitoring role of the Corporation and regulate both sets of landlords. There are moves at a Government level to focus investment activity on neighbourhood renewal strategies which necessitate a multi-agency approach. There are also suggestions for a new funding agency which would bring together all forms of public funding on housing.

The legal position of housing associations is unsatisfactory in a number of ways. First, their constitutional structures are diverse and complex, rendering a general statement about them almost impossible. Secondly, they seem to be both public and private bodies. Those that are registered with the Housing Corporation are treated as public bodies yet in relation to their tenants they are treated in law as private

---

[68] Coleman, "Private rented housing: the next steps" in Best, R. et al. (eds.) *The Future of Private Renting: Consensus and Action* (1992).
[69] Coleman, *ibid.*

bodies because the relationship with tenants is based on contract and property law. *Peabody Housing Association v. Green* (38 P. & C.R. 644), decided in 1978, remains the authority that the activities of housing associations as landlords are private law matters and not subject to judicial review even though associations are publicly funded and operate under Government regulation. The distinction between powers conferred directly by statute and powers which formally derive from contract is somewhat artificial in the present context of housing association relationships. Since *Peabody* there have also been substantial developments in the scope of public law which might cast doubt on the judgment.[70] A matter is now regarded as one of public law if it involves the exercise of powers of a kind peculiar to government. It is therefore possible that for some activities housing associations could be regarded as bodies exercising public functions or services.

There is some support for this position from *R. v. West Kent Housing Association, ex p. Sevenoaks D.C. (Inside Housing* October 28, 1994). This case concerns a housing association established specifically in relation to a large scale voluntary transfer of local authority stock. The authority had reserved seats on the management board for councillors. Later the board decided to dispense with these seats and changed their rules with the approval of the Housing Corporation to achieve this end. The council applied for judicial review against the association and the Corporation. The High Court granted leave but the action was withdrawn before the court was able to consider the issues involved.

## Conclusion

The origins of the present day housing associations lie in the nineteenth century (and before) when renting relations were centred on the property relations encapsulated in the lease. The philanthropic and voluntary nature of these landlords overlaid this relationship with

---

[70] See in particular *R. v. Takeovers and Merger Panel, ex p. Datafin* [1987] 1 W.L.R. 1520. There are also developments within European law on the nature of state bodies which will in time have a bearing on this issue see *Foster v. British Gas plc* [1991] 1 Q.B. 405.

a philosophy of social responsibility towards their tenants but independence from the state.

The regulatory context which emerged in the 1960s gave housing associations a social policy role. This focus has sharpened over the last 30 years so that housing associations are presently seen as central to state housing policy. This role has been funded and regulated by the state through the Housing Corporation. The state involvement although late in comparison to the other rented sectors has significantly affected the power relations within the tenurial spheres. The general regulatory sphere has come to dominate relations generally.

The construction of these landlords through statute has reflected the changing roles assigned to them and the nature of this form of landlordism. Tenants, although reliant on the individual property relations in the tenancy, were initially excluded from statutory protection because their landlords were seen as socially responsible. Housing association tenants were included in the statutory protection offered to local authority tenants as state landlords lost legitimacy and thus were less responsible in the 1970s. Housing associations have subsequently been redefined as private landlords for protection purposes now that certain private landlords are being seen as capable of social responsibility.

This construction of socially responsible independent landlords is, however, heavily regulated by the state, leading to considerable ambiguities over the forms of accountability within the spheres of relationships.

# Chapter Six

# Horizontal Concerns: Tenure, Accountability and the Law

## Introduction

Those concerned with housing use tenure as an organising concept. For policy makers there are four main tenures: owner-occupation, the private rented sector, housing associations and council housing. These tenures are a product of their political histories within the welfare state and are, therefore, affected by the substantial upheavals and policy changes which have occurred in the last 20 years. Tenure in this housing policy sense has been the subject of political struggle over the period under consideration in this book.

Discussion has been dominated by the relative size and merits of each of these sectors. Government policy has consistently encouraged the growth of owner-occupation and the reduction of council housing. The privatisation of state provided housing through the right to buy local authority dwellings was the first of these initiatives which offered individuals a stake in the property-owning democracy. Where funding for the provision and maintenance of the local authority stock formed the basis for many of the battles fought between central and local government in the eighties.

Policies in relation to housing associations and the private rented sector have been more a product of intervention in the other two sectors. Until very recently, the political opposition and most housing professionals saw the private rented sector as an anathema – to be phased out as painlessly as possible. The Government support was strong, although predominately rhetorical rather than practical. Housing associations had their own passionate supporters but were on the margins of housing policy, envied by local authorities for their generous funding but not mainstream players. Then they became the vehicle through which the social market in housing was to develop, offering an alternative choice for the majority of potential tenants, against the wishes of many public sector providers.

By 1995 the political struggles around these tenures seemed to have been won or lost, because policy makers and commentators are suggesting that tenure is becoming insignificant in itself. Now Merrett argues that "all the existing major tenures should be regarded as legitimate vehicles in eradicating housing poverty", including private renting (Merrett, 1992). The three rented sectors are increasingly being subsumed under the heading of social renting signifying a continuum from the privately owned (private and housing association landlords) to the publicly owned social housing sector.

The pace of change has been greatest within the local authority and housing association areas: the former's role as producer of rented housing has almost disappeared and its role as landlord is changing rapidly, while the latter have moved centre stage as developers of new rented housing and recipients of existing rented dwellings. Political enthusiasm for housing associations seems to be waning, so it is uncertain how long they will continue to fulfill these roles. Much depends on the development of a politically acceptable and financially viable private rented sector.

The aim of these developments is diversification.

> "New types of landlord will provide and run social housing alongside traditionally structured housing associations: local housing companies and commercial developers and landlords. Existing housing associations may increasingly expand their commercial arms."[1]

Changes within the wider economy, rather than legislation, have had a significant effect on the owner-occupied sector, although the deregulation of building societies in the mid-eighties contributed

---

[1] DoE, *Our Future Homes. Opportunity, Choice, Responsibility: The Government's Housing Policies for England and Wales* (1995), Cmnd. 2901.

substantially to the impact of these changes. The institutional structure of the building society movement is likely to undergo further change in the near future with the transformation of a number of the largest societies into banks. Mergers are also continuing to reduce the number of institutional lenders available. The financial difficulties experienced by a significant minority of mortgagors in the early eighties has undermined the sense of economic advantage which had been a key attraction of the owner-occupied sector.

As we have seen in each of the preceding chapters this diversification has necessitated considerable repositioning within the politics and economics of housing provision and involved high levels of government intervention in each area. The result has been changed relationships within each sector. These changes have had significant impact on the specific regulatory and accountability sectors for each sector as well as the organisational patterns of the providers. These in turn have affected the relationships between providers and occupiers.

The legal concept of tenure is very different from that used by housing professionals. Within legal discourse there are two main "tenures" (more precisely estates in land): the fee simple freehold and leasehold. These conceptual divisions give rise to a variety of social statuses such as an owner-occupier or a tenant. The law also creates divisions between the public and the private which do not necessarily reflect the usage within housing policy.

I have argued that tenure is a layered concept which can be unpicked to reveal shifts in power relations. I have sought to distinguish three spheres of interacting relationships contained within the concept of tenure and then applied them to a variety of occupational groupings. The preceding chapters have charted the interactions between the various spheres within specific groupings. The relationships have been discussed "vertically". The concern of this chapter is to look across the sectors to see the changes within each of our conceptual spheres.

Generally, the individual property relationships are becoming more significant in all rented groupings at the expense of individual statutory regimes based on concepts of state protection. Instead the statutory regimes have emphasised the development of market relationships. Historically, for owners purchasing property with a mortgage, statutory protection has not been of particular significance because of the dominant ethos of this type of property ownership. The statutory protection afforded to some residential tenancies during the twentieth century has recognised that tenants are vulnerable to unequal power relationships. The vulnerable occupier with a mortgage has not been recognised in the same way.

Greater emphasis on this sphere of individual property relationships does not automatically result in the balance of power shifting against the occupier, as can be seen in relation to the exiting rights of local authority tenants, although we have seen the practical difficulties experienced by tenants who have bought long leasehold interests in flats formerly owned by the local authority.

While legally presented as protecting weaker parties, the statutory regimes have also constructed different categories of landlords and mortgagees. Thus, local authority landlords only provided "secure" tenancies after the Housing Act 1980. Tenants before 1980 were, therefore, legally insecure. Housing associations after 1989, housing the same constituency of tenants, now provide not "security" but "assurance" as private landlords in line with their newly constructed role in the "social" sector. Tenants of private landlords are assured to no longer need "fair" rents after 1988. Mortgagors of building societies are deemed to be not in need of the same protection as lenders from other institutions. Unpicking the statutory distinctions exposes the assumptions upon which power relations are constructed.

The greatest realignment in relationships have occurred as a result of changes in the regulatory frameworks. These have expanded substantially in all areas from increased supervision by the Building Societies Commission to the extensive powers of the Housing Corporation. Again, this is part of the process of constructing market relationships and exposing providers, and therefore occupiers, to the financial consequences of the market. We have seen the interaction of the term in mortgage agreements which requires the mortgagor to pay any interest charged over the term of the mortgage, at a time when societies are exposed to the full rigours of the international financial market. Equally, we have seen that assured tenants of housing associations are required by their agreements to pay a rent stipulated by their landlords but unregulated by statute, when associations are being exposed to market risks for the first time.

Tenants of local authorities pay rent which is structured by the demands of market-based financial accounting made necessary by the regulatory framework.

This leads to a more general discussion of the construction of this new social landlordism which increasingly seems to encompass the activities of local authority, housing association and certain types of private landlord. What relationship is expected of a social landlord with their tenants? Does it include wider responsibilities, for the anti-social behaviour of tenants for instance, or is it a more limited role of providing a choice of landlord offering a market-related rent?

The accountability of market related housing costs is undermined by individual subsidies to occupiers. Changes in these subsidy systems are of vital significance to occupiers, whether they concern mortgage interest paid via the social security system, the withdrawal of income support from owner-occupiers or housing benefit. We have seen how the contests over rent have been transformed into contests over these subsidies. Building societies are not exempted from these contests. They succeeded late in 1991 in obtaining direct payment of interest when the mortgagor is dependent on state welfare, a facility already available to some landlords. In exchange, they agreed to co-operate in "rescue" schemes for indebted mortgagors. The transformation of the rent officer into a guardian of the public purse, applying the strict criteria laid down in the benefit regulations, is just another element in the centralisation necessary to further the market. Arguably, challenging unaccountable welfare regulations, is more problematic than referring a rent to the rent officer.

The power of the regulators to transform relations within the other spheres becomes clear. The Housing Corporation is the most obvious example of a regulator affecting the relations between landlord and tenant. The collective elements within the local authority landlord and tenant relationship have been transformed by central government's housing finance regime, compulsory competitive tendering and audit requirements. The regulators centralise to construct markets forms.

Finally, there is the role of the courts in this evolving world. Occupiers will be obliged to rely more on private law forms which, in theory, gives them access to the legal system to provide some redress and landlord accountability. On present performance, it is unlikely that the courts will be able to provide much leverage to occupiers unless some of the limitations of the present system of public law are tackled.

The remainder of the chapter will develop these issues in more detail, starting with consideration of the general regulatory context, before moving on to consider the changing contribution of statutory protection and the consequences of these changes for individual property relationships.

## General Regulatory Context

Three institutions play key roles in the regulation of the various occupational groupings. They are differently positioned in relation to the bodies they regulate but a comparison between them raises interesting questions, in particular the extent of their accountability. Not surprisingly, given the nature of owner-occupation, the key regulatory bodies are concerned with the regulation of the financiers. Building societies and banks are neither providers nor managers of housing but financiers which nevertheless have considerable impact on occupiers. Their policies determine who will enter the sector and, in the case of mortgage default, who will leave it. The regulators are concerned with financial opprobium of the lenders, not housing management performance.

The other two bodies are concerned with the non-profit sectors. Both the Audit Commission, in relation to local authority activity, and the Housing Corporation, in relation to housing associations, not only oversee the financial activities of their respective sectors but are increasingly concerned with performance monitoring and quality assurance. Their accountability, however, is not directly to the occupiers in their respective sectors. The profit making private rented sector presently has no overarching regulatory body.

In 1991, the building societies accounted for 61 per cent of outstanding mortgages, the banks, 28 per cent and the centralised lenders for 8 per cent.[2] The banks and centralised lenders are subject

---

[2] Pryke and Whitehead, "An Overview of Mortgage-Backed Securitisation in the U.K.", *Housing Studies* (1994), Vol. 9, No. 1, p. 77.

to regulation under the Banking Act 1987, the Companies Act 1985 and the Financial Services Act 1986. The banks come under the prudential regulation of the Bank of England. The building societies are regulated via the 1986 Building Societies Act and the 1986 Financial Services Act.[3] I intend here to concentrate on the system of regulation within the building society sector.

The 1986 Building Societies Act established a new system for the regulation of building societies. This legislation was necessitated by the changed conditions within which the building societies operated. The 1980s had seen a marked increase in competition in both the retail deposit market and the mortgage market and the societies were restricted in their ability to compete by their existing legal powers.

> "Furthermore, a general structural change has been taking place which has resulted in traditional demarcations between financial institutions and markets being eroded and a trend towards the development of financial conglomerates."[4]

The Building Societies Act 1986 defines the permissable activities of the building societies, extending their powers to meet the new conditions. They are now able to hold up to 40 per cent of their total assets in non-retail funds and have been enabled to offer a wider range of consumer services. The societies, with assets over £100m, can diversify by lending small unsecured loans, second mortgages and non residential loans and by investing in subsidiaries and associates.[5]

The Act, however, leaves many of the detailed provisions to be dealt with through regulations and orders at the instigation of the new statutory body responsible for the prudential supervision, the Building Societies Commission (BSC). The BSC is also given powers to modify certain requirements within the Act, subject to the approval of Parliament. Regulation is achieved through the activities of the BSC, which can give direction through statutory instruments and guidance notes.

---

[3] The extended financial services offered by the societies bring them within the domain of the Financial Services Act 1986, the aim of which is to provide investor protection. These activities do not relate directly to our concerns and will therefore not be dealt with here. (For more details see Drake, 1989: Chap. 4).

[4] Drake, *The Building Society Industry in Transition* (1989), p. 82.

[5] These powers are to be extended to permit societies greater opportunities to diversify under a Treasury proposal announced in 1995.

The BSC takes over the regulatory function previously exercised by the Chief Registrar of Friendly Societies. The BSC is now serviced by the Registry of Friendly Societies, a non-ministerial government department and funded though a levy of building societies. Commission members (between 4 and 10) are appointed by the Treasury. The general functions of the BSC are set out in section 1 of the 1986 Act: to promote the protection by societies of the investments held with them; to promote the financial stability of the societies; to ensure that societies carry out their principal purpose; to administer the system of regulation under the Act; and to advise and make recommendations to the Treasury or other departments.

The BSC is obliged to report on its activities annually to the Treasury and to Parliament (section 4) and to present its accounts annually to the Public Accounts Committee (section 3). It has wide ranging powers laid out in Part 6 of the Act. A core requirement is to ensure that the directors of societies manage prudentially (section 45). The BSC provides guidance on prudential management through the issue of prudential notes.

The BSC has not been given the power to wind up a society. For this to occur, the BSC must petition the court. A society may appeal against certain of the commission's decisions (section 46) to a tribunal constituted under the Act (section 47), thereafter on point of law to the High Court.

The Building Societies Act 1986 introduced a new system for mergers, including provisions to cover opposed mergers, as well as providing a novel procedure by which a society can convert into a public limited company (see Drake, 1989: Chapter 4 for more details). The Abbey National was the only building society in the 1980s to make use of the new powers contained within the Building Societies Act 1986 to convert to a public limited company. It faced opposition from a vocal minority of its members. The details of the proposed conversion were also the subject of litigation between the society and the Building Societies Commission (*Abbey National Building Society v. Building Societies Commission* [1989] 5 BCC 259).

However, in the competitive climate of the 1990s, there is growing interest among societies in merging with other financial organisations. In the first significant move of this sort, the Lloyds Bank Group sought to take over the Cheltenham and Gloucester Building

Society. The Building Societies Commission considered that the proposed terms for the take over were outside the powers of the Cheltenham and Gloucester and unlawful. The main concern was the proposal that a parent company within the Lloyds Bank Group would pay a cash bonus to all Cheltenham and Gloucester members. Section 100(9) of the 1986 Act stipulates that a successor company can only offer such payments to members of two years' standing. The Cheltenham and Gloucester Building Society sought a declaration that the proposals were lawful in an action against the Commission. In *Cheltenham and Gloucester Building Society v. Building Societies Commission* [1994] 4 All E.R. 65, the court held that the proposal did contravene section 100 and was therefore unlawful. The court was also called upon to clarify the meaning of section 100(8) of the Act in relation to the proposed merger between the Halifax and the Leeds (the combined group then intends to convert) in litigation with the Building Societies Commission (*Building Societies Commission v. Halifax Building Society* [1995] 3 All E.R. 193).[6]

The BSC is not concerned with the consumer interests of mortgagors and is not required to have representatives of housing consumers on its board, instead the Building Societies Act 1986 stipulated that a complaints procedures be established to which all building societies must belong. The BSC role is limited to the establishment and subsequent general oversight of such schemes. As we shall see below, however, this aspect of their activities was very much tacked on to the core prudential supervisory role.

The societies themselves undertake a degree of self regulation through collectively agreed codes of conduct and statements of practice. These are drawn up by the Building Societies Association and the Council of Mortgage Lenders (the former is the trade association solely for building societies, the latter includes other mortgage lenders) or jointly by those bodies and the regulators.

---

[6] The question was whether the distribution of free shares to members other than two-year shareholders was restricted by s.100(8) of the 1986 Act, which provided that rights to acquire shares in priority to other subscribers' could lawfully be conferred only on members who had held shares in the society throughout the period of two years expiring on the qualifying day specified in the transfer agreement. Mr Justice Chadwick held that the particular agreement under consideration did not infringe the restriction.

These codes include a statement of practice on the handling of mortgage arrears which represents the aspirations of the most responsible lenders.

The BSC therefore restricts its activities to the prudential management of societies and does not concern itself with performance review or social responsibility. Its accountability is essentially to the financial community, leading some to argue that there is a need for greater public accountability given the impact of financiers on housing provision (Hawes, 1986; NACAB, 1993).

Hawes (1986) suggests that there are four goals of public accountability: to ensure that the collective impact of the personal sector financial investments into owner-occupied housing is in accordance with other social investments; to ensure that the pattern of investment into housing is equitable within the owner-occupied sector and between spatially defined areas; to create an orderly supply of mortgage finance; and to ensure that there is equity between savers and borrowers within building societies.

In contrast, the two other statutory bodies involved with the regulation of the non-profit making sectors have increasingly become involved in performance monitoring as well as prudential management. Both in different ways are concerned with issues of accountability, their own and also that of the bodies with which they are concerned.

The Housing Corporation was established by the Housing Act 1964 but its powers were significantly expanded in the Housing Act 1974 and are now contained primarily within the Housing Associations Act 1985 (as amended by the Housing Act 1988 and the Local Government and Housing Act 1989). The Corporation is required to promote, finance and supervise the voluntary housing movement. Since 1988 it has additional powers in relation to local authorities. As we have seen it is a non-elected public corporate body whose board members are appointed by the Secretary of State. As a non-departmental public body, it has wide discretionary powers but its decisions are not generally subject to any right of appeal. It is not required by statute generally to publicise its policies, to give reasons for its decisions nor to consult interested parties (although in practice it does all of these).

"Its general principles, policies and rules can be discovered only by perusing the entire range of relevant literature, including in particular the Corporation's circulars and annual reports and DOE circulars."[7]

It has limited parliamentary accountability in that the Secretary of State must lay its annual report and accounts before Parliament (Housing Associations Act 1985, section 78). Its accounts are subject to parliamentary supervision via the Comptroller and Auditor General (section 79 of the Housing Associations Act 1985). It is subject to scrutiny by the Public Accounts Committee. The Government is responsible for setting the major policy aims and its essential priorities. Its accountability to government is defined through the Management Statement and a linked Financial Memorandum which "focuses mainly on the Corporation's responsibilities for expenditure programmes" (House of Commons, 1993, Memorandum by DoE: 7). It has at its disposal very substantial government funds to induce associations to comply with its priorities. It also has considerable regulatory powers in relation to registration of associations, a prerequisite to eligibility for public funds, and supervisory powers in relation to the financial and management performance of associations. It thus regulates associations through "dominium" as well as "imperium", to use Daintieth's terminology.[8]

The Corporation has not proven popular with any constituency. Coleman who supports market provision of housing sees it thus:

"Despite the great and good capitalists parachuted in to take over its direction, it resembles a large free floating local authority, devoted to the public sector ethos, to the minutiae of control, with a growing obsession with contract compliance for race relations purposes which threatens to overshadow its responsibilities for housing."[9]

He shares the view of others representing very different political views on housing that the present mix of functions is a contradiction

---

[7] Alder and Handy, *Housing Association Law* (2nd ed., 1991), p. 215.

[8] Daintieth uses these terms to distinguish the ways in which governments can induce people to change their behaviour. A government can use legal commands backed by force, imperium, or it can employ its wealth to offer incentives to comply, dominium (1994).

[9] Coleman, "Private rented housing: the next steps" in Best, R. et al. (eds.) *The Future of Private Renting: Consensus and Action*, (1992).

of the principle of the separation of powers and that the financing and regulatory roles should be separated (Alder and Handy, 1991; Institute of Housing, 1992; NFHA, 1995). The Association of Metropolitan Authorities has demanded complete abolition and, perhaps not surprisingly, the transfer of the quango's funding to councils (Blake, 1995c).

The Corporation has been the subject of considerable official review in recent years by among others, the National Audit Office (1994), the Public Accounts Committee (1994), the Environment Select Committee (1993) and the Department of the Environment under the Housing Corporation Prior Options Study (1995). The most recent of these official reviews concludes that "There would be little to be gained, and much to be lost, if funding and regulation were to be performed by seperate organisations . . . The Corporation's funding and regulatory rules are deliberately and inextricably linked, but there are tensions between the two rules."[10]

There is general unease about the Corporation's lack of accountability (Birch, 1994b and 1995c). There is also considerable concern within the housing association movement that the emphasis on prudential supervision is at the expense of its other functions.

> "Paragraph I of the section (of the Management Statement) dealing with the constitution of the Corporation and the role of the Board indicated the duty of the Corporation to 'promote and regulate the work of housing associations registered by it'. . . . The remainder of the Management Statement demonstrates a complete absence of objectives and systems which would fulfil the statutory duty to promote associations."[11]

In their report on regulation and accountability in social housing, Day, Henderson and Klein suggest that regulatory systems have three main aims: first, a public accountability function, ensuring that the resources invested in housing associations are used economically, efficiently, and effectively; secondly, a good stewardship function, ensuring that associations provide adequate standards of management

---

[10] DoE, Housing Corporation Prior Options Study (1995), p. 3.
[11] Evidence of the National Federation of Housing Associations to the Environment Select Committee, House of Commons (1993), p. 98.

and service provision to their tenants; thirdly, the social policy function, ensuring that associations carry out national social policy objectives.[12] They argue that "developments have been largely driven by the public accountability function, reinforced by the need to provide assurance to potential private lenders and that the system of financial monitoring which has developed is largely satisfactory".[13]

They, however, point to four general regulatory dilemmas which emerge from their research on housing corporation inspectorial visits. The first is whether to be selective or comprehensive in the selection of associations for monitoring. The second is the style of inspection, the Corporation, unlike many other agencies, emphasises managerial structure and process rather than outcomes: they examine the process by which the associations will assess outcomes. Arguably, this approach is a result of the desire to see associations as autonomous private bodies with responsible management committees. The third issue is whether the Corporation acts as policer or a consultant. Official policy is to deny a consultancy role but some associations would like assistance. If the aim is to encourage the growth of co-operatives and ethnic associations then there will be a greater need for this function. The fourth issue is whether the regulatory process is changing the nature of the association movement. The demands of the regulatory system are likely to encourage the growth of large associations with adequate managerial capacities at the expense of the less orthodox associations who nonetheless fulfill needs. The stream-lined financial monitoring system introduced by the Corporation in response to the mixed funding regime and the reviews of its activities is geared to the supervision of the large development led associations. In 1995 the Corporation published a set of performance indicators for 350 of the larger associations for the first time. "[T]he price of growing dependence on state financing is . . . increasing conformity with national policy objectives"[14] which some associations see as a threat to their autonomy.

They argue that "whereas in the past the regulatory system was itself shaped by its constituency, it is now increasingly shaping the

---

[12] Day et al., Home Rules: Regulation and Accountability in Social Housing (1993), p. 35.
[13] ibid. p. 35.
[14] Day et al., op. cit., p. 38.

housing association movement. The notion of regulatory capture . . . has been turned on its head".[15] There is also disquiet about the social policy element of the regulation because the objectives to be met are vague and seemingly not clear to the regulators, particularly in the area of tenant participation. On "affordability" the regulators are at the mercy of other governmental policy in the social security and benefits system.

Accountability to tenants is achieved primarily by the Corporation ensuring that the landlord operates appropriately including adopting proper procedures for consultation, participation and for dealing with complaints. We have seen that the regulator itself is more hesitant about the first two. Complaints procedures have been strengthened by the development of the ombudsman scheme which has the limitation of being under the auspices of the regulator (although proposed legislation will provide independence (DoE, 1995b)). To summarise, regulation by the Housing Corporation of the housing association sector is extensive but formal accountability is primarily to the funders, both public and now private, rather than to the occupants of housing association dwellings or the wider constituencies affected by their activities such as local authorities.

If we now turn to the local authority housing sector we see a different combination of regulation and accountability. In the case of local authorities the line of accountability runs to the voters who elect them, although this constitutional independence from central government has been substantially eroded in the 1980s. Local authorities are multi-purpose and as such the housing function is not generally regulated separately from other functions. Nonetheless we have seen the specific ways in which the Department of the Environment has intervened in the affairs of local authority housing. In this chapter we are not concerned with this relationship as such but with regulation by the body charged with oversight of local authority performance, the Audit Commission.

Traditionally, the financial regulation of local authorities has been undertaken by the District Auditor Service. In 1972 the Local Government Act placed the audit of local authorities in England and Wales under a single statutory regime. District auditors were paid and

---

[15] *ibid.* p. 38.

appointed by the government but they did not carry out their duties on behalf of ministers. They exercised their powers in their own right: they were answerable to the courts but not to ministers. Nonetheless, there was still some anxieties about their independence.

The Audit Commission was established by Part 3 of the Local Government Finance Act 1982: to appoint auditors; to prepare and review a code of audit practice; to undertake studies designed to improve the economy, efficiency and effectiveness of local authority services; to report on the impact on the economy, efficiency and effectiveness of statutory provisions and ministerial directions and guidance. However, the Commission itself does not determine whether an authority acted unlawfully and it is not within its power to initiate procedures. The auditors, whose functions remains separate and distinct, continue to exercise these powers.[16] Thus the auditors remain accountable in law to the courts for the exercise of their statutory duties.

Auditors have a different relationship with the Audit Commission to Inspectors with the Housing Corporation. The latter are directly responsible to the corporation. Nonetheless, the Commission exercises considerable influence over the auditors. The Commission has drawn up a Code of Audit Practice with which the auditors must comply. Included in the Code is the stipulation that the auditor's reappointment is dependent upon the Commission's judgment of his or her discharge of duties under the Act and the Code. Further, auditors are required to take account of the Commission's advice. Generally, the Commission exercises considerable influence by way of advice, training and quality control reviews.

The Commission, unlike the Corporation, is independent of central government. It is not dependent on government for funding, it relies on auditing fees. It is not a Crown body and its staff are not Crown servants (1982 Act, Sched. 3, para. 2) (this is also the case with the Corporation). Nevertheless, its members are appointed by the Secretary of State (section 11) who is empowered, among other things, to give the Commission directions which it is obliged to follow (Sched. 3, para. 3). As Radford points out the government

---

[16] Much of the discussion on the Audit Commission relies on the work of Radford, "Auditing for Change: Local Government and the Audit Commission, *Modern Law Review* (1991), Vol. 54 No. 6, p. 913.

"has considerable potential to influence the Commission but there is no convincing evidence that it has attempted to do so".[17] The Commission is not directly accountable to Parliament because this was thought to confuse the appropriate lines of accountability in relation to local government which is accountable to its own electorate. However, the Code of Audit Practice is subject to approval by resolution of both Houses every five years and the Commission is required to produce an annual report which is laid before Parliament by the Secretary of State (Sched. 3, para. 15).

The Commission itself sees three strands to its accountability: to satisfy Parliament that it is carrying out its statutory duties; to satisfy local government that it is making proper and beneficial use of its resources; and to provide ratepayers and other interested parties with a summary of its work. However, as Radford points out it is ultimately not responsible to any single institution for the way in which it carries out its duties, "a situation which has been described as placing it in a 'political vacuum'".[18]

Originally, the purpose of the local authority audit was regularity: to ensure that proper accounting procedures had been adopted and expenditure was within the law. The 1982 Act adds the responsibility for auditors and the Commission to promote value for money. This latter function involves a closer relationship with the authority and has encouraged the Commission to offer "an individual advice service". This has resulted in first the Commission and its auditors developing a complex relationship with local authorities "acting both as independent watchdogs, with all the powers of inspection and enforcement which that entails; and at the same time as professional advisers, seeking to assist and serve their 'clients' who pay for their services".[19] In ways similar to that described early in relation housing associations, Radford describes a process whereby the Audit Commission has played a significant part in defining and indeed limiting the activities of local government in a period of change and uncertainty. He describes the way in which the commission's understanding of appropriate practice in relation to "creative accountancy" was significantly narrower than that of the law itself.

---

[17] Radford, *op. cit.*, p. 916.
[18] *ibid.* p. 916.
[19] Radford, *op. cit.*, p. 918.

Secondly, Radford suggests that the Commission influences the way in which authorities conduct their affairs by issuing advice in which its interpretation of the law is set out. In the case of the interpretation of the competitive contracting provisions in the 1988 Local Government Act, this advice was more restrictive than necessary for legal compliance with the Act.

Thirdly, the Commission has a duty to undertake studies (comparative or otherwise) leading to recommendations for improving economy, efficiency and effectiveness in the provision of local authority services. The auditors have a separate duty to ensure that the local authority has made proper arrangements for securing economy, efficiency and effectiveness in its use of resources. In practice, "the Commission has linked its own powers . . . with the auditors' role.[20] There has been criticism that the Commission has concentrated on economy and efficiency at the expense of effectiveness, which is a measure of outcomes not inputs. The Commission has attempted to tackle this issue but it leads them into consideration of policy which can lead to considerable controversy.

The Commission has moved away from audit and accountancy towards a management consultancy role. It is increasingly "using its position to influence the way in which local government itself develops"[21] and to "setting the agenda".[21a] It is these developments which can sit uneasily with democratic accountability. "Although accountants and management consultants can make a contribution to assessing how the body politic operates, there is a need for caution lest they transform local government in their own image".[22]

The Audit Commission has few formal sanctions at its disposal unlike the Housing Corporation which, in particular, has the ability to withhold finance. It has, however, carried out a number of very influential value for money audits into aspects of local authority housing, including capital financing, repairs systems, arrears and allocation (see for example Audit Commission 1986; 1989; 1992). It has been influential in the development of performance indicators (under the Citizen's Charter provisions in the Local Government Act

---

[20] *ibid.* p. 926.
[21] *ibid.* p. 930.
[21a] *ibid.* p. 932.
[22] *ibid.* p. 932.

251

1992) which are now published to demonstrate comparative performance between authorities.

As we have seen, local authorities are heavily dependent on Department of the Environment policy and practice in the area of financial allocation for housing. The DoE also specifically regulates the housing functions of local authorities through the legislative requirement to publish annual housing reports which contain specified performance indicators (Local Government and Housing Act 1989, section 167).

The existence of two regulatory systems for social housing and a comparision between them has led some to argue that there could be harmonisation or indeed takeover by one or other body. If housing associations and local authorities serve common goals, could they not be subject to the same regulatory regime?[23] The Institute of Housing (1992) has proposed that the development and regulatory functions of the Housing Corporation (and its Scottish and Welsh equivalents) should be split. Then there could be two national agencies, a National Housing Agency dealing with funding for all social housing and a Standards Agency to regulate all social housing landlords. These proposals would transfer considerably more power into the hands of non-elected bodies.

Day et al. have suggested a more piecemeal development whereby the two systems would gradually converge on standard specification rather than institutional framework. "The logic of [recent] developments could be pushed further by ensuring that common performance standards are applied to both local authorities and housing associations".[24] While there are similarities, there are also differences.

"The main impetus behind the production of performance indicators for local authorities has been to make them more accountable to voters by insisting on the publication of the information. The driving force behind the development of standards and performance indicators for housing associations has been to make them more accountable to government, through the regulators".[25]

---

[23] Day et al., Home Rules: Regulation and Accountability in Social Housing (1993), p. 40.
[24] ibid. p. 41.
[25] ibid. p. 41.

Neither system is designed to make the landlords accountable to the tenants. "Unlike the electors or the regulators, they do not have sanctions. They may be able to exercise voice but . . . they do not usually have the option to exit."[26]

The missing element in this discussion is a regulator for the private rented sector. Regulation of the "old" private rented sector is essentially achieved through policing in the courts on the assumption that the landlords are potentially socially irresponsible as we have seen in Chapter 3. However, there is the potential for development of a "new" private rented sector engaged in the provision of social housing and as such eligible for public subsidy. There are plans for housing associations to develop commercial arms and for the development of local housing companies. In this context there are suggestions that the privately owned rented sector should be the subject of regulation particularly where the landlord receives a public subsidy. The present proposal is that the Housing Corporation's supervision should be extended to cover new forms of social landlords, including landlords receiving transferred local authority stock. The Housing Corporation will licence all profit making landlords who will be eligible to receive public funds for the provision of social housing. All independent social landlords will be expected to deliver a "social housing product". This product is defined as: dwellings of an appropriate standard; tenancies allocated in accordance with government policy; sub-market rents; and specified rights and levels of service:

> "Taken together this package of 'outputs' defines the social housing 'product' which Government is 'buying' either with grants to subsidise new-build or rehabilitation or by approving the transfer of local authority stock at a price designed to enable purchasing landlords to deliver this 'product'."[27]

If there is large scale transfer of local authority stock to housing companies, thereby removing housing from democratic control, one regulatory body for all social renting would seem appropriate. The

---

[26] Day et al., *op. cit.*, p. 42.
[27] DoE, *More Choice in the Social Rented Sector*. Consultation paper linked to the Housing White Paper *"Our Future Homes"* (1995), p. 20.

only unregulated rented constituency would be the "old style" private landlords. It would not be impossible to see further developments whereby the financiers of home ownership could be incorporated into a regulatory system which concentrated on consumer accountability.

## The Governance of Providers: Landlords and Lenders

The focus for the previous section was primarily on regulation and the accountability of the bodies responsible for this function. In this section we consider what could broadly be described as the governance of the providing bodies. This will involve a brief consideration of the constitutional structures of the key providers, building societies, housing associations, local authorities and private landlords. All of these bodies are presently facing, in their different ways, pressures to change their constitutional structures.

Economic pressures are encouraging a trend towards more traditional private forms, in particular, that of the company. However, at the same time for building societies, private and housing association landlords, there are pressures to develop accountability to a wider constituencies than at present. Local authorities, facing very substantial upheavals in their housing function, are obliged to rethink their traditional methods of accounting. Landlords generally are obliged to consider these governance issues in the context of market-oriented provision.

We will review the position of the various providers before moving to consider the consequences for users and the attempt to transform mortgagors and tenants, differentiated by tenure and statute, into homogoneous consuming citizens.

The constitution of any building society must comply with the requirements of Part 2 of the Building Societies Act 1986.[28] Any 10 persons can establish a society through drawing up a memorandum of its purpose, the adoptable powers which it has adopted and any restrictions which it has assumed on its powers.[29] The building

---

[28] The constitutional detailed requirements are set out in Sched. 2 and those covering management are set out in Pt. 7 of the Building Societies Act 1986.
[29] The extended powers available to societies with an asset value over £100m under the Act must be adopted by the society. They are not automatically granted.

society must comply with its principal purposes and be incorporated under the Act by registration with the central office of the Registry of Friendly Societies. To raise funds, the society must also be authorised by the Building Societies Commission to do so. Its rules must also comply with the statutory requirements set out in Schedule 2 and include the rights of members.

Each society must hold a register of members who are defined as including any person who for the time being holds a share in the society (section 119). Members are entitled to receive a copy of the summary financial statement, the annual accounts and the annual business statement. They are entitled to vote in an election of directors and on a resolution of the society. There is a limited right to inspect the register. A member can obtain access if s/he wishes to communicate with fellow members on matters relating to the society where the Building Societies Commission considers it to be in the interests of the members as a whole. Members are also given rights to obtain particulars of members and rights to demand a poll. A minimum holding of £100 entitles a member to receive documents and vote. A requisite number (50 or 10 according to whether a society has or has not a qualifying asset holding) of members who move resolutions at a general meeting can have a document circulated in support and there is an equivalent power for members who seek election to the board.[30]

The requirements in relation to directors of the society are set out in Part 7 of the 1986 Act. There is a minimum requirement of two directors who must be elected either by postal ballot or at the annual general meeting, although co-option is permitted (sections 58 and 60). The directors must appoint a chief executive and secretary (section 59). This Part of the Act also regulates the activities of directors. Thornton and McBrien suggest however that the key to probity is contained within section 45 which sets out the criteria for prudent management. They also suggest that the standard required is a "lot higher than is the case under company law".[31]

In practice, the power of the membership to influence the board is very diffuse: large building societies have millions of members.

---

[30] Thornton and McBrien, *Building Society Law: Cases and Materials* (1988), p. 35.
[31] *ibid.* p. 16.

There have been some isolated attempts to achieve the election of a director nominated by dissident members, but these have not been successful. The most concerted and organised campaign was stimulated by the conversion of the Abbey National Building Society into a company. The board of directors was obliged to fight a very public battle with a minority of its members (Abbey National Members Against Flotation) who attempted to make use of the powers available to members under the Act.[32] The process exposed the limitations of member power. They have been described as

"Oligopolistic financial giants which are emerging at the top end of the industry and which cannot continue masquerading as mutual institutions responsible to and controlled by their members."[33]

The Treasury is proposing to increase the accountability of building societies by improving the information given to members of building societies and the transparency with which societies conduct their affairs, particularly the procedures for electing directors to boards (Treasury, 1995). The measures include giving borrowing members (mortgagors) broadly the same voting rights as shareholders. The interest in greater accountability is stimulated by the present climate of merger, takeover and conversion to public limited company.

In the highly competitive conditions of the 1990s there is a strong business incentive to obtain the greater flexibility offered by the company structure, but there are also those who argue that the company structure offers more opportunity for accountability to shareholders and less political interference. Shareholders in companies can vote with their feet and inefficient companies fear takeovers. However, the mass of home owning mortgagors are not necessarily likely to be substantial shareholders in such companies (although the conversion process does offer shareholding to former

---

[32] See coverage in the *Financial Times* in 1988 including July 25, September 27, October, 1, 6–8, 15, December 15, also The *Guardian* May 18, 1989. The group attempted to force the board to hold an extraordinary meeting to discuss the matter and to recognise the group so that it could publicly represent the opposition case. Members of AMAF attempted to stand against existing board members at the Annual General Meeting. They also referred the matter to the industry's ombudsman. At all stages they were thwarted.

[33] Hawes, *Building Societies—The Way Forward*, Occasional Paper 26, School for Advanced Urban Studies (1986), p. 43.

members—see Lucas, 1995 for the arguments for and against conversion).

Housing associations are at the other end of the spectrum to these financial giants, although evolving out of the same tradition of voluntary, self-help, non-profit based involvement with housing. Generally they are small, local organisations dedicated to providing homes in specific localities. Nonetheless the company structure is also being considered for their future development.

At an administrative level, as we have seen, the Housing Corporation's new financial monitoring system introduced in the context of mixed funding schemes requires company account formats. Some, like Coleman, would still see them as overly protected by government and advocates exposure in the market with company status for the associations. He argues that the voluntary status of boards is no longer adequate to attract further talented membership and that there is a case for allowing associations which would wish to diversify by "privatising" themselves, attracting shareholder capital, making profits, issuing dividends and attracting corporate talent to run them by paying boards.[34]

Housing associations are responding to the pressures placed upon them by the reduction in public funds by forming profit-making subsidiaries, limited companies to undertake schemes that are not permissible for either charitable or non-charitable associations.

> "Some argue, however, that such involvement will eventually have a detrimental effect upon the voluntary housing movement and that it cannot continue to embrace two such different cultures. Can a single organisation even with properly structured subsidiaries maintain an ethos that is compatible with both charitable and commercial objectives?"[35]

This split identity is illustrated in the recent ombudsman case (see later for discussion of the housing association tenants' ombudsman scheme) against Bradford & Northern Housing Association Ltd[36]

---

[34] Coleman, "Private rented housing: the next steps" in Best, R. et al. (eds.) *The Future of Private Renting: Consensus and Action* (1992).
[35] Cope, *Housing Associations—Policy and Practice* (1990), p. 298.
[36] Report on investigation into complaint No. 0032/93 against Bradford & Northern Housing Association Ltd.

which concerned the sale of a shared-ownership property. The Housing Association's asking price was £78,000, although the building society's valuation was £68,000. The prospective purchaser had asked the association to reduce the price but it had declined. Two weeks after completion, the association dropped the price for the remaining properties to £70,000. The ombudsman made the following remarks in his decision which found no maladministration.

> "The introduction of shared ownership schemes and the need for associations to raise private finance, has increasingly meant that associations have to operate in a commercial atmosphere, taking into consideration market forces and financial returns on money borrowed. When selling property, associations have to take into account the same factors as any other property developer and they are required to take commercial decisions based on a fluctuating housing market. The public may consider that associations, involved in the sale of residential properties, should operate on a different basis to private property developers, but I do not regard this as realistic."[37]

The relentless pressure on the associations to compete for private funds for development as the level of housing association grant casts a spotlight on their traditional constitutional forms, emphasising the need for business management skills on management committees. On the other hand there are pressures for greater public accountability of these independent bodies now that they are the main vehicle for public social housing provision.

The responsibility for this balancing act lies with the voluntary management committee of the association which is legally responsible for all association activities. Under the model rules provided by the NFHA, which most societies adopt, the society has corporate status, a common seal and limited liability like a company. As we have seen the majority of associations are registered as industrial and provident societies and therefore must comply with the rules of incorporation. As such, it must conduct its business either for the benefit of the community or for the benefit of members (if it is a mutual society). It must have a minimum membership of seven but

---

[37] Housing Association Tenants' Ombudsman Service, *Report on Investigation into Complaint No. 0032/93 against Bradford and Northern Housing Association Ltd* (1995), p. 16.

there is no prescribed maximum. Each member purchases a nominal £1 share which entitles them to attend the annual General meeting, to vote at the meeting and to receive the annual report.[38]

Committee members are elected at the annual general meeting. The governing body is the committee of management. The model rules prescribe that the committee is elected from the membership at the AGM and that the committee consists of between seven and 15 members. They also permit the addition of five co-opted members. Cope argues that:

> "These particular electoral regulations lead in many cases to the same members being elected year after year. This is particularly true where the pool of members is limited and not very active. This has led to criticism of associations as being 'self-perpetuating oligarchies'. The lack of truly democratic representation in comparison with local councils is one of the greatest weaknesses of the housing association movement."[39]

A 1985 National Federation of Housing Associations commissioned survey of 287 associations and 242 Abbeyfield Societies[40] found that two-thirds of associations had less than 50 members (Crook, 1985); four had over 1,000; seven per cent had elections; the average size of management committee was 12; 1,000 tenants served on management committees out of a total of 30,000 volunteers; 25 per cent of associations had some form of tenant representation on the management structure.[41]

More recent research into the composition of management committees and membership of associations reveals:

> "the remarkable extent to which housing associations with development programmes are governed by committees of management with relevant skills and experience. The typical committee member is a male, well qualified, working or retired, professional or manager from the private sector. . . . it appears on paper that associations have committees of management who should have the skills and experience necessary to achieve business efficiency and good management performance."[42]

---

[38] Cope, *op. cit.*, p. 42.

[39] *ibid.* p. 43.

[40] Abbeyfield Societies are a specialist section of the housing association movement catering for the needs of the frail elderly.

[41] Cope, *Housing Associations—Policy and Practice* (1990), p. 45.

[42] Kearns, *Going by the Board: The Unknown Facts about Housing Association Membership and Management Committees in England* (1994), p. 33.

They might seem competent to deal with the business matters but they look weak in terms of accountability. The committee members have similarities in background to local authority councillors but they are obviously not balanced committees, with almost no representatives from manual working groups, unemployed or women who undertake unpaid domestic labour. Further, their electoral credibility is far weaker than local councillors (themselves elected on a relatively small vote). As Kearns points out:

> "Housing associations are membership organisations without many members. . . . The paucity of the situation is revealed by the fact that in half the developing associations studies, the ratio of total shareholding members to actual committee members was no better that 2:1 and in only eight cases was a ratio of 10:1 achieved."[43]

Thus membership power cannot offset the over reliance on certain groups on the management committees, thereby weakening the legitimacy of the organisations. "[D]ue attention needs also to be given to popular credibility and accountability, to be achieved in large measure (though not entirely) through greater involvement of shareholding members".[44] Tenants seem to figure very little in these equations.

The National Federation of Housing Associations' Inquiry (1995) into the governance of housing associations identified a number of these weaknesses, including the uncertainty about the appropriate role of shareholding members who in industrial and provident societies elect the board (its preferred term for the committee of management). Membership has not been an effective accountability mechanism. Board members have not always adapted to the increase in size and complexity of their association. Few boards have formal processes for the selection of board members and the appraisal of the board's performance. The governing instruments (rules) of associations are inadequate in not providing for delegation to staff.[45]

There have been calls for professional committees and moves to adopt corporate models of governance following the Cadbury Com-

---

[43] *ibid.* p. 35.
[44] *ibid.* p. 36.
[45] NFHA, *Competence and Accountability: The Report of the Inquiry into Housing Association Governance*, 1995, pp. 10–11.

mittee of Inquiry into the Financial Aspects of Corporate Governance (Cadbury, 1992). The argument is that not only in business terms, but also in accountability terms, the private company structure offers advantages. This would involve more power to the chief executive officer and reduce the input of the board. It would also probably involve the chief executive becoming a full voting member of the board of associations (Kearns, 1994b).

The Inquiry considered that "there were strong arguments against associations becoming private sector companies that can distribute profits to shareholders".[45a] As the assets of housing associations are mainly derived from public or charitable funds and are invested in tenanted property, they thought it inappropriate for them to be managed for the benefit of shareholders and that this might undermine the security of the tenants. The Inquiry also found no justification for proposing that housing associations become public or statutory bodies, considering such a status incompatible with the independence and diversity of associations. They recommend therefore that the independent and non-profit distributing status should be perserved.[46]

The NFHA report, however, does make a number of far reaching proposals to improve the competence and accountability of housing associations which includes a clearer definition of the role of the board of management and that of the employed managers (where there are any). The Inquiry was not satisfied that the current arrangements provided adequate accountability to residents in the areas not covered by statute. It considered that expanded access to board membership was not sufficient and recommended the development of much wider accountability structures, in particular through consultation with recognised residents' associations. Relationships with local authorities would be strengthened by the development of written agreements stating each party's obligation to consult about policy. It recommends implementation of all these measures through a Code of Governance which would be adopted by the National Federation of Housing Associations and would also be incorporated into the regulatory framework of the Housing Corporation (NFHA, 1995).

---

[45a] *ibid*. p. 12.
[46] *ibid*. p. 12.

Unlike housing associations, local authorities are multifunctional and as such not specialists in housing. Housing provision is the responsibility of elected local councillors who sit on a range of service committees and do not necessarily develop particular skills in relation to housing matters. Housing has traditionally been the responsibility of a specific committee, although in some authorities this is combined with other services such as social services or public health. The introduction of compulsory competitive tendering (under the Local Government Act 1988 and the Leasehold Reform, Housing and Urban Development Act 1993) for housing management, which splits housing functions into service procurers and providers, introduces major changes in the relationship of councillors and managers. Councillors will still be responsible of policy development, service specification and monitoring but will have less "hands on" involvement with service delivery in the future.[47]

Changes to the structure of provision of housing finance as seen in Chapter 4, above, have also had their impact on the management of housing budgets. The Housing Revenue Account is now ring fenced, free standing in relation to other budgets and increasingly a rent flow account rather than based on historic cost. Councillors are responsible for a specific revenue budget which is separate from the overall council budget and one that receives no direct subsidy from local council tax payers. The structure of the budget, the need to comply with the regulators requirements of value for money and the specification procedures for compulsory competitive tendering are encouraging market-oriented forms of accounting.

The pressure to find ways of attracting funds, which are defined not as public sector for the purposes of the public sector borrowing requirement, continues. The simplest way would be not to count borrowing for council housing investment as part of public expenditure. This would place councils in the same position as housing associations.[48] However, Wilcox et al. argue that there is a clear logic for the current inclusion of council borrowing within the definition of public spending because "[a]lmost by definition it is hard to

---

[47] Brooke, "The Enabling Authority", *Public Administration* (1991), Vol. 69.
[48] As Wilcox et al. point out quoting Sir Leo Pliatzky "the PSBR is a creation of the Treasury's — the concept is not used at all in France or the United States, for instance — and it is what the Treasury says it is . . ." (1993: 32).

sustain the argument that housing borrowing by (local) government should somehow be excluded from General Government Expenditure".[49] Local authority housing departments are integral to local government and they do not operate on a wholly commercial basis (unlike for instance British Petroleum Company which was always excluded from the figures during its state-owned period). Such an action would also offend core international and United Kingdom accounting conventions.[50]

Therefore the other options all involve moving the stock out of local authority ownership. To date the most popular method has been the voluntary transfer of stock to housing associations which, despite its name, involves a capital payment for any value the stock may have. The new owners are obliged to raise this on the private market, while the local authority must remit a proportion of the receipt to central government as a way of offsetting the increase in the housing benefit bill which results from privatisation. A further drawback for some is the restriction on local authority representation on the new body to 20 per cent.

Recently there has been considerable interest in the idea of transfer to a local housing company. Under some proposals, local authority stock would be transfered to a new landlord body as a going concern. Such an arrangement would allow access to private finance for repairs and improvements without the need to raise funds for a capital payment. The government's recent proposals are based on the assumption that at least some transfer will involve a positive receipt for the outgoing landlord (DoE, 1995b; DoE, 1995e).

Any company must avoid the specifications within sections 68 and 69 of 1989 Local Government and Housing Act in relation to local authority controlled and influenced companies:

"A controlled company is defined, by a number of criteria, as a company where the local authority effectively has majority control over its operations. An arms-length company is a particular form of controlled company. An influenced company is defined as one where 20 per cent or more of the voting rights over the company are effectively

---

[49] Wilcox et al., Local Housing Companies: New Opportunities for Council Housing (1993), p. 32.
[50] *ibid.* p. 33.

held by 'persons associated with the authority', and where there is a 'business relationship' between the company and the authority".[51]

Both of these types of company are considered to be in the public sector. It is perfectly possible to establish a company which provides a substantial degree of continuing council influence but falls outside these definitions and therefore within the private sector. (The company would, however, still be defined as a minority interest company which is subject to regulation under the 1989 Act.) While this type of proposal is driven by the need to find new sources of investment, it has significant consequences for accountability which will be achieved through representation on the committee or board of the company. One model would be five committee members nominated by the local authority and ten members elected by tenants, another, one-third membership local authority, one-third tenants, one-third professionals with relevant skills (Wilcox et al. 1993). Thus local accountability both to the local authority and to tenants is achieved through "stakeholder" representation rather than democratic process. The Government intends, however to scrutinise any arrangement carefully to ensure that the local authority does not exercise a "dominant influence". While the presence of developers suggests independence, tenant representatives does not.[52]

Housing association accountability is often compared unfavourably with that of local authorities for its lack of democracy. However, there is considerable criticism of representational democracy for offering low levels of accountability to citizens; little public influence on decision making; offering uniform services with standard rules to diverse citizens; and failing to represent diverse, multi-cultural interests.[53] In particular there is an argument that councillors represent citizens generally rather than housing users specifically and have failed to develop the necessary accountability towards this constituency (Birchall, 1992). Local authority landlords have tended to be resistant to tenant participation (see Chapter 4, above). Tenants have

---

[51] Wilcox et al., p. 42.
[52] DoE, More Choice in the Social Rented Sector. Consultation paper linked to the Housing White Paper "Our Future Homes" (1995), p. 17.
[53] Kearns, On Considering the Governance of Social Housing: Putting the Horse Before the Cart (1994), p. 24.

not been encouraged to form tenants' associations or to be involved in the decision-making process. Tenant representation on housing committees with voting rights has been almost non-existent and now the Local Government and Housing Act 1989 prevents co-optees of housing committees and sub-committees from voting, although they can attend in an advisory capacity.

A growing support for "stakeholder" or constituency based memberships approaches to accountability can be seen in both the National Federation of Housing Association Inquiry recommendations and in the local company proposals to replace open membership systems or local democracy.

Once again we find that the stimulus for change is coming from the social sector landlords, but proposals to develop the private sector also involve encouraging the development of corporate landlordism rather than relying on individual landlords. These developments suggest a broadly based trend, encompassing widely different political positions, towards seeing the private company as an appropriate form through which to provide housing across the whole sector. These companies would range from the huge financial giants providing finance to owner-occupiers to the small local company providing subsidised rented dwellings.

## Statutory Protection and the Contracting State

In the previous chapters we have seen the way in which individual statutory arrangements have provided rights and entitlements to such matters as security of tenure, rent regulation, the provision of information and protection from unlawful eviction. We have also argued that these statutory regimes have constructed and positioned the various relations within the broader provision of housing.

Owner-occupiers with mortgages from building societies have been deemed as in less need of statutory protection than others, although they have the benefit of the court's discretion when they are faced with possession proceedings. Those renting from private landlords as protected tenants have been entitled to security of tenure and a fair rent, those renting as assured tenants have less security and must pay a market rent. Eventually in the eighties those renting from

265

local authority landlords were deemed in need of security specifically as users as opposed to as general citizens and, therefore, became secure tenants under the Tenants' Charter, while rents continued to be required to be reasonable. Housing association tenants have been constructed as quasi-public tenants, as secure tenants but with fair rents until 1988 and now quasi-private tenants with assured tenancies and market rents.

The very substantial changes which we have documented in each of the sectors in the 1980s have been aimed increasingly at creating greater competition and encouraging market methods of provision. There has been an attempt to strengthen the social market in renting. The different economic and political positions of the landlords based on historical developments are a barrier to the creation of the market. The council sector has had relatively low levels of rents which are a product of historic cost funding, collectivism and local politics. Local authority landlordism encompassed much more than private landlordism. Housing associations have had a very preferential development regime, rent regulated by a rent officer and in the main high standards of management, again a product of their history. Private landlords have operated in a market which regulates rents but not physical standards with very little direct subsidy. As political pariahs for most of the twentieth century, they have been policed by a variety of public agencies rather than regulated.

These differences which are reflected in the individual statutory regimes are dissolving through the construction of a market. Both local authority and housing associations, although having different legal contexts for rent determination, are moving towards market provision. Housing associations now set rents to cover the costs of their borrowing in the market. The 1989 financial regime for local authorities has a similar effect on rents. "At a stroke, the historic cost system of rent setting is being rendered nugatory, without the problem of abolishing it".[54] The audit demands of economy, efficiency and effectiveness in both sectors are having their impact: rents are becoming prices rather than charges[55] (Harden, 1992).

---

[54] Coleman, "Private rented housing: the next steps" in Best, R. et al. (eds.) *The Future of Private Renting: Consensus and Action* (1992).

[55] Charges are user fees which are not necessarily set by market forces but which may be compulsory. Charges occupy the ground that separates taxes from prices in relation to services provided by a public body under statutory powers (Harden, 1992).

Public landlordism has had strong collectivist elements within which it recognised needs. Housing management within the public and housing association sector has increasingly involved considerations of the social welfare of tenants. Perceived often as paternalism in earlier decades, these broader responsibilities have led to the development of policies in relation to harassment and anti-social behaviour and equal opportunities and housing advisory services. Yet the financial regimes developing in both sectors have emphasised value for money and company accounting structures. Housing Revenue Account items are now more tightly specified; the inclusion of social welfare items such as advice on homelessness and sheltered housing wardens must now be justified as an appropriate charge on a rent account. There is an argument to suggest that these welfare elements associated with collective provision will need to be externalised, or at least costed separately from rent payments, if comparison is to be made with the private rented sector, if a market based landlordism is to become the norm.

The competing demands of financial audit and quality service provision are exacerbated by the changing composition of the social rented sector. Many point to the residualisation which is occurring in both the local authority and housing association sectors. The population living in council or housing association homes is increasingly concentrated in the poorest income groups.

"66 per cent of social housing tenants (in 1990) but only 5 per cent of home buyers have household incomes in the lowest three deciles. But four out of five households with incomes in the fourth decile and above own their own homes".[56]

Further, the incomes of new tenants of housing associations were not just lower, but much lower, than existing tenants with 54 per cent deriving their incomes wholly from state benefits or pensions and only one in four tenants is in any kind of work.[57] Page documents a parallel, but not identical, change taking place throughout the decade among the tenants of local authorities.

"At the beginning of the decade, the average council tenant income was 73 per cent of the national average: by 1990 this had fallen to only 48

---

[56] Page, *Building for Communities: A Study of New Housing Association Estates* (1993), p. 27.
[57] *ibid.* p. 30.

> per cent while the average for housing association tenants was only 45 per cent of that for all incomes. . . . What is clear . . . is that social housing now accommodates a very high proportion of people who are poor, unemployed or otherwise disadvantaged and that this proportion is increasing."[58]

While this social and economic process has been going on, the emphasis has been on creating market-based approaches to protecting the interests of occupiers. We have noted in all sectors the increased emphasis on individual contractual obligations. The administrative benevolence of the building societies is being replaced by greater emphasis on the rights of the mortgagee under the mortgage. Housing association tenants with assured tenancies do not have access to the statutory rights of their secure counterparts. Assured tenants and assured shorthold tenants in the private-rented sector theoretically negotiate their contractual terms including rent. Local authority tenants still enjoy the statutory rights if they remain in the sector, but, as we have seen, there is increasing pressure to transform the status of the local authority landlord. At one remove from the tenants, but directing affecting them, housing management is now subject to compulsory competitive tendering so that services to tenants are undertaken through a service contract with the landlord.

## Constructing the Housing Consumer

Arguably, contractual arrangements are replacing direct statutory entitlements based on legally differentiated providers. These contracts are overlaid with a variety of regulatory mechanisms which seem to be more consistent with market provision, such as codes of conduct, either self imposed or imposed by the regulators.

Occupants differentiated by sector are being reconstructed as consumers of housing. This is part of a much wider change in the nature of state provision of services. As we have seen there developed in the 1970s a crisis of legitimacy in the provision of state services which the political right tackled through "Thatcherism": a belief in

---

[58] Page, *op. cit.*, p. 31.

market solutions which led to attacks on the direct provision of state services through privatisation, deregulation and competition. In the 1990s this project has taken the form of the Citizen's Charter (1991). It pursues themes (value for money, increased competition, privatisation, greater emphasis upon performance measurement, etc.) that were already well in train by the time Mr Major took over from Mrs Thatcher as Prime Minister. It reaffirms the Government's commitment to privatisation, to contracting out and compulsory competitive tendering but also emphasises the need to make the remaining public services more consumer oriented.

While these initiatives have evolved out of a radical right agenda, the democratic left have also responded to the crisis of legitimacy in the state. Both have wanted effective countervailing power to that of public bureaucracies. The right has taken the route of the market, in Hirschman terms, exit, the left has been keener to strengthen public involvement in the decision-making processes, to empower through voice.

The charter initiative seems to take some account of the alternative agenda. In relation to the provision of public services, it offers higher standards, more openness, more information, a commitment to non-discrimination, greater responsiveness to consumer needs and better procedures for the redress of grievances.[59]

Both the concept of "citizen" and "charter" carry their own meanings.

> "The public is seen as having acquired rights to services through the payment of taxes rather than community membership. The model of the state's relationship with citizens is one of contract rather than embodying any idea of commitment or responsibility."[60]

Barron and Scott also make the point that "citizen" is grafted onto the identity of the consumer, who is not the bearer of needs but an economic actor.

> "What this suggests, in turn, is that the consumer's legitimate expectation of quality in the context of contracts for services may in fact be

---

[59] Drewry, "Mr Major's Charter: empowering the consumer", *Public Law* (1993), pp. 250–251.
[60] Stewart and Walsh's "Change in the Management of Public Services", *Public Administration* (1992), Vol. 69, p. 507.

akin to a constitutional right where those services are provided by public sector agencies".[61]

The concept of a charter is also novel: it sounds legalistic, contractual, but does not directly imply the conferment of legal entitlements.[62] The objectives of the Citizen's Charter initiative are met through a wide range of specific charters such as the Public Sector Tenants Charter. The first edition document revealed the ambiguity over enforceability. Its introduction explained "Some of the *rights* mentioned here are rights you have in law — they are printed in red. Some of them are things your council should do as a matter of good practice — they are printed in blue. Things the government plans to do in the future are printed in green." (DoE, 1992) There was a considerable amount of blue ink in the booklet. The second edition perhaps wisely separates "rights" and expectations into development sections.

We have seen in the case of *Palmer v. Sandwell District Council* (1988) 20 H.L.R. 74 the confusions which arise when landlords produce their own versions of these booklets, merging expectations with statutory rights. The courts in the mid-1980s adopted a restrictive approach to the issue relying on traditional concepts of contract rather than developing more appropriate concepts of legitimate expectations.

Broadly speaking the Citizen's Charter approach has at its heart the consuming citizen. Hambilton and Hoggett suggest that:

> "Although the charter type initiatives clearly contain elements of exit and voice, they should be more correctly be considered as an aspect of the 'new managerialism' and thus lacking the radicalism of the politically inspired empowerment strategies of the Right and Left of the early 1980s."[63]

Lewis also sees these initiatives as concerned with managerialism but sees them to be of far reaching significance.

---

[61] Barron and Scott, "The Citizen's Charter Programme" (1992) 55 *Modern Law Review*, pp. 526–546 at 543.

[62] Drewry, *ibid.* p. 252.

[63] Hambilton and Hoggett, "Rethinking Consumerism in Public Services", *Consumer Policy Review* (1993), Vol. 3, No. 25, p. 108.

"The Citizen's Charter is not what it started out to be. Its tentacles are extending into areas previously unconsidered when the idea was first mooted. It is now becoming part of both a philosophy of government and a *means* of government. Taken together these may in future be seen as constituting a real break with the past. It may even be viewed as a way of governing."[64]

He points to the influence of the ideas of Osborne and Gaebler (1992).

"The state (central or local) cannot govern effectively by becoming involved in the minutiae of service delivery. What it must do instead is empower a myriad of providers to compete and innovate in delivering on policies/mission statements chosen by the state whose task is the task of governance rather than governing."[65]

Many of these changes of governance are to be brought about through the state contracting with a wide range of agencies to provide the specified services. Harden has considered the consequences of the "contracting" state. While seeing this development as potentially positive because it can promote constitutional values through the institutional separation of functions, by distinguishing the provider from the purchaser, he does suggest that that the contract cannot work the same magic for public services as it does for private. Public contracts are not like commercial contracts but much more like delegated legislation.

The debates over the advantages and disadvantages of the wider issues will continue. We will look specifically at the implications for the legal system later but first we return to consider their impact on the users of housing services. Partington has taken up the theme in relation to the housing sector. He notes quite correctly in relation to the existing patterns of legal regulation that "[t]here is no doubt that the present level of complexity is quite self defeating. Neither the intended beneficiaries of the law nor those potentially regulated by it take sufficient notice of the law, because of its complexity".[66] He

---

[64] Lewis, "The Citizen's Charter and Next Steps: A New Way of Governing?" *Political Quarterly* (1993), p. 36.

[65] *ibid.* p. 317.

[66] Partington, "Citizenship and Housing", in Blackburn (ed.), *Rights of Citizenship* (1993), p. 135.

suggests that the consumer movement associated with manufactured goods and services, particularly financial services, have obtained substantial benefits and protections for consumers.

"By contrast, housing has not formerly been perceived in this way. . . . (there are) piecemeal measures, not part of what could be described as a coherent package of measures to protect those — whether owner-occupier or tenants — who 'consume' housing services. . . . A 'consumerist' perspective on housing would encourage the bringing together of the provisions that currently exist and their expansion with a view to ensuring that all citizens are guaranteed proper standards of housing service".[67]

He argues that this approach, which would rely on industry-wide codes of practice or standards overseen by a body akin to the Office of Fair Trading, would be more politically neutral in sensitive areas such as rent levels.

We can see the move away from reliance on statutorily defined rights to greater interest in the use of consumerist, market based approaches. We have touched on the public sector tenant's charter which overlays the rights granted under the 1985 Housing Act to secure tenants with a range of expectations of good practice by the landlord, some of which are based on the requirements placed upon the landlord by the regulators. Indeed the tenant would probably obtain a very good service if these expectations were entitlements. Much store is placed upon the tenants' abilities to exit.

The same pattern, but more pronounced, can be seen in relation to the housing association sector. Tenants entering the sector since 1989 have become assured tenants and as such do not have access to the same statutory rights as their secure counterparts. Nonetheless these entitlements are offered to tenants via the regulator's (the Housing Corporation) Code of Guidance. Thus the basic statutory rights which construct tenants as private sector tenants are overlaid by entitlements which, if offered in statutory form, would construct them as public sector tenants. The National Federation of Housing Association's model tenancy agreement translates many of the guidance aspirations into contractual obligations, thus transforming them into more recognisably market forms.

---

[67] *ibid.* pp. 132–133.

The Housing Corporation's Code of Guidance is statutorily sanctioned by section 36A of the Housing Associations Act 1985. The extent to which it is followed will be taken into account by the Corporation when it considers whether an association has mismanaged its affairs. In contrast, the document which covers the handling of mortgage arrears and possessions by mortgage lenders is described by the industry as a statement of practice. Originally the Council of Mortgage Lenders had issued two statements in 1990 in response to requests from the Department of the Environment, one on arrears practice, the other on possession. In 1992 the Council of Mortgage Lenders issued a consolidated statement.[68] The Building Societies Association and the Council of Mortgage Lenders argue that voluntary codes of practice are better that regulations imposed by statute. The BSA-CML describe a statement of practice as a common practice in a given area of activity. "Thus the statement of practice on handling mortgage arrears and possession. . . . describes what most lenders do when borrowers fall behind in their payments but such a statement, although endorsed by the CML is not sanctioned in a formal or legalistic way".[69] These codes are not incorporated into the regulatory process. Although the Building Societies Commission is empowered to regulate by means of statutory instruments (paragraph 12, Schedule 1 of the Building Societies Act 1986), it limits its activities to prudential management.

The codes described above are specific to occupational groupings, although they point in the direction of generic consumer rights and protections. The public-sector tenant's charter and the code of guidance cover the same ground and arguably could be extended to other assured tenants, most notably those in the private-rented sector. Therein lies a problem, however, which we have discussed above. These codes do assume high performance by landlords of the sort normally associated only with social landlords. However, it would not be impossible to imagine a code of practice which ensured that consumers of housing services who fall into difficulties, such as over rent or mortgage arrears, were subject to procedures that gave

---

[68] BSA–CML (Building Societies Association/Council of Mortgage Lenders), *BSA and CML Statements and Codes of Practice* (1994), p. 1.
[69] BSA–CML, *op. cit.*, iii.

them appropriate opportunities to extricate themselves from these difficulties.[70]

The Commission for Racial Equality (CRE) provides an example of a body responsible for ensuring practices across sectors. The Housing Act 1988, section 137, and the Local Government and Housing Act 1989, section 180, provide the CRE with the power to introduce codes of practice in the field of non-rented and rented housing. (Both provisions amend section 47 (1) of the Race Relations Act 1976.) The CRE have issued two codes: a code of practice in rented housing (CRE, 1991) and code of practice in non-rented (owner-occupied) housing (CRE, 1992), both of which are described as for the elimination of racial discrimination and the promotion of equal opportunities. The codes do not have full force of law, failure to observe them does not render a person liable for any proceedings. However, in any proceedings under the Race Relations Act before a court, the codes are admissable in evidence. It is possible that a failure to adhere to the provisions might amount to a presumption of unlawful discrimination (Handy, 1993).

Some argue that a strategy of changing approaches through exhortatory codes, rather than using the formal powers of investigation available to the CRE, has been successful in producing changes of practice among the housing providers. Others are more sceptical about the effectiveness of the CRE's general strategy. McCrudden (1988), considering the CRE code of practice in relation to employment, argues that they lack legitimacy because they are made by an agency rather than Parliament and that agency is itself relatively marginalised. The legal status of the code is uncertain and weak and as such is generally ignored by lawyers.

These codes, however, need to be seen in the context of the statutory duties imposed upon local authorities (section 71 of the Race Relations Act 1976) and the Housing Corporation (section 75 (5) of the Housing Associations Act 1985) to eliminate unlawful discrimination and to promote equality of opportunity and good race relations. A failure to set up appropriate arrangements would amount to a breach of a local authority's statutory duty. The Corporation can pass on this general duty to housing associations through administrative control only.

---

[70] Partington, *op. cit.*, p. 134.

There has been a general trend towards the use of informal rules of which codes of practice, guidance notes and circulars are a part. Whether this trend can be attributed generally to the new form of governance is perhaps debateable; the use of administrative rule making has been prevalent for some time, predating the Citizen Charter initiative. In any case there are those who are less enthusiastic about these developments arguing that "informal rules are too free from control by Parliament, executive, judiciary or any other source and that this freedom is increasingly open to exploitation".[71]

We have discussed a number of ways in which responsibilities towards occupiers have developed, through statutory and contractual rights and more indirectly through the powers of the various regulators and the codes of practices. Now we turn to redress systems, concentrating on the three relevant ombudsman schemes which deal with complaints from tenants of local authorities and housing associations and for mortgagors of building societies.

## The Role of the Ombudsman

Here again we see a developing uniformity of approach through the use of grievance systems outside the court system which emphasise due process. Originally a way of dealing with public administrative malpractice, these bodies have spread to the private sector partly because many nominally private organisations exercise monopolistic (or oligopolistic) economic powers over access to services.

> "Once it is realised that these powers are in essence governmental, the quest of lawyers to graft forms of legal accountability onto their exercise is predictable but nonetheless justifiable."[72]

The spread of these redress systems also reflect a marked shift away in the commercial arena from courts imposed resolution of disputes

---

[71] See Baldwin and Houghton, "Circular Arguments: The Status and Legitimacy of Administrative Rules", *Public Law* (1986), p. 240; Baldwin and McCrudden, *Regulation and Public Law* (1987).

[72] Morris, "The Banking Ombudsman's, *Journal of Business Law* (1987), Part 1, pp. 130–136.

to more flexible and informal modes of extra-judicial dispute settlement, most notably consultation, complaints procedures, conciliation and arbitration (Cotterell, 1992). Although ombudsman schemes generally act as arbitors of individual complaints they do have also, in some instances, a more reformatory role as auditors of administrative practice.

The essential characteristics of the office of ombudsman are independence from the institutions concerned; accessibility for the individual complainant; cheapness and with adequate powers to investigate and require information. The first scheme was introduced into the United Kingdom in 1967 when the office of Parliamentary Commissioner for Administration was set up to investigate complaints from individual citizens who alleged that they had suffered injustice as a result of maladministration within a central government department. The Local Government Ombudsman was subsequently introduced under the Local Government Act 1974 following an influential Justice report in 1969. The public sector ombudsman lack enforcement powers; having found a complaint to be justified they can only make a recommendation as to appropriate redress. The institution has now been extended to the private sector where some schemes allow an ombudsman to investigate the merits of a decision, not simply issues of maladministration, and also allow the ombudsman to direct a remedy.[73] The Building Societies Ombudsman Scheme was the first to be imposed by statute on a private sector industry.[74-75]

Individual schemes have their own accountability structures: the local ombudsman (Commission for Local Administration), until the passing of the Local Government and Housing Act 1989, reported directly to a representative body which was made up of representatives of the local authority associations who funded the scheme, and about whom complaints were investigated. After adverse comment by

---

[73] James et al. "Building Societies, Customer Complaints, and the Ombudsman", *Anglo-American Law Review* (1994), Vol. 23 at p. 216.

[74-75] For background on the creation of the statutory scheme, see James and Seneviratne, "The Building Societies Ombudsman Scheme", *Civil Justice Quarterly*, esp. pp. 158–160. The other financial services sector schemes were set up on a voluntary basis. The Insurance Ombudsman Bureau was established in 1981, the Banking Ombudsman was introduced by the banks in 1986.

*inter alia* the Widdicombe Committee the representative body was abolished under section 25 of the 1989 Act.[76]

The Housing Association Tenant Ombudsman Scheme is presently established under the powers of the Housing Corporation giving rise to doubts about its independence. In 1994 an advisory panel was appointed by the Housing Corporation to act as a buffer between the Housing Corporation and the Ombudsman: to safeguard the independence of the service, to provide general oversight and also guidance where appropriate and to recommend to the board of the Housing Corporation the appointment of Ombudsman. It can also recommend changes to the jurisdiction of the Ombudsman to the board. The Ombudsman has also established a Chief Executives' Forum which meets biannually to discuss matters which have arisen.

A company (the Building Societies Ombudsman Company Limited) established by the industry provides the main funds for the scheme. It has ultimate oversight of the budget and the scheme's operation. The company set up the independent Building Society Ombudsman Council with powers to appoint the ombudsman with the approval of the board of the company and to oversee the day to day running of the scheme. The council presents annual accounts to the company and requires its agreement for each year's budget. The Council is headed by an independent chairman and currently comprises four independent members and three building society members; all are appointed by the board. The council recommends any amendments to the board as they see fit and respond to any proposals relating to the scheme from the board.[77]

The National Consumer Council has doubts about the independence of these private sector schemes.

"The structure of the private sector schemes has been designed to put an independent council with a majority of lay members, as a 'buffer' between the industry board of directors and the ombudsman. So on the face of it, a structural mechanism exists to ensure that the ombudsman is able to act independently. On a fundamental level, it could be argued

---

[76] James et al., *op. cit.*, p. 246.
[77] James and Seneviratne, *op. cit.*, p. 162.

that the ombudsman schemes that are funded by the industries they are investigating can never be truly independent."[78]

The NCC, therefore, recommend that there should be an independent organisation with a majority of public interest/consumer representation to oversee all the ombudsman schemes. The United Kingdom Ombudsman Association established in 1991 with the objective among others of deciding who can use the name of ombudsman (James et al., 1994) is not thought to provide sufficient independence to monitor the operation of the various schemes, but it could develop to take this on board by becoming a statutory body.

We will now consider the three schemes individually in a little more detail. The Building Societies Act 1986 (section 83) provides that an individual building society must be a member of a recognised scheme which gives individual customers the right to have complaints investigated (see Edell, 1990). Failure to be a member would result in criminal penalties (section 84 (8)). The Act requires the scheme to be administered by an independent body (Schedule 12, Part 1, para. 1). Any scheme has to be approved by the Building Societies Commission: there is only one established and approved in 1987, largely modelled on the non-statutory insurance and banking ombudsman schemes in relation to basic constitutional matters.

The regulatory body for the industry, the Building Societies Commission, has to "recognize" the BSO Scheme in the first place to ensure that it complies with the provisions of the 1986 Act (section 83(8)) and has responsibility with the consent of the Treasury, for making any variations to the terms of reference of the scheme, (section 83(7)).[78a] The BSO scheme is very much "tacked on" to the Commission and is only of minor significance to its overall work. We have seen in an earlier section that the Commission's work is directed at prudential supervision and there is little to encourage it to consider the consumer interest directly. The jurisdiction of the BSO covers shares and deposit accounts, borrowing of any kind, banking

---

[78] Sched. 12, Pt. 2 of the Building Societies Act 1986 (as amended by the Building Societies (Investigation of Complaints) Order 1990, S.I. 1990 No 2203) sets out the minimum conditions for a scheme.

[78a] National Consumer Council, *Ombudsman Services: Consumers' views of the Office of the Building Societies Ombudsmen and the Insurance Ombudsman Bureau* (1993), p. 84.

services, trusteeship, executorship. Originally, this jurisdiction did not include most complaints about events occurring before the mortgage was completed or the relevant investment made. This led almost immediately to difficulties particularly in relation to valuations and surveys. The BSO Council made a formal proposal to the Commission in November 1988 that the Ombudsman's terms of reference should be extended to cover allegations of negligent valuations and surveys where loans were eventually completed and the valuer of surveyor was an employee of the society.[79] This proved to be a contentious issue which could not be resolved within the industry and led eventually to testing in court.[80] In *Halifax Building Society v. Edell* [1992] 3 All E.R. 389, Morritt J. held that in the case of a basic valuation, the surveyor or valuer was acting within the scope of his employment for which the society was responsible. His actions were in relation to the grant or refusal to grant a further loan. Thus the actions were covered by the scheme. In relation to a house buyer's report and valuation and a full structural survey prepared by an employee, the provision of the report to the borrower was an action by the building society in relation to the grant or refusal to grant a further loan and therefore within the scheme. Subsequently the directors of the Building Societies Ombudsman Company Limited decided that the scheme's jurisdiction should be extended to cover "pre-completion" complaints as long as the contemplated transaction is in fact completed.[81]

Under the scheme the societies are obliged to comply with the decision unless they take the "publicity option" (section 84(4) of the Building Societies Act 1986). This entails the society publicising the fact that it is not complying with the ruling, together with its reasons, in whatever way the Ombudsman requires.[82] The office of the Ombudsman publishes annual reports outlining cases and setting out its approach to issues but not individual decisions. Research by the National Consumer Council (1993) found that less than half the complaints concern consumers as mortgagors. However, the

---

[79] James and Seneviratne, "The Building Societies Ombudsman Scheme", *Civil Justice Quarterly* (1992), p. 163.

[80] National Consumer Council, *op. cit.*, pp. 63–65 for more detail.

[81] Annual Report of the Building Societies Ombudsman (1993–94), p. 26.

[82] This has only been used by one society, The Cheshunt (James et al., 1994: 237).

Ombudsman's annual report 1993–94 reveals that the number of complaints concerning mortgages has increased: initial complaints about mortgages were up by 11.4 per cent and cases increased by 15.5 per cent. Complaints about mortgage repayments have now become most prolific source of work: initial complaints being up by 59.9 per cent and cases by 61.7 per cent on the previous year.[83]

Consumers are in general satisfied with the scheme (James et al, 1994 and NCC, 1993). One key problem, the restricted jurisdiction which did not cover pre-completion matters such as surveys, has now been tackled. Another is knowledge of the internal complaints procedures and the Ombudsman service. A society's internal complaints system must be exhausted before the Ombudsman can intervene. There is no statutory requirement for building societies to publicise the existence of the Ombudsman.

There is much less consumer satisfaction with internal Building Society complaints procedures (NCC, 1993). Legislation requires societies to have such procedures but sets down no minimum requirements and does not require that individual internal complaints procedures be approved by the Ombudsman.[84] However, since the introduction of the Code of Banking Practice in March 1992 (now 1994), each society is required to have formal internal complaints procedures, to publicise it and to publicise the existence of the Ombudsman.

It is clear that some societies have not been overly enthusiastic about publicising their complaints procedures or providing publicity for the Ombudsman (Graham et al., 1993; Building Societies Ombudsman Scheme, 1994). However, the situation seems to be improving particularly since the introduction of the Banking Code. There also tends to be a greater awareness that, in a highly competitive situation, there are market advantages in operating an efficient and effective complaints scheme.

James et al. have argued that the functions of the Ombudsman Scheme are twofold: the fair resolution of individual disputes and the raising of standards. They are particularly concerned to explore the extent to which the experiences of the Ombudsman are reintroduced

---

[83] Building Societies Ombudsman Scheme, *Annual Report 1993/94* (1994), p. 10.

[84] James et al., "Building Societies, Customer Complaints, and the Ombudsman", *Anglo-American Law Review* (1994), p. 221.

into the organisational structure of the organisations and thereby improve the quality of the service.

> "Our research indicates that building societies are convinced of the wisdom of effective complaint handling for managerial and instrumental reasons. By contrast, the Ombudsman's impact on societies' procedures, and more importantly, policies, has been relatively muted. In part this is due to the scheme's constrained terms of reference and, as recent litigation indicates the societies have not been willing to consent to a liberal interpretation of the Ombudsman's jurisdiction."[85]

After flotation date in 1989, the Abbey National, formally one of the largest societies, was no longer within the Building Societies Ombudsman Scheme but joined the Banking Ombudsman Scheme.[86]

The public-sector ombudsman schemes have been in existence for longer. The Parliamentary Commissioner for Administration does not concern us too much here although the work of the Department of the Environment and the Housing Corporation is subject to his/her jurisdiction (the latter by virtue of the Parliamentary and Health Service Commissioner Act 1987, section 1) The Commissioner can be approached only through a Member of Parliament and has no enforcement powers, merely reporting to Parliament. S/he has no jurisdiction to investigate complaints relating to the substance of Housing Corporation or DoE decisions but must confine him/herself to injustice caused by maladministration.[87]

---

[85] James et al., *op. cit.*, pp. 247–248.

[86] (James and Seneviratne, "The Building Socieites Ombudsman Scheme", *Civil Justice Quarterly* (1992), p. 17. The scheme covers the wholesale mortgage market also. The Banking Ombudsman Scheme follows a similar approach to that of the building societies. It also has three-way structure: the office of the ombudsman which is an unregistered limited company, a board of the office of the Banking Ombudsman and independent Ombudsman Council. The board is made up of banking interests. It raises the funds for the Scheme via levies on the participating banks, it appoints the banking representatives on the Council, approves the Council's appointment of the Ombudsman and monitors overall budgetary control. The Council operates as a buffer between the two other elements. It has a simple majority of lay members on it (4:3) (Morris, 1987: 135). The Ombudsman is not able to command access to documents in his investigation unlike the building society scheme, under which such disclosure is made mandatory by statute. It seems unlikely that the Ombudsman in this scheme will move away from the role of independent arbitor of individual claims towards a more proactive administrative audit role (Morris, 1987).

[87] Alder and Handy, *Housing Association Law* (2nd ed., 1991), p. 215. For further discussion of the Ombudsman, local and central, see McEldowney, 1994: 432–444.

The Local Commissioners for Administration appointed under the Local Government Act 1974 are of greater relevance to our discussion. Originally there was a councillor filter equivalent to the Member of Parliament filter. This requirement was removed, following a recommendation by the Widdicombe Report (1986), by the Local Government Act 1988. The Widdicombe Committee also recommended that the Local Government Commissioners (LGC) be given powers to initiate investigations on their own behalf. The Government did not accept this but subsequently the LGC has been given powers under the Local Government and Housing Act 1989 to issue codes of practice on good administrative procedures for local authorities. Section 31 empowers the Secretary of State to publish such a code (the National Code of Local Government Conduct) which has been approved by resolution of each House of Parliament.[88] Failure to comply with this code may be evidence of maladministration.

The remedies available to the LGC are relatively weak: they rely on the goodwill of the authority to take account of the recommendations.[89] They consist of a report of the investigation showing maladministration which must be publicly available. If the authority fails to respond then section 26 of the Local Government and Housing Act 1989 requires the authority to consider it and to respond within three months. If still not satisfied, the LGC can require the publication of the report in a local newspaper with the authority's reason for not implementing it — the publicity option. Under section 5 of the same Act, a local authority must appoint a monitoring officer to report on findings of maladministration.

The role of the ombudsman is now being questioned in the context of privatisation and market testing in particular through compulsory competitive tendering. The LGC has no jurisdiction over contractual or commercial matters which lie at the heart of the new approach to local government and, in particular, to the provision of housing services. There is a great danger that the ombudsman will be marginalised, to be replaced by regulation based on contractual concepts and on audit in particular.

---

[88] McEldowney, *Public Law* (1994), p. 441.
[89] For more details on the role of the LGC in housing matters, see Hughes and Lowe, 1995: 153–159.

The LGC argued long and hard to obtain jurisdiction over the New Towns and the Urban Development Corporations. The service was also eventually granted jurisdiction over their housing functions and over the Housing Action Trusts by section 26 of the Local Government and Housing Act 1989. They also wanted jurisdiction over housing associations but were denied it.

There is evidence to suggest that there is considerable satisfaction with the LGC (Lewis et al., 1987). The same authors found that internal complaints procedures were patchy. However, the Widdicombe Committee heard evidence of the extensive system of internal complaints procedures within local authorities.[90] Housing complaints form a substantial proportion of the ombudsman referrals particularly on matters of allocation and repairs (Hoath, 1978). The author has found that housing departments are well aware of the potential for ombudsman referrals and treat them seriously when they occur.[91]

Can the LGC play a role in co-ordinating internal complaints or developing administrative audit in a similar way to the Audit Commission in addition to its traditional individual complaint role? The LGC seems to concentrate on the latter, although the powers given under the 1989 Act hint of a different role. However, it is clear that in comparison to the Audit Commission the LGC has a far less proactive role (see Crawford, 1988 for a discussion on these issues).

The final ombudsman to be considered is that established recently for the housing association movement. The government's intention to provide such a service appeared in the first annual report on the Citizen's Charter (1992). The Housing Corporation in its consultation document, *Resolving Housing Association Tenants' Complaints: The Way Forward*, February 1993, proposed to establish the ombudsman service within the Housing Corporation.

The Environment Select Committee detected:

---

[90] McEldowney, *op. cit.*, p. 444.

[91] There findings result from research into the power of law in municipal politics conducted under the Economic and Social Research Council's local governance programme by Davina Cooper and Ann Stewart.

"almost universal support for the Government's intention to create an ombudsman . . . but found an almost total absence of support for the Corporation's published proposal."[92]

There was considerable suspicion that the service would not be or, would not be seen to be, independent. This lack of independence would be particularly apparent in a context where the Corporation's actions would play a significant part in the matter under consideration, for example when an association has acted on the instructions of the Corporation. There was also concern over the lack of enforcement powers under such a scheme. The Ombudsman is obliged to rely on the Corporation's existing range of sanctions to enforce the decision and on the Corporation's statutory powers of investigation.[93]

The main reason identified for the establishment of a non-statutory scheme under the auspices of the Corporation was the lack of Parliamentary time to introduce the primary legislation which would be necessary to establish a fully independent service. Although the service is presently retained within the jurisdiction of the Corporation (Housing Corporation, 1993b), the Government proposes to provide a separate statutory base for the service (DoE, 1995b). It also proposes:

"that although the Independent Housing Ombudsman will operate within a statutory framework, the intention is that the scheme itself will not be prescribed by statute, although its basic requirements will be laid down. . . . The statutory framework envisaged is that for the Building Societies Ombudsman."[94]

At present the Ombudsman publishes an annual report and individual decisions. The terms of reference are widely drawn (HATOS).[95] The main prerequisite for complainants is that they exhaust the Housing Association's internal complaints procedures.

The first annual report of the service goes to considerable lengths to provide reassurance on the anxieties expressed by critics. The

---

[92] House of Commons, The Environment Committee Session 1992/3, second report on the Housing Corporation (1993), para. 198, p. xlix.
[93] House of Commons, Environment Committee, *op. cit.*, para. 201, p. 1.
[94] DoE, More Choice in the Social Rented Sector. Consultation paper linked to the Housing White Paper *Our Future Homes* (1995), p. 44.
[95] See Housing Association Tenants Ombudsman Service (HATOS) Annual Report (1993–94), Appendix 2.

Ombudsman stresses first, that he is independent of the parties in dispute, the tenants and associations, secondly that housing associations are obliged to take part in the scheme and to publicise it to their tenants. These stipulations are contained in the Housing Corporation Guidance (Circular 39/93) issued under section 36A of the Housing Associations Act 1985 which also makes it clear that housing associations will be monitored on their performance in relation to the scheme. Thirdly, the Ombudsman argues that he is wholly free to conduct his functions and fourthly, that the Advisory Panel guarantees independence which despite being appointed by the Corporation, is not responsible to it.[95a]

However, the first reported decision of the Ombudsman make clear some of the potential difficulties of his position (Housing Association Tenants Ombudsman Service, 1994). The housing association had applied to the rent officer for a regular increase in rent under the Rent Act 1977. They asked as usual for about 10 per cent, a figure which was acceptable to the tenant. The rent officer increased the rent by over 40 per cent. The housing association supported the tenant's appeal to the rent assessment committee which confirmed the rent officer's determination. The housing association began to charge the tenant the new rent. The tenant complained about the level of rent and was told that the association was expected by the Housing Corporation to maximise its rental income by charging the registered rent. The landlord was under no statutory obligation to do so, the Rent Act merely stipulates that the registered rent is the maximum legally chargeable and indeed is also under an obligation from the Housing Corporation to charge an affordable rent.

The Ombudsman made it clear in his decision that under his terms of reference he could not consider the merits of the decision, *i.e.* the rent level or the Housing Corporation guidance. He therefore restricted himself to considering whether the association had conducted itself appropriately in relation to the tenant after the rent level had been fixed. He concluded that they had. Within its terms of reference this is probably a satisfactory decision. However, the tenant could conclude that the only reason why he was paying 30 per cent more rent than either he or his landlord wanted was because of the

---

[95a] HATOS Annual Report (1993–94), pp. 1–8.

policy of the Corporation against which he had no redress. (Subsequent to this decision the Housing Corporation has introduced a degree of flexibility into its guidance to associations: an association is able to charge an equivalent assured rent if it is lower than the registered rent.)

The Ombudsman also raised in his report the possibility of extending his jurisdiction to cover other landlords. In particular he mentioned the pressure from the Association of Retirement Home Managers, which represents both registered housing associations and private sector providers of retirement homes, to extend his jurisdiction to cover their private-sector members. Recently, a private landlord, the Peveril Group which manages retirement homes, has taken the initiative and set up its own ombudsman scheme.[96] The Government now proposes to extend the HATOS jurisdiction to cover all "independent social landlords," but not to the remaining private rented sector (DoE, 1995e).

The annual report suggests that the Ombudsman would want to develop his role as monitor of good practice as well as arbitor of good practice. The Ombudsman stresses the importance of the internal complaints procedures and is collecting a copy of each of these to provide a resource base for analysis of good practice.

There seems to be considerable satisfaction with this type of grievance redress system across the sectors, although it is rather early to tell with the Housing Association Tenants Ombudsman. While there is an expansion in the use of ombudsman schemes within the private sector as the institutions come to see dispute resolution systems as part of a marketing strategy in a tightly competitive market, the Local Government Ombudsman looks increasingly vulnerable particularly in relation to housing services. The introduction of compulsory competitive tendering of housing management services highlights the jurisdictional difficulties faced by the LGC.

Strengthening the jurisdiction of the LGC and extending the revamped HATOS jurisdiction to include non-social private landlords would seem to merit consideration.

To summarise, we have seen a move to the use of regulatory agencies to oversee various parts of the housing market, a reduction

---

[96] Simmons "Where the buck doesn't stop", *The Guardian* (1995), p. 9.

in the significance of rights granted to specific sections of the market based on occupational differences, a growing desire to see users of public services as consuming citizens and at the same time for users of housing services whether public or private to be treated in a similar way by industry wide codes of practice and redress systems such as ombudsman schemes. We have seen the growing use of market mechanisms and terminology, companies and contracts, value for money and performance audit across the occupational sectors.

These developments lead to a discussion of the role of the specific regulatory bodies. If these trends continue the argument in favour of one overarching body responsible for housing standards and one for distributing public money would grow stronger, particularly if local authority housing moved out of the public domain into the hands of housing companies. Such a development would raise serious issues over the regulatory power and accountability of such bodies. The present Housing Corporation model would seem unsuitable.

Yet at the same time, and many would argue because of the growing use of the market, there has been a significant social and economic residualisation within both the council rented and housing association sectors. With the growth in the owner-occupied sector to become a majority sector, it now houses within it a much wider cross section of the population including the economically vulnerable. This sector has growing disparaties within it which are masked by a rhetoric of the property-owning democracy. The processes which are breaking down the distinctions between the groupings mask the substantial social and economic divisions which continue to exist and to intensify.

In what ways will the consumer of the various housing services be able to exercise any control over their providers? Given their social and economic vulnerability many consumers are not in a position to choose between providers and in any case are dependent upon state benefits to pay housing costs.

## Governance and Law

Finally, we come to the implications for law, raised by this chapter.

The move to market forms of regulation and accountability has its impact on the legal position of tenants and owner-occupiers. The

287

greater reliance on contractual obligations, it could be argued, should improve the position of those involved within them. The advantages of contracts are that they embody clear and, on the whole, provide enforceable rights and obligations. Mortgagors in relatively large numbers have experienced the full rigours of the obligations of the mortgage in the early 1990s. Mortgagees have relied on the terms of their mortgages to seek and obtain possession against mortgagors in debt. We have also seen that substantial numbers of tenants have also been the subject of possession actions resulting from their obligations under the tenancy. The contractual obligation to pay the financial charge is very clear, despite the many codes, circulars and official exhortations in relation to good practice in the debt recovery process.

Enforcing the developing consumer rights is not so straight forward. While there has been a move towards the rights and responsibilities of the consuming citizen there has not been a similar move towards harmonising the legal frameworks in which the various occupational groupings operate. This brings us to the debates over public law. The traditional mantra is that we do not have a distinctive system of public law.

> "As we enter [the] last decade the ideas on which this tradition is founded seem to hold little plausibility. The courts now make a conceptual distinction between matters of public law and private law and a special procedure — the application for judicial review — is used to process disputes concerning public law issues."[97]

The distinction between public and private law is significant as we have seen throughout the foregoing chapters. First, council tenants can use public law to challenge the collective responsibilities of their landlords, housing associations tenants seemingly cannot. The status of housing associations as private bodies is under question at the moment. There is considerable pressure from various constituencies to see them as "public" bodies at least to the extent that judicial review is available against them, given their reliance on public money and also their role in the social marketplace. Yet there is considerable anxiety from housing associations that if they were classified in this manner that it would have a very damaging impact on their ability to

---

[97] Loughlin, *Public Law and Political Theory* (1992), p. 1.

obtain funds from the private market. Those advocating changing the status of council landlords into companies would recognise the difficulty. They would wish to move the stock out of the domain of the public precisely in order to obtain access to private funds (see McEldowney 1994: Chap. 15 for more detailed discussion of judicial review).

Secondly, we have seen the development of administrative law making and what seems to be its 1990s manifestation as part of a move to a new form of governance based on state contracts and specifications to diverse providers of services. In the housing context, we have seen the move to centre stage of the Housing Corporation, a body with few accountability structures and considerable power over thousands of providers of housing. We have seen its use of a code of guidance to ensure good housing management. What is not so clear is the extent to which it is possible to obtain judicial review on the basis of non-compliance with self-imposed or regulator-imposed rules. This is related to the development of the, as yet rather confused, concept of "legitimate expectations" within both public and indeed private law.

Thirdly, we have seen the development of the "contracting" state which some argue brings with it the possibility of greater accountability. However, there are trenchant criticisms to be made of the new contractualisation in relation to the existing state of redress through public law. As Freedland argues "the law, especially in its public aspect, seems to remain one step behind, even out of step with, this set of new realities, frequently denying their contractual or corporate significance".[98] He sees a tension between public law and the new patterns of public administration. He argues that:

> "[the] orientation of judicial review towards specific decisions may be thought unremarkable, uncontroversial, or even in large measure inevitable; but I suggest that it can significantly constrain the capacity of the courts to look at the fundamental workings of government by contract."[99]

It is also a problem over the jurisdiction of the public sector ombudsman.

---

[98] Freedland, "Government by Contract and Public Law", *Public Law* (1994), p. 90.
[99] *ibid.* p. 97.

"Although a spate of private world ombudsman has occurred in recent years, it must be time to take stock of our classical ombudsman systems when so much public sector activity has been privatised or contracted out. . . . Now the office holders say that they can look at services provided 'for or on behalf of' the public sector bodies but it should be remembered that their governing statutes exclude the right to investigate commercial or contractual matters."[1]

The implication is that there will be far less access to supervision by the courts unless public law develops in line with these new movements. The world of private law, based on the narrow concept of a discrete bargain encapsulated into an agreement is not suitable to deal with the multi-layered world of the provision of housing. Users, even if defined as consuming citizens, will be reliant on their consumer power. Given that the social and economic composition of the rented sector and those who tend to be affected by the actions of mortgagees, they would seem to have little of it. Few tenants have realistic exit powers, fewer still have the capacity to pay directly for their service but must rely on state support, very few have effective voice powers, the neglected aspect of consumer power.

## Conclusion

The last chapter discussed a range of issues which emerged when the tenurial spheres discussed in the proceeding chapters were looked at in a different manner. This conclusion continues the process of cross-cutting the tenurial spheres by reflecting on the categories themselves. The tripartite division has been used to chart the way in which the law is involved with residential ownership and occupation. I would like to argue that these spheres represent examples of the plurality of legal forms of regulation in the modern state which is described by De Sousa Santos (1987) as interlegality. I have attempted to demonstrate that the differential combination of legal and non-legal relations present within particular types of relations

---

[1] Lewis, "The Citizen's Charter and Next Steps: A New Way of Governing?" in *Political Quarterly* (1993), pp. 324–325.

affects the different forms of legal relations depending on the social practices and institutions to which they relate (Hunt, 1987).

The individual property relation discussed in each occupational grouping represents the classical form of liberal legality within modern western legal doctrine. All are equal subjects before the law. Each relates to the other through agreement. Legal subjects are seen as owning assets which are conceptually distinct from themselves. "Private law guarantees the right of all citizens to own property and engage in lawful transactions with it".[2] Inequalities are seen as "arising from the free exercise of uniform rights which all subjects have because of their fundamental legal equality".[3] The private law assumptions of freedom of contract and sanctity of property help to externalise the relations of private power present in property relations. We have seen three forms of these private property law concepts in operation: the trust, the mortgage and the lease. We have attempted to chart the way in which the nature of property has changed over time in the dynamic social and economic contexts in which they operate. This process reveals the power relations involved.

Property is not only a framework and mystification of power, it is also important as security—as a form of protection (Cotterell, 1987). I would like now to elaborate a little on the concept of property as a relation of power but also as a basis for security by exploring the economic and social dimensions of the residential property context under consideration in this book. By looking at the way in which the property relations in the trust, mortgage and lease have evolved in the setting of a residential housing market increasingly dominated by a particular form of owner occupation we can see the dynamic relations between property as security and as economic power.

Let us commence by equating the "property as power" concept with claims to ownership based on sanctity of property and freedom of contract, *i.e.* abstract ownership of an asset, and "property as a basis for security" as associated with the use and occupation of property as a home. Chapter 2 charted the changing social and economic conditions of home ownership, particularly the increasing

---

[2] Cotterell, "Power, property and the law of trusts: A partial agenda for critical legal scholarship", *Journal of Law and Society* (1987), p. 83.
[3] *ibid.* p. 83.

claim for recognition of property rights based not on abstract ownership but on social and economic contributions to homemaking, coupled with occupation. We have seen the gendered nature of these differing claims to property. We have also seen that they have been debated within the legal construct of the trust—whether there is a constructive or implied trust for sale created by a woman's contributions. Some judges have taken an equitable approach based on the fulfilment of expectations to recognise claims, others, seemingly in the ascendancy at the moment, have taken an approach more firmly rooted in the abstract concept of contract. This difference can be characterised as Denning doing justice to women occupying dwellings owned by men who have deserted them versus Lord Bridge looking for an agreement between the parties which embodied their mutual intentions over the asset value of the property (Bottomley, 1993).

We also saw in chapter 2 the attempts by those with claims to property based on occupation and contributions towards the home to resist the property claims of mortgagees. We see recognition of claims constructed in this way in *Williams & Glyn's Bank v. Boland* [1980] 2 All E.R. 408 before the courts move back to a more formalistic position based on the technicalities of the trust for sale concept (*City of London Building Society v. Flegg* [1988] A.C. 54). We see a similar struggle for the recognition of the consequences of the property as power relation in the case law on undue influence and misrepresentation involving the claims of predominately male owners of property and their financial advisers and those of their female spouses and partners. Here women's lack of familiarity with the consequences of using property as security against business indebtedness rather than as a family home emerges, but struggles for recognition in the courts.

Home ownership as it has emerged since the 1960s in the United Kingdom has combined both aspects of property, abstract ownership of the freehold with the security of occupation of the home. The former has offered access to wealth, the latter social freedom. Most owner occupiers purchase their properties with a mortgage. We have seen the social and legal evolution of this property concept, particularly the way in which it was moulded in the courts to become a security instrument rather than a devise for property transfer. However, in the late twentieth century many owners of property find that their status as mortgagors jeopardises their continued ownership of their homes. Although mortgagees are not legal owners of the dwellings, the economic and social context of mass home ownership has transformed them into often reluctant possessors of homes. This reluctance stems from the development of housing financiers as mutual building societies. We have seen that the relationship between most building society mortgagees and mortgagors has not relied significantly on the legal form of the mortgage rather on administrative processes. Mutuality has structured the way in which the mortgage operates.

Recent economic conditions coupled with the government's overwhelming encouragement for the extension of home ownership has placed strains on relationships leading the mortgagees to seek public company status and to utilise their property and contractual rights in the mortgage. They have met considerable resistence to the exercise of their powers as mortgagees precisely because of the combined strength of owner occupation's property as power and security concepts. These responsible mortgagees have been encouraged to continue to pursue administrative not legal solutions to their financial relations with owners.

The landlord and tenant relations embodied in the lease reveal a separation of ownership and occupation. In chapter 3 we argued further that the rent relation involves continuing economic and social expectations and constraints. We have seen that there are both sale and hire connotations within the lease—landlords sell the right to occupy until the lease terminates while tenants hire the continuing right to occupy a decent home. We have seen the way in which different types of landlord reflect in their activities different balances between the economic imperative and the continuing social relationship with their tenants. For informal landlords, most of whom are letting space within their own homes, the rent relation is very different to that of trader landlords whose business is centred on the profit to be made from sales and for whom renting to tenants is simply a prelude to that activity. Equally the social relations of the tenancy are very different. Attitudes to investment and to legal rights and obligations also differ. Occupying space in the landlord's home involves a very different set of expectations to occupying a house owned by a company. Nonetheless, both sets of relations are tenancies (although the former can sometimes be construed as a licence).

In sharp contrast to the private landlords, local housing authorities share a common history and philosophy of housing according to need. Differences in political control have had little impact on this philosophy until very recently where a minority of mainly shire authorities have decided to dispose of their stock altogether and cease to carry out a landlord function. We have seen in chapter 4 that public landlordism has been dominated by the consequences of state ownership. The welfare orientation has swamped the property relations to the extent that the concept of tenancy almost disappeared. Indeed, the Law Commission concluded in 1987 that:

> "It may no longer be satisfactory to treat the arrangements between the owners and occupiers of municipal housing as tenancies governed by the general law of landlord and tenant, . . .[4]"

Property as security therefore was very underdeveloped in this relation. We have seen the way in which the courts differentiated the needs of public sector and private sector tenants for security of tenure. So security for tenants in the public sector was provided until the 1980 Housing Act by the assumption of political and administrative responsibility. The Housing Act Tenants' Charter which granted legal security rests uneasily on an assumed landlord and tenant property relation. The changed political and economic context of public landlordism in the late 1980s and 1990s is leading to a greater emphasis on the property aspect of the relationship as the pressure to privatise the stock increases.

Housing associations share a diversity of form with private landlords but a greater shared philosophy with public landlords. The property form of the lease is more developed than in the public sector although access to property as security has not featured in this relatonship either to any extent. Again, security has been provided by the socially responsible nature of the landlord which like its local authority counterpart has not been motivated by profit. Housing association landlordism is also being moulded by the changed

---

[4] Law Commission, Landlord and Tenant: Reform of the Law (1987), Cmnd. 145, p. 8.

economic and political context in which it operates. In particular, their absorbtion into state housing policy has had a major impact on their property relations.

Landlord and tenant law does not differentiate between these forms of landlordism. Thus we can see that, although conceptually there are no legal differences between the relationships of these landlords with their tenants because property law assumes them all to be autonomous parties entering into an agreement over the use of an asset, the power of the lease depends very substantially on the social, political and economic context of its operation.

The evolution of the claim to enfranchise provides a specific illustration of the way in which claims based on property as power have been challenged by claims based on property as security emerged. It also demonstrates the interaction between legal form and the social, economic and political environment. Compulsory enfranchisement features in each of the rented sectors but in different contexts. We charted the way in which the demand for enfranchisement emerged in the private rented sector in chapter 3. With the development of an owner-occupied market based on asset values, long leaseholders began to pay premiums related to that market for the right to occupy premises. We have seen the way in which the competing claims to property of the freeholder and the occupying long leaseholder were made. The former relied on the economic aspect of the abstract property relation, the latter on occupational rights in a housing market dominated by owner occupation. The long-leaseholder unable to enfranchise would lose his/her home for which s/he had paid an owner-occupiers price, irrespective of the contractual arrangement entered into at the time of assignment or the sanctity of the freeholder's property. This claim to property was recognised in the Leasehold Reform Act 1967. In the Leasehold Reform, Housing and Urban Development Act 1993, a similarly based claim was recognised in relation to flat-dwelling long leaseholders after a market in flats emerged, although we have seen the differing strengths of the freeholder's claim to their property reflected in the purchase prices.

The right to buy was granted to qualifying public sector tenants in the 1980 Housing Act. In contrast to the private sector enfranchisers, these tenants held short term, predominately periodic, tenancies.

Their claim to enfranchise was based on the central government political priority of extending individual home ownership at the expense of public ownership. The insignificance of the lease, and with it concepts of the landlord's sanctity of property and freedom of contract, meant that the heavily discounted prices for the dwelling were not seen so much as expropriating the landlord in violation of their property rights as compensating the tenants for their occupation.

A similar measure in relation to housing association property was resisted because the property relation was stronger and also because the political position of housing associations in 1980 was different from that of local authorities. As we have seen in chapter 5, charitable housing associations were excluded from the right to buy, other housing association landlords could offer tenants cash or an alternative property. The 1995 white paper (DoE) sets out the government's proposals to introduce a wider right to buy for the housing association sector. However, unlike the public sector, the landlord's property right is more clearly recognised in these proposals: the tenants will not be entitled to a discount from their landlords rather they will receive a central government grant towards the purchase price.

The evolution of the concept of property, particularly the growth of the idea of property as security based on occupation, can be seen through developments within the lease itself. We discussed the dual nature of the lease, based on proprietary concepts but also on contractual terms in chapter 3. Using Bright and Gilbert's (1995) analysis we saw the way in which the contractual elements of the lease which tend to represent the continuing social dimension of the leasehold relationship, such as carrying out repairing obligations, are being given greater prominence by the courts in the context of the urban residential letting. These developments are not necessarily occurring because of a recognition of the power relation between landlord and tenant, although clearly individual judgments are motivated by a desire to improve the position of tenants. They could equally be seen as a desire to classify short term residential lettings as non-property relationships, as personal contracts. Although the mortgage contains a similar duality we have not seen judicial development of a specific contractual base in relation to residential mortgages within the private law area. However, the Law Commission (1991) has recently recommended such an approach.

This private property law response takes place within the development of legislation based on the welfarist principles of protection of the weaker party. In the residential property sector this protection has taken a number of forms but has been based primarily on protecting occupation and regulatory rents. This type of legal intervention constructs differences, creates categories which represent interests. These interests are graded in relation to others.[5] We have seen these statutory constructs in each of the sectors. Certain private tenants have been entitled to rent regulation and security of tenure. Certain tenancies are included and then excluded particularly in the context of rent deregulation. Distinctions change—furnished tenancies had less protection at one stage than unfurnished, tenants with residential landlords presently have less protection than tenants without.

Tenants of local authority landlords were not considered in need of statutory security of tenure until 1980 because of the overwhelmingly public nature of their landlord. When they obtained protection it was on different terms to private tenants. Equally, housing association tenants have been distinguished both from public sector tenants and private rented sector tenants at various stages in their history. These interventions have recognised the power of property in the range of private property relations. Specific statutory regimes have been built upon the social and economic histories of the different forms of provision. Other individual statutory measures have been less specifically related to one form of landlordism such as protection against harassment and unlawful eviction and the provision of information in rent books, nonetheless the usefulness of these measures is heavily related to the form of landlordism. Harassment and unlawful eviction by or on behalf of the landlord occurs in certain sections of the private rented market but it is not a feature of public or housing association landlordism. Indeed, these landlords are obliged to tackle harassment of their tenants by others.

The owner-occupied sector reflects the range of interests seeking to be protected in its fragmentary statutory approach. Occupational protection is needed primarily by those owners financing their purchase on borrowed money. As we have seen in chapter 2, for the

---

[5] Ewald, "A concept of social law", pp. 41–75 in Teubner (ed.) *Dilemmas of Law in the Welfare State* (1986), p. 46 .

majority of borrowers the limited protection offered is access to court possession proceedings under the Administration of Justice Acts 1970 and 1973. The district judge then has discretion to intervene on behalf of the mortgagor in arrears to enable repayment to take place. Those with secured loans under the Consumer Credit Act 1974 can seek court assistance via another route. The two systems are separate, reflecting different interests—the first system is aimed at those with first mortgages with "mainstream" lenders such as building societies, banks and the centralised lenders, the second is aimed at second loans by less mainstream lenders. The vulnerability of owner occupiers based on a recognition of unequal power relations within property concepts has not been recognised until recently.

Owner-occupation has not generated such an interest partly because only a minority of the whole sector is affected at any one time. However, with the segmentation of the sector, the interests of particularly vulnerable constituencies might emerge and gain specific recognition. Presently these interests are being resisted by government which argues that owner-occupiers are responsible for securing their own protection in the market through such mechanisms as mortgage indemnity insurance. This resistance reflects the growing trend, associated with what we described in the introduction as the crisis of legitimacy, for the state to wish to limit the interests which receive support.

We have seen the way in which particular combinations of individual property relations and state sponsored statutory regimes have constructed particularised regulatory contexts. These are embodied in the forms of landlordism, public, housing association and private. These landlordisms hold different values although again we have seen that these values shift over time. Public landlordism is socially responsible, private landlordism is not. Housing associations are socially responsible but in different ways to public landlords. These particularised regulatory contexts reflect political and economic histories and amalgams of power. We have charted their evolution but also the increasingly complex regulatory contexts in which they are located which at the same time blur these distinctions.

We have seen the nature and impact of these wider regulatory contexts on the specific occupational groupings in chapters 2 to 5 and also across the groupings in chapter 6. They are examples of the increasing spread of law and legal constructions into social life which have been noted more generally by legal theorists. The significance of this process has also been the subject of considerable discussion which cannot be summarised adequately here.[6] Instead we will consider the developments in the context of our more specific study of housing. We have seen what Loughlin describes as the juridification of relations between central and local government. He suggests there are two forms. First:

> "To the extent that conventional practices lose their authority, the institutions of central government and local government inevitably, and in many cases for the first time, turn to the legal framework in order to determine their rights, duties, powers and liabilities. In this sense, the relationship becomes legalised and, in so far as the institutions look to law as a source of guidance we might talk of juridification of the relationship."[7]

The second form of juridification:

> "envisages that local authorities will, more than hitherto, be rule-bound agencies subject to a much greater degree of judicial supervision and that the central-local relationship will be reconstructed in an authoritative, hierachical form."[8]

We have seen the impact on tenancy relations of this increasing use of law to structure the relationship between the landlord and central government, particularly in the area of housing finance. We saw in chapter 4 the way in which the rent relation has been juridified not directly through rent control but through subsidy regimes and the restructuring of the Housing Revenue Account by legislation in 1989. The greater use of formal legal interventions is also often accompanied by the grant of considerable legal discretion to the Secretary of State. We have seen a number of examples of the use of this

---

[6] Cotterell (1992: particularly chaps. 5 and 9) and Hunt (1993: particularly chap. 13) provide good general discussions of these developments. See also the contributions in Teubner (ed.) (1986); Habermas (1976); De Sousa Santos (1985); Luhmann (1985); Nonet and Selznick (1978).

[7] Loughlin, "The Restructuring of Central–Local Government Relations", Jowell and Oliver (eds.) *The Changing Constitution* (1994), p. 278.

[8] *ibid.* p. 278.

discretion in relation to the sale of council dwellings, both individually and collectively, in the processes of regulating housing subsidies and in specifying the content of Housing Revenue Accounts.

At the same time we have seen the proliferation of adminstrative rule making and the use of administrative codes of practice across the housing sector. There are codes to combat racial discrimination in owner-occupied housing, in rented housing, guidance on homelessness, codes of practice on rent arrears in the public sector, practice statements on mortgage arrears in the private sector. There are charters for public sector tenants and guarantees for housing association tenants. The list could go on. The legal status of these documents is often ambiguous. Some are voluntary, some have evidential effect in a court, breach of some have legal or financial consequences for landlords. The ability of the occupier to utilise them as a basis for a legal action is often particularly ambiguous.

The boundaries between state and civil society are increasingly blurred in this proliferation of forms of regulation "discretion and rules reinforce each other to extend regulatory jurisdictions into realms of policy formation often beyond the preview of judicial review."[9] We have seen the consequences for housing association tenants of this particular extension of regulatory scope. The status of housing associations provides a good example of the outcome of this confusion. They look like public bodies, act like them and are subject to regulation like them but constitutionally they are private bodies. The Housing Corporation's tenants guarantee is designed to regulate landlord and tenant relationships but tenants are unable to enforce its terms directly unless they have been incorporated into their tenancy agreement because judicial review is not available to them.

The ambiguity of the guarantee points to another outcome of this regulatory invasion which is confused accountability. Accountability is generally directed towards the regulators rather than occupiers. This is often not obvious to occupiers because the language of these regulatory documents tends to be consumerist in orientation.

The proliferation of state involvement in civil society not only calls into question the boundaries between the two but also the legitimacy of the intervention. We have argued that the housing policies of the

---

[9] Cotterell, *The Sociology of Law* (1992), p. 291.

1980s and 1990s are a response to a perceived crisis of state legitimacy in the 1970s. The political and financial cost of meeting increased expectations over housing through the state in the 1970s was tackled by withdrawing state support for council housing and redirecting expectations into a social market. This was part of a wider attempt by government to strengthen civil society and to re-establish the boundaries between state and civil society. So attempts were made to reinforce the position of housing associations as private bodies through changed security of tenure and funding regimes. The private rented sector was decontrolled. Private bodies were encouraged to take over local authority housing stock. Owner-occupiers are now being urged to seek private insurance to cover risk.

Yet this process has led to greater regulatory invasion of civil society (Cotterell, 1992). Government has insisted on the adoption of voluntary codes on mortgage arrears by mortgage lenders. The Housing Corporation has increased its powers to regulate existing housing associations and is about to extend its power to oversee parts of the privtate rented sector. Complaints mechanisms such as ombudsman services, some on a self-regulatory basis, have come into being.

We can illustrate some of these trends through a discussion of the development of independent social landlordism. While the individual property relations and statutory codes contributed to the production of particularised landlordism which reflected their history and power relations, this new construction silences specific histories. It is gradually becoming associated with all forms of renting, irrespective of landlord history, philosophy or form of ownership. Transferred local authority stock will be subsumed within it as will part of the private rented sector, leaving only the rump of the private rented sector outside. This landlordism is constructed as economically efficient and socially effective. It delivers a social housing product defined by government through the Housing Corporation but delivered in a social market in which the landlords are all deemed to be private bodies. It is taking extensive government intervention to create.

The language of its creation is market oriented and consumerist. Tenants are consumers of housing products. Once this construction is achieved, it is quite possible to see the way in which it could be extended to cover owner-occupiers, who also consume housing products in the form of mortgages. On one level this move to a consumerist approach can be seen as a welcome rationalisation of the plethora of overlapping legal and administrative provisions. On another this approach masks in a new but equally effective way the power disparities between providers of housing and occupiers and between different types of occupiers. Contract might be replacing property as the language of residential occupation but it holds within it the same abstract notion of equals bargaining for products.

At the same time we have seen the growth in social and economic divisions which are increasingly based on occupational grouping. Local authorities now house poorer and more socially disadvantaged occupiers than ever in their history. The consequences of this concentration of disadvantage are materialising in anxiety over lawless estates and deep insecurity for tenants provoked by anti-social behaviour. Housing associations are also housing concentrations of poorer residents and face similar pressure. The proposals to tackle the social consequences of this residualisation involve withdrawing security of tenure from newcomers to both sectors (as a deterrent presumably) and speedier mechanisms for eviction. The commensurate growth in the owner-occupied sector has led to millions feeling insecure because of actual or potential debt within a sector which is supposed to offer economic and social security.

In the end whether the relationship of residential occupiers to their providers is couched in the language of contract or property, insecurity is produced by wider social and economic vulnerabilities which cannot be regulated away.

# Index

# Introduction to
# Modern Virology